THE FAMILY LETTERS OF THOMAS JEFFERSON

EDITED BY

EDWIN MORRIS BETTS AND JAMES ADAM BEAR, JR.

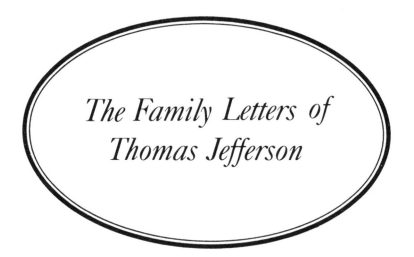

The Family Letters of Thomas Jefferson

PUBLISHED FOR

BY THE UNIVERSITY PRESS OF VIRGINIA
CHARLOTTESVILLE

Preface

Thomas Jefferson was a prolific letter writer in a great letter-writing age: it has been estimated that he wrote and received as many as fifty thousand letters. Writing these was a great burden, especially in his later years when old age and rheumatism rendered writing slow and difficult. He then complained that to fill a single page was the work of almost an entire day. Correspondence with his children and grandchildren, however, could at no time of his life have been considered anything but pleasant. For, next to being with his family, hearing from and about them was his delight.

The family letters are not limited to family matters, but deal with local affairs in Paris, Philadelphia, New York, Washington, and Albemarle County, Virginia, or wherever the correspondents happened to be. They are also concerned with farm problems, the construction of the house and gardens at Monticello, and innumerable other subjects, including the perils of ennui, the fine arts, and poignant suggestions on how to get along with one's neighbors. It is the family relationship, however, that commands the interest and makes the letters as entertaining to the general reader as they are instructive to the scholar.

Jefferson could write with facility and authority on subjects ranging from agriculture to architecture, from philosophy to history, but it was in the role of parent and grandparent that he wrote with most assurance and pleasure. As such he believed in telling his correspondents something worth while, and he ran the gamut of parental prerogatives by proposing stern regimens of occupation and improvement while confidently advising on how to ensure happiness in the married state or on the nursing of children. Amid such parental dicta one does not lose sight of the fact that Jefferson was a loving and excellent father, if a possessive and precise one.

mrs, and *miss,* are altered to *Mr., Mrs.,* and *Miss.* The ampersand is expanded to *and* in all cases except when used with the names of business firms, as, *Farrel & Jones.* No attempt has been made to alter spelling, even with respect to proper names. Punctuation is maintained as far as possible as it appears in the original, but periods are inserted where needed and dashes removed. No attempt has been made to identify or distinguish between a recipient's copy and a file draft, the present purpose being only to use a complete and legible text when available.

The locations of the 570 manuscripts included in this correspondence are not given; these may be found by consulting the photocopies of the Alphabetical and Chronological Checklists of Jefferson Manuscripts (including letters to him) prepared by The Jefferson Office, Princeton University, Princeton, New Jersey, and those placed in a number of research centers throughout the United States. I wish, however, to acknowledge permission to use these letters as having been granted by the Alderman Library of the University of Virginia, Charlottesville, Virginia (ViU); Colonial Williamsburg, Inc., Williamsburg, Virginia (ViWC); the Henry E. Huntington Library and Art Gallery, San Marino, California (CSmH); The Jefferson Office, Jervis Library, Rome, New York; The Library of Congress, Washington, D.C. (DLC); Massachusetts Historical Society, Boston, Massachusetts (MHi); The Pierpont Morgan Library, New York, New York (NNP); Princeton University Library, Princeton, New Jersey; The University of North Carolina, Chapel Hill, North Carolina; and Gordon Trist Burke, Omaha, Nebraska; John Randolph Burke, Bryn Mawr, Pennsylvania; Harold Jefferson Coolidge, Washington, D. C.; James H. Eddy, New Canaan, Connecticut; Mrs. Robert Graham, Alexandria, Virginia; Robert H. Kean, Charlottesville, Virginia; Mrs. Page Taylor Kirk, Charlottesville, Virginia; Mrs. A. Slater Lamond, Alexandria, Virginia; Cecil Eppes Shine, Jr., Miami, Florida; Walter C. Stearns, Ridgefield, Connecticut; Miss Olivia Taylor, Charlottesville, Virginia; and Mrs. Harold M. Wilson, Miami, Florida. The texts of a number of letters are from Sarah Nicholas Randolph, *The Domestic Life of Thomas Jefferson* (New York, 1871); this is also an excellent account of the personal side of Jefferson.

I wish to express my sincere appreciation to those persons who very kindly have assisted in a greater or lesser degree in the editing of these letters: Francis L. Berkeley, Jr., Mrs. Edwin M. Betts, Miss Anne E. H. Freudenberg, Donald R. Haynes, Herbert Gantner.

Contents

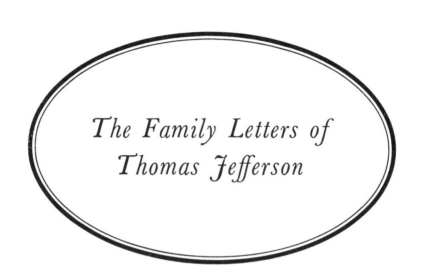

The Family Letters of
Thomas Jefferson

Introduction

Monticello was the place beyond all others where Jefferson could enjoy the supreme satisfaction of family associations. Often while burdened with public office he found it difficult to believe that existence could be a blessing, except when something called to mind his family and farm. Of the two, it was the "ineffable pleasures . . . of family society" which always came first in his affections.[1]

During his happiest years, his daughters Martha and Mary,[2] with his wife, the former Martha Wayles Skelton, made the contented household at Monticello where literary and agricultural projects were eagerly pursued. This contentment was shattered by the tragic death of Mrs. Jefferson on September 6, 1782, a few months after the birth of their daughter Lucy Elizabeth. The bereavement welded an enduring bond between ten-year-old Martha and her father, while it caused Mary, aged four, and the infant Lucy to be sent to live at Eppington[3] with Aunt Elizabeth and Uncle Francis Eppes — the only early home and parents these children were ever to know. Little Lucy was not to know them long, for she died at two, while her father was abroad.

Besides inducing him to resume the chores of public life sooner

1. Thomas Jefferson to Martha Jefferson Randolph, June 8, 1797, Coolidge Collection, Massachusetts Historical Society. Hereafter cited as MHi. Jefferson will be referred to as TJ.
2. Since these children were called by different names at different times during their lives, they will be referred to in this work by their given names, Martha and Mary. Martha, named for her mother, was sometimes called Patsy and especially so as a child. Mary, in the family, was Pol or Polly, in France, Marie or Mademoiselle Polie, and after returning home, Maria. They addressed each other as Sister Patsy or Polly and their father as Papa. As Martha grew older she used the more conventional Father, but Mary was no more consistent in addressing her father than in corresponding with him.
3. Elizabeth Wayles Eppes and Martha Wayles Jefferson were half sisters; John Wayles of The Forest, Charles City County, was their father. Eppington, the Eppes home, was located on the Appomattox River in southern Chesterfield County.

ter, wrote that her father always accompanied her on the rather hectic visits to the mantuamaker, the staymaker, and the dressmaker. For the convent school, Abbaye Royale de Panthemont, which she entered prior to August 24, she required a uniform that she described as "crimson made like a frock, laced behind, with the tail, like a robe de cour, hooked on, muslin cuffs and tuckers." This sounds like a formal costume for a child not yet twelve, but the tone of the convent was not so pompous as to prevent her sixty schoolmates from calling Martha "Jeff" or "Jeffy."

The Jeffersons had not been more than a month in France when Lucy, Mary, and several of the Eppes children in Virginia contracted the whooping cough to which Lucy succumbed. She died about October 13, 1784, but Mrs. Eppes's letter informing her brother-in-law of his loss did not reach him until May 6, 1785.[6] Jefferson, already anxious to reunite his family, began to accelerate plans to have Mary sent to France as soon as possible.

After apprising the Eppeses of his wishes, Jefferson instructed Francis Eppes relative to the conditions to be met before Mary could undertake the voyage. First, on account of the equinoctial storms, she must sail from Virginia only "in the months of April, May, June or July." Next, a responsible person must attend her, "A careful negro woman, as Isabel . . . if she has had the smallpox, would suffice under the patronage of a gentleman." Finally, a safe vessel, one that should have made one voyage and be no more than five years old, must be found.[7]

In writing to Mary, her father said, "I wish so much to see you that I have desired your uncle and aunt to send you to me . . . you shall have as many dolls and playthings as you want." To this, Mary, now nearly nine, realizing that her secure position in the Eppes family was threatened, responded with a truthfulness and tenacity reminiscent of her father: "I don't want to go to France, I had rather stay with Aunt Eppes."[8]

One by one the obstacles that must at times have seemed insurmountable to the anxious father were removed, albeit with difficulty. The danger from Algerine pirates was to be avoided by sending Mary only in a ship that, being English or French, would be immune from attack. Elizabeth Eppes, having little desire to send her niece on such a trip, wrote her brother-in-law that she

6. Julian P. Boyd and others, editors, *The Papers of Thomas Jefferson* (Princeton, 1950——), VII, 441–42. Hereafter cited as *Papers*.
7. TJ to Francis Eppes [August 30, 1785], *Papers*, VIII, 451.
8. September 20, 1785, *Papers*: VIII, 532–33; [ca. May 22, 1786], IX, 560–61. 560–61.

quil, sturdy, and self-reliant as her father, and like him was dis-
tinguished-looking rather than handsome. Martha's granddaughter Sarah Nicholas Randolph wrote of her as "a sweet girl,
delicacy and sensibility are read in her every gesture, and her
manners are in unison with all that is amiable and lovely," and
although "not handsome at twelve she was tall and aristocratic
looking."

Mary, unlike Martha in physical appearance as in temperament,
was timid and clinging and often forgetful of her father's stern
directions respecting the studies he urged her to master and report
on to him. She has been described as singularly beautiful and delicate physically; in this no doubt she resembled her mother. Miss
Randolph's description, based on family tradition, noted her
great-aunt as having been "rather a querulous little beauty." [16]

After the return voyage to America the family disembarked at
Norfolk on November 23, 1789. Mary was now a child of eleven
and Martha a grownup of seventeen. If the younger was not entertaining thoughts of the opposite sex, apparently the elder was,
and probably during the trip to Monticello the spark of love was
ignited. When and where she and young Thomas Mann Randolph, Jr., her third cousin, met and courted remains something
of a mystery. Jefferson's account book, which listed the itinerary
to Monticello, failed to record a visit to Tuckahoe, Randolph's
Goochland County home. They could have met while Jefferson
was in Richmond, or it is possible, as Malone suggests, that they
might have spent several days at Tuckahoe on a side trip from
Richmond. William Gaines, in his fine dissertation on Randolph,
expresses the opinion that Thomas Mann began to court Martha
during the Christmas season of 1789–1790, and this would have
been their first meeting since his childhood at Edgehill, his father's
Albemarle County farm, several miles east of Monticello.

Despite the lack of details, we know that they were impressed
with each other, and by January 30, 1790, they had become engaged. [17] Jefferson did not attempt to influence the romance, since
in the case of young Randolph, his fears were groundless that his

16. Sarah Nicholas Randolph, "Mrs. Thomas Mann Randolph," in Mrs.
O. J. Wister and Miss Agnes Irwin, editors, *Worthy Women of Our First
Century* (Philadelphia, 1877), 16, 17, 23.
17. William H. Gaines, "Thomas Mann Randolph" (unpublished dissertation, University of Virginia, 1950), 60. Hereafter cited as "Gaines."
The trip up country took nearly a month from Norfolk. They arrived at
Monticello December 24, 1789. It is interesting to note that family tradition
maintains that the two met in Paris; however, neither Gaines nor Dr. Boyd
in the *Papers* shows evidence to support the tradition. See Account Book 1789
for their itinerary from Norfolk to Monticello.

to both sides of the family.[21] Grandpapa, as he was soon to be called, first saw the baby at Monticello in September, when she was eight months old.

On October 12, 1791, Jefferson left Monticello for Philadelphia, taking Mary with him so she could be placed in school. Until his resignation as Secretary of State in 1793, Jefferson, sometimes accompanied by Mary, commuted between Albemarle and the capital several times a year. During his Philadelphia residence additional grandchildren were being born at Monticello. The second, Thomas Jefferson Randolph, arrived September 12, 1792, and on August 30, 1794, came Ellen Wayles Randolph, Martha's only child to die in infancy. The second of this name was born October 13, 1796.[22]

The year 1797 was important for the Monticello family. For Jefferson it brought his return to public life as Vice-President,[23] and for Mary it was the time of her marriage to John Wayles Eppes, the eldest of Uncle and Aunt Eppes's children, her half first cousin and childhood playmate at Eppington. Jefferson hailed the union with "inexpressible pleasure," for he had known "Jack" from infancy and superintended his schooling when the boy was in Philadelphia. He confided to Martha that Jack "could not have been more to my wishes if I had had the whole free earth to have chosen a partner for her."[24]

The happy father, as possessive of Mary as of Martha, prophesied, "I now see our fireside formed into a group, no one member of which has a fibre in their composition which can ever produce any jarring or jealousies among us. . . . In order to keep us all together . . . I think to open and resettle the plantation of Pantops for them." He then advised Mary that "harmony in the marriage state is the very first object to be aimed at . . . that a husband finds his affections wearied out by a constant string of little checks and obstacles."[25] The ceremony took place at Monticello on October 13, 1797, and was perfunctorily noted in the account book: "My daughter Maria married this day."[26]

Unlike the Randolphs, the Eppeses did not remain in Albemarle

21. TJ to Martha Jefferson Randolph, March 17, 1791. Edgehill Randolph Papers, University of Virginia. Hereafter cited as EHR.

22. *Jefferson's Prayer Book*, vii.

23. His Vice-Presidential term began Saturday, March 4, 1797.

24. June 8, 1797. MHi.

25. January 7, 1798. MHi.

26. Malone, *Jefferson and the Ordeal of Liberty* (Boston, 1962), 239–40, gives the best account of the wedding.

heart, dying in 1804 at twenty-six[30] and leaving two children, Francis, aged three, and an infant, Maria Jefferson, who did not survive many months. Mary Eppes's death, indeed, as that of Mrs. Jefferson, was caused by complications following the birth of a daughter. Mary had become an Eppes by association in 1782, and one in name in 1797. Of the "happy family" dispersed in 1782, she was the second to return after death to Monticello, where she was buried near her mother in the family cemetery on the lonely slope of the mountain.

From 1797 to 1809, during Jefferson's terms as Vice-President and President, his chief communication with his relations was by the post to and from Monticello, Edgehill, or Bermuda Hundred Often he complained of its irregularity and of the long intervals between letters. Besides maintaining a large, burdensome official correspondence, he wrote regularly to the Eppes and Randolph families and later to those grandchildren who could read and write. By the time Jefferson left Washington for all time, his grand-children included seven young Randolphs — Anne Cary, Thomas Jefferson, Ellen Wayles, Cornelia, Virginia, Mary, Benjamin Franklin, and James Madison.

Retirement meant happy days at Monticello for Jefferson and for Martha, who experienced infinite pleasure at seeing herself and her children established under the kindly and benevolent influence of her father. These were good years for the children also, as they now had someone to fill the void in their lives caused by their father's prolonged absences and apparent lack of interest in their welfare.

As the six older Randolphs passed from childhood others arrived to take their places: Meriwether Lewis in 1810, Septimia Anne or "Tim" in 1814, and George Wythe in 1818. Jefferson's living grandchildren now numbered eleven Randolphs and one Eppes. Her grandfather's influence in naming Septimia is not so easily discernible as in the cases of the other Randolph children. However, family tradition has it that by the time she was born, no girls' names having immediately sprung to mind, as the seventh granddaughter she was called Septimia, perhaps at Jefferson's suggestion.[31]

The children at Monticello provided constant pleasure and in-

30. She died at Monticello on "April 17. 1804 between 8. and 9. A.M." Account Book 1804.
31. "Mrs. Septimia R. Meikleham, Jefferson's Granddaughter," an undated clipping (probably from a Washington, D. C., newspaper) in the Septimia Randolph Meikleham Folder at Monticello.

interruption of studies and filling our houses with children are consequences of early marriage."[34] His grandson married the girl anyway; notwithstanding the objections of his father and grand-father, Francis Eppes at twenty-one married Mary Elizabeth Cleland Randolph, a fourth cousin, on November 28, 1822.[35]

Jefferson's last year opened badly for him. He was oppressed "with disease, debility, age and embarrassed affairs."[36] Indeed, his pecuniary difficulties had by now reached such a state that an appeal was made to the state legislature for permission to hold a lottery to dispose of certain lands. After permission had been granted by a very reluctant legislature, the family decided to seek succor from a public subscription; however, as encouraging as the results were for the moment, this device fell far, far short of the need.

In March Jefferson made his will, leaving Poplar Forest to Francis Eppes and, after several small bequests, devising the remainder of his estate in trust to Jefferson Randolph, Nicholas P. Trist, a grandson-in-law, and Alexander P. Garrett, for the sole benefit of Martha and her children. Jefferson's one desire was to prevent Randolph's creditors from laying claim to an inheritance Martha might have to share with her husband; he was not moved by antipathy to a son-in-law who by his own acts had set himself apart from his family. In this same month, Jefferson's financial situation had become so distressing that he wrote an old schoolmate that he would "welcome the hour which shall once more reassemble our antient class."[37]

The hour was not long in coming. On July 4, at fifty minutes past the meridian, Jefferson died in his bedroom at Monticello. His death was caused by the complications of old age. Jefferson Randolph, Trist, his trusted body-servant Burwell, and Dr. Robley Dunglison had maintained the bedside vigil since the venerable patriot had lapsed into a stupor on July 2. When it became apparent that he was dying, other members of the household were called in to pay their last respects. During the immediate forenoon

34. TJ to John Wayles Eppes, July 28, 1822. CSmH.
35. Walter Lewis Zorn, *The Descendants of the Presidents of the United States of America* (Monroe, Michigan, 1955), 58.
The bride was the daughter of Jane Cary Randolph, Thomas Mann Randolph, Jr.'s sister, and Thomas Eston Randolph, a cousin. Randolph was a merchant and postmaster at Milton and resided at Ashton, across the Rivanna River from Milton.
36. Joseph C. Vance, "Thomas Jefferson Randolph" (unpublished dissertation, University of Virginia, 1957), 94–106. Also, Randall, III, 527–29.
37. To Thomas Walker Maury, March 3, 1826. ViU.

THE JEFFERSON FAMILY

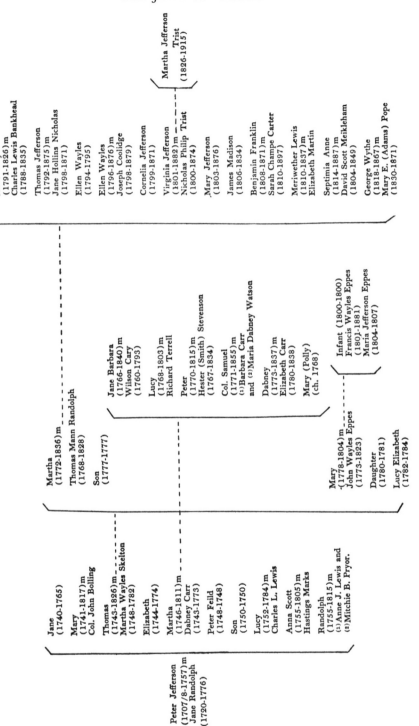

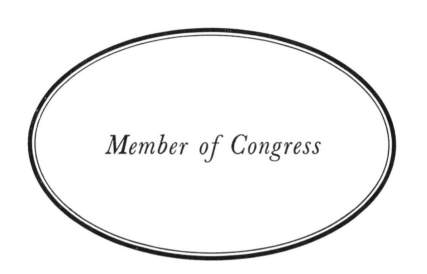

Member of Congress

To Martha Jefferson

Annapolis Nov. 28. 1783

My dear Patsy

After four days journey I arrived here without any accident and in as good health as when I left Philadelphia. The conviction that you would be more improved in the situation I have placed you than if still with me, has solaced me on my parting with you, which my love for you has rendered a difficult thing. The acquirements which I hope you will make under the tutors I have provided for you will render you more worthy of my love, and if they cannot increase it they will prevent it's diminution. Consider the good lady [1] who has taken you under her roof, who has undertaken to see that you perform all your exercises, and to admonish you in all those wanderings from what is right or what is clever to which your inexperience would expose you, consider her I say as your mother, as the only person to whom, since the loss with which heaven has been pleased to afflict you, you can now look up; and that her displeasure or disapprobation on any occasion will be an immense misfortune which should you be so unhappy as to incur by any unguarded act, think no concession too much to regain her good will. With respect to the distribution of your time the following is what I should approve.

from 8. to 10 o'clock practise music.

from 10. to 1. dance one day and draw another

from 1. to 2. draw on the day you dance, and write a letter the next day.

from 3. to 4. read French.

from 4. to 5. exercise yourself in music.

from 5. till bedtime read English, write &c.

Communicate this plan to Mrs. Hopkinson and if she approves of it pursue it. As long as Mrs. Trist [2] remains in Philadelphia cultivate her affections. She has been a valuable friend to you and her good sense and good heart make her valued by all who know her and by nobody on earth more than by me. I expect you will write to me by every post. Inform me what books you read, what tunes

every week yet it will not be amiss for you to enquire at the office every week. I wrote to Mr. House[1] by the last post. Perhaps his letter may still be in the office. I hope you will have good sense enough to disregard those foolish predictions that the world is to be at an end soon. The almighty has never made known to any body at what time he created it, nor will he tell any body when he means to put an end to it, if ever he means to do it. As to preparations for that event, the best way is for you to be always prepared for it. The only way to be so is never to do nor say a bad thing. If ever you are about to say any thing amiss or to do any thing wrong, consider before hand. You will feel something within you which will tell you it is wrong and ought not to be said or done: this is your conscience, and be sure to obey it. Our maker has given us all, this faithful internal Monitor, and if you always obey it, you will always be prepared for the end of the world: or for a much more certain event which is death. This must happen to all: it puts an end to the world as to us, and the way to be ready for it is never to do a wrong act. I am glad you are proceeding regularly under your tutors. You must not let the sickness of your French master interrupt your reading French, because you are able to do that with the help of your dictionary. Remember I desired you to send me the best copy you should make of every lesson Mr. Cimitiere[2] should set you. In this I hope you will be punctual because it will let me see how you are going on. Always let me know too what tunes you play. Present my compliments to Mrs Hopkinson, Mrs. House and Mrs. Trist. I had a letter from your uncle Eppes[3] last week informing me that Polly is very well, and Lucy[4] recovered from an indisposition. I am my dear Patsy your affectionate father,   TH: JEFFERSON

1. Samuel House of Philadelphia.
2. Pierre Eugène du Simitière was Martha's art tutor. Note the various spellings of his name used by TJ: Cimitiere, Simetiere.
3. Francis Eppes.
4. Mary and Lucy Elizabeth Jefferson were TJ's younger daughters.

To Martha Jefferson

Annapolis Dec. 22. 1783

MY DEAR PATSY

I hoped before this to have received letters from you regularly and weekly by the post, and also to have had a letter to forward from you to one of your aunts as I desired in my letter of Novem-

TO MARTHA JEFFERSON

Annapolis Jan. 15. 1784.

MY DEAR PATSY

Your letter by the post is not yet come to hand, that by Mr. Beresford[1] I received this morning. Your long silence had induced me almost to suspect you had forgotten me and the more so as I had desired you to write to me every week. I am anxious to know what books you read, what tunes you can play, and to receive specimens of your drawing. With respect to your meeting Mr. Simitiere at Mr. Rittenhouse's,[2] nothing could give me more pleasure than your being much with that worthy family wherein you will see the best examples of rational life and learn to esteem and copy them. But I should be very tender of obtruding you on the family as it might perhaps be not always convenient to them for you to be there at your hours of attending Mr. Simitiere. I can only say then that if it has been desired by Mr. and Mrs. Rittenhouse in such a way as that Mrs. Hopkinson shall be satisfied they will not consider it as inconvenient, I would have you thankfully accept it and conduct yourself with so much attention to the family as that they may never feel themselves incommoded by it. I hope Mrs. Hopkinson will be so good as to act for you in this matter with that delicacy and prudence of which she is so capable. I have so much at heart your learning to draw, and should be uneasy at your losing this opportunity which probably is your last. But I remind you to inclose me every week a copy of all your lessons in drawing that I may judge how you come on. I have had very ill health since I came here.[3] I have been just able to attend my duty in the state house, but not to go out on any other occasion. I am however considerably better. Present my highest esteem to Mrs. Hopkinson and accept yourself assurances of the sincere love with which I am my dear Patsy Yours affectionately,

TH: JEFFERSON

1. Possibly a delegate to the Continental Congress from Maryland. See *Papers*, VI, 437, 465.

2. David Rittenhouse was the celebrated Philadelphia scientist, patriot, and friend of TJ's.

3. TJ wrote to James Madison on January 1, 1784: "I have had very ill health since I have been here and am getting rather lower than otherwise." (*Papers*, VI, 438.) He is not explicit in alluding to his ailment; however, about March 1 he suffered an attack of the periodical headache, which was probably migraine. Whatever the causes of his illnesses, he was restricted in reading and writing as well as in public pursuits until about mid-April. See "Medical Chronology of Thomas Jefferson," a typescript in the Monticello Files of excerpts from Jefferson manuscripts and other sources relating to his health; hereafter cited as "Medical Chronology."

I send herewith Mr. Zane's[1] present of the looking glass which I dare say he intended for you. Wait upon Mrs. House and let her know, if she should not have heard from Mrs. Trist lately, that we have received a letter from her by a gentleman immediately from Fort Pitt. She is very well and expects to leave that place about the first of April.[2] Present me in the most friendly terms to your patroness Mrs. Hopkinson and be assured of the love with which I am Dr. Patsy yours affectionately,

TH: JEFFERSON

Mr. Maury[3] will deliver you this, who is lately from Virginia and is my particular friend.

1. Isaac Zane, a friend of TJ's, was proprietor of the Marlboro Iron Works in Frederick County, Maryland.
2. Mrs. Trist was traveling from Philadelphia to New Orleans. The late Gordon Trist Burke, a Trist and Jefferson descendant who lived in Omaha, Nebraska, owned the manuscript diary of her trip.
3. James Maury was the son of the Reverend Mr. James Maury and a classmate of TJ's at the Reverend Mr. Maury's classical school in Albemarle County. TJ was three years older than his friend. Malone, *Jefferson the Virginian* (Boston, 1948), 40–44.

FROM MARY JEFFERSON

Eppington April 1. 1784.

MY DEAR PATSY

I want to know what day you are going to come and see me, and if you will bring Sister Patsy, and my baby[1] with you. I was mighty glad of my sash's, and gave Cousin Booling[2] one. I can almost read. Your affectionate daughter,

POLLY JEFFERSON

1. Possibly a doll.
2. Martha Bolling Eppes was a daughter of Elizabeth and Francis Eppes.

TO MARTHA JEFFERSON

Annapolis Apr. 4. 1784.

MY DEAR PATSY

This will be handed you by Genl. Gates,[1] who going to Philadelphia furnishes me with the opportunity of writing to you. I am again getting my health, and have some expectations of going to Philadelphia ere long; but of this am not certain. I have had no letters from Eppington since I wrote you last, and have not received one from you I think these two months. I wish to know what you read, what tunes you play, how you come on in your

Minister to France

FROM MARY JEFFERSON

[Eppington ca. 13 Sep. 1785?] [1]

DEAR PAPA

I want to see you and sister Patsy, but you must come to Uncle
Eppes's house.   POLLY JEFFERSON

1. Date from *Papers*, VIII, 517.

TO MARY JEFFERSON

Paris Sep. 20. 1785.

MY DEAR POLLY

I have not received a letter from you since I came to France.
If you knew how much I love you and what pleasure the receipt
of your letters gave me at Philadelphia, you would have written
to me, or at least have told your aunt what to write, and her goodness would have induced her to take the trouble of writing it. I
wish so much to see you that I have desired your uncle and aunt
to send you to me. I know, my dear Polly, how sorry you will be,
and ought to be, to leave them and your cousins but your [sister
and m]yself cannot live without you, and after a while we will
carry you back again to see your friends in Virginia. In the mean-
time you shall be taught here to play on the harpsichord, to draw,
to dance, to read and talk French and such other things as will
make you more worthy of the love of your friends. But above all
things, by our care and love of you, we will teach you to love us
more than you will do if you stay so far from us. I have had no
opportunity since Colo. LeMaire [1] went, to send you any thing:
but when you come here you shall have as many dolls and playthings as you want for yourself, or to send to your cousins whenever you shall have opportunities. I hope you are a very good girl,
that you love your uncle and aunt very much, and are very thank-
ful to them for all their goodness to you; that you never suffer
yourself to be angry with any body, that you give your playthings
to those who want them, that you do whatever any body desires

FROM MARY JEFFERSON

[ca. 22 May 1786?] [1]

DEAR PAPA

I long to see you, and hope that you and sister Patsy are well; give my love to her and tell her that I long to see her, and hope that you and she will come very soon to see us. I hope you will send me a doll. I am very sorry that you have sent for me. I don't want to go to France, I had rather stay with Aunt Eppes. Aunt Carr, Aunt Nancy [2] and Cousin Polly Carr [3] are here. Your most happy and dutiful daughter,   POLLY JEFFERSON

1. Date from *Papers*, IX, 560–61.
2. Anna Scott Jefferson Marks (Mrs. Hastings) was TJ's youngest sister and the twin of Randolph, his only brother. She was known in the family as Nancy. Malone, *Jefferson the Virginian*, [426]–31.
3. Mary or Polly Carr was TJ's niece and daughter of Martha Jefferson Carr.

TO MARTHA JEFFERSON

[Nov. 1786]

I will call for you today, my dear between twelve and one. You must be dressed, because we drink tea with Mrs. Montgomery.[1] Bring your music and drawings. Adieu my dear Patsy.

1. Mrs. Dorcas Montgomery was a Philadelphian who went to France in 1780/1. See *Papers*, X, 282–83.

TO MARTHA JEFFERSON

Saturday Nov. 4. [1786]

MY DEAR PATSY

Two of your country-women, Mrs. Barrett [1] and Mrs. Montgomery, will dine with me tomorrow. I wish you could come and dine with them. If you can obtain leave let me know in the morning and I will come for you between one and two o'clock. You must come dressed. Adieu my dear Patsy your's affectionately,

TH: J.

1. Mrs. Nathaniel Barrett was the wife of a commercial agent representing a group of Boston merchants in France. Lester J. Cappon, *The Adams-Jefferson Letters* (Chapel Hill, 1959), I, 73.

he charged TJ 144 livres. See Account Book 1789, May 2, and Arthur Loesser, *Men, Women and Pianos* (New York, 1954), 317.

5. Titus Livius, *History of the Roman People*. This is possibly the Jacopo Nardi translation of 1562. See E. Millicent Sowerby, *Catalogue of the Library of Thomas Jefferson* (Washington, 1952–1959), Number 53; hereafter cited as Sowerby. The Sowerby editions are not always those mentioned in these letters.

6. Madame de Béthisy de Mézières was abbess from 1743 until 1790. It is presumed Martha sat at her table.

7. Reference is to the speech of Louis XVI to the Assembly of Notables wherein he expressed an inclination to consult with them on affairs of the kingdom.

8. Arthur Richard de Dillon, Bishop of Narbonne.

9. Sister Jeanne-Louise de Stendt de Taubenheim, who had taken the veil at the Abbaye Royale de Panthemont in 1750, was the Maîtresse des Pensionnaires, or Mistress of Boarding Pupils, when the Jefferson girls were at the convent. She was of Saxon origin. Although her name is variously spelled by the correspondents here, the correct spelling is Taubenheim. Information through the courtesy of Howard C. Rice, Jr., of the Princeton University Library, a scholar well versed in the history of this school.

From Martha Jefferson

March 25th, 1787.

My dear Papa

Though the knowledge of your health gave me the greatest pleasure, yet I own I was not a little disappointed in not receiving a letter from you. However, I console myself with the thought of having one very soon, as you promised to write to me every week. Until now you have not kept your word the least in the world, but I hope you will make up for your silence by writing me a fine, long letter by the first opportunity. *Titus Livius* puts me out of my wits. I can not read a word by myself, and I read of it very seldom with my master; however, I hope I shall soon be able to take it up again. All my other masters go on much the same, perhaps better. Every body here is very well, particularly Madame L'Abbesse, who has visited almost a quarter of the new building, a thing that she has not done for two or three years before now. I have not heard any thing of my harpsichord,[1] and I am afraid it will not come before your arrival. They make every day some new history on the Assemblée des Notables. I will not tell you any, for fear of taking a trip to the Bastile for my pains, which I am by no means disposed to do at this moment. I go on pretty well with Thucydides, and hope I shall very soon finish it. I expect Mr. Short every instant for my letter, therefore I must leave you.

master for the summer, you must increase your other exercise. I
do not like your saying that you are unable to read the antient
print of your Livy, but with the aid of your master. We are always
equal to what we undertake with resolution. A little degree of
this will enable you to decypher your Livy. If you always lean
on your master, you will never be able to proceed without him.
It is a part of the American character to consider nothing as desperate; to surmount every difficulty by resolution and contrivance.
In Europe there are shops for every want. It's inhabitants therefore have no idea that their wants can be furnished otherwise.
Remote from all other aid, we are obliged to invent and to exe-
cute; to find means within ourselves, and not to lean on others.
Consider therefore the conquering your Livy as an exercise in the
habit of surmounting difficulties, a habit which will be necessary
to you in the country where you are to live, and without which
you will be thought a very helpless animal, and less esteemed.
Music, drawing, books, invention and exercise will be so many
resources to you against ennui. But there are others which to this
object add that of utility. These are the needle, and domestic
oeconomy. The latter you cannot learn here, but the former you
may. In the country life of America there are many moments when
a woman can have recourse to nothing but her needle for employment. In a dull company and in dull weather for instance.
It is ill manners to read; it is ill manners to leave them; no card-
playing there among genteel people; that is abandoned to black-
guards. The needle is then a valuable resource. Besides without
knowing to use it herself, how can the mistress of a family direct
the works of her servants? You ask me to write you long letters.
I will do it my dear, on condition you will read them from time
to time, and practice what they will inculcate. Their precepts will
be dictated by experience, by a perfect knowledge of the situation
in which you will be placed, and by the fondest love for you. This
it is which makes me wish to see you more qualified than common.
My expectations from you are high: yet not higher than you may
attain. Industry and resolution are all that are wanting. No body
in this world can make me so happy, or so miserable as you. Retirement from public life will ere long become necessary for me.
To your sister and yourself I look to render the evening of my
life serene and contented. It's morning has been clouded by loss
after loss till I have nothing left but you. I do not doubt either
your affection or dispositions. But great exertions are necessary,
and you have little time left to make them. Be industrious then,

tion to useful pursuits. I will venture to assure you that if you inculcate this in her mind you will make her a happy being in herself, a most inestimable friend to you, and precious to all the world. In teaching her these dispositions of mind, you will be more fixed in them yourself, and render yourself dear to all your acquaintance. Practice them then, my dear, without ceasing. If ever you find yourself in difficulty and doubt how to extricate yourself, do what is right, and you will find it the easiest way of getting out of the difficulty. Do it for the additional incitement of increasing the happiness of him who loves you infinitely, and who is my dear Patsy your's affectionately,

TH: JEFFERSON

FROM MARTHA JEFFERSON
Panthemont, April 9th, 1787.

MY DEAR PAPA

I am very glad that the beginning of your voyage has been so pleasing, and I hope that the rest will not be less so, as it is a great consolation for me, being deprived of the pleasure of seeing you, to know at least that you are happy. I hope your resolution of returning in the end of April is always the same. I do not doubt but what Mr. Short has written you word that my sister sets off with Fulwar Skipwith[1] in the month of May, and she will be here in July. Then, indeed, shall I be the happiest of mortals; united to what I have the dearest in the world, nothing more will be requisite to render my happiness complete. I am not so industrious as you or I would wish, but I hope that in taking pains I very soon shall be. I have already begun to study more. I have not heard any news of my harpsichord; it will be really very disagreeable if it is not here before your arrival. I am learning a very pretty thing now, but it is very hard. I have drawn several little flowers, all alone, that the master even has not seen; indeed, he advised me to draw as much alone as possible, for that is of more use than all I could do with him. I shall take up my Livy, as you desire it. I shall begin it again, as I have lost the thread of the history. As for the hysterics, you may be quiet on that head, as I am not lazy enough to fear them. Mrs. Barett has wanted me out, but Mr. Short told her that you had forgotten to tell Madame L'Abbesse to let me go out with her. There was a gentleman, a few days ago, that killed himself because he thought his wife did

continue all my masters and am able now to take only some of
them, those that are the least fatiguing.[1] However I hope soon
to take them all very soon. Mde. L'abesse has just had a fluxion
de poitrine and has been at the last extremity but now is better.
The pays bas[2] have revolted against the emperor who is gone to
Prussia to join with the empress and the venitians to war against
the turcs. The plague is in spain. A virginia ship comming to
spain met with a corser of the same strength. They fought And
the battle lasted an hour and a quarter. The Americans gained
and boarded the corser where they found chains that had been
prepared for them. They took them and made use of them for the
algerians them selves. They returned to virginia from whence
they are to go back to algers to change the prisoners to which if
the algerians will not consent the poor creatures will be sold as
slaves. Good god have we not enough? I wish with all my soul
that the poor negroes were all freed. It grieves my heart when I
think that these our fellow creatures should be treated so teribly
as they are by many of our country men. A coach and six well
shut up was seen to go to the bastille and the baron de Breteuil[3]
went two hours before to prepare an apartment. They supose it
to be Mde. De Polignac[4] and her sister, however no one knows.
The king asked Mr. D'harcourt how much a year was necessary
for the Dauphin.[5] M. D'harcourt [aft]er having looked over the
accounts told [him] two millions upon which the king could [not]
help expressing his astonishement because each of his daughters
cost him nine, so Mde. de Polignac has pocketed the rest. Mr.
Smith[6] is at Paris. That is all the news I know. They told me a
great deal more but I have forgot it. Adieu my dear papa believe
me to be for life your most tender and affectionate child,

M. JEFFERSON

1. Since Martha was well on April 9, she must have become ill between
then and May 3. William Short wrote TJ on May 8 (*Papers*, XI, 357) that she
had been only "indisposed" but recovered; on the 14th he reported her perfectly recovered (*Papers*, XI, 362). An article by D. P. Thompson, "A Talk
with Jefferson," *Harper's New Monthly Magazine*, XXVI, 833–35, suggests "a
typhus fever" as her ailment, but this is unsupported by any evidence. The
physician is believed to have been Dr. Richard Gem, an eminent Parisian
practitioner.

2. The Low Countries, that is, the Netherlands.

3. Louis-Charles-Auguste Le Tonnelier, Baron de Breteuil, a minister in the
King's household.

4. Governess of the children of the royal household and close friend of
Marie Antoinette.

5. Eldest son of the King of France. M. d'Harcourt was his tutor.

6. William Stephens Smith.

To Martha Jefferson

May 21. 1787.

I write to you, my dear Patsy, from the Canal of Languedoc, on which I am at present sailing, as I have been for a week past, cloudless skies above, limpid waters below, and find on each hand a row of nightingales in full chorus. This delightful bird had given me a rich treat before at the fountain of Vaucluse. After visiting the tomb of Laura at Avignon, I went to see this fountain, a noble one of itself, and rendered for ever famous by the songs of Petrarch who lived near it. I arrived there somewhat fatigued, and sat down by the fountain to repose myself. It gushes, of the size of a river, from a secluded valley of the mountain, the ruins of Petrarch's chateau being perched on a rock 200 feet perpendicular above. To add to the enchantment of the scene, every tree and bush was filled with nightingales in full song. I think you told me you had not yet noticed this bird. As you have trees in the garden of the convent, there must be nightingales in them, and this is the season of their song. Endeavor my dear, to make yourself acquainted with the music of this bird, that when you return to your own country you may be able to estimate it's merit in comparison with that of the mocking bird. The latter has the advantage of singing thro' a great part of the year, whereas the nightingale sings but about 5. or 6 weeks in the spring, and a still shorter term and with a more feeble voice in the fall. I expect to be at Paris about the middle of next month. By that time we may begin to expect our dear Polly. It will be a circumstance of inexpressible comfort to me to have you both with me once more. The object most interesting to me for the residue of my life, will be to see you both developing daily those principles of virtue and goodness which will make you valuable to others and happy in yourselves, and acquiring those talents and that degree of science which will guard you at all times against ennui, the most dangerous poison of life. A mind always employed is always happy. This is the true secret, the grand recipe for felicity. The idle are the only wretched. In a world which furnishes so many emploiments which are useful, and so many which are amusing, it is our own fault if we ever know what ennui is, or if we are ever driven to the miserable resource of gaming, which corrupts our dispositions, and teaches us a habit of hostility against all mankind. We are now entering the port of Toulouse, where I quit my bark; and of course must conclude my letter. Be good and be industri-

received letters from America as late as March assuring me that your sister shall be sent this summer. At that time however they did not know certainly by what occasion she could come. There was a hope of getting her under care of the French Consul and his lady, who thought of coming to France. The moment and place of her arrival therefore are still incertain. I forgot in my last letter to desire you to learn all your old tunes over again perfectly, that I may hear them on your harpsichord on it's arrival. I have no news of it however since I left Paris, tho' presume it will arrive immediately as I had ordered. Learn some slow movements of simple melody, for the Celestini stop,[1] as it suits such only. I am just setting out for Lorient, and shall have the happiness of seeing you at Paris about the 12th. or 15th. of this month, and of assuring you in person of the sincere love of Your's affectionately,   TH: JEFFERSON

1. A mechanism that produces different levels of tonal quality and is operated by a set of knobs on the front board of the harpsichord. See Loesser, *Men, Women and Pianos,* 13–14, and for the operation of this particular stop, see Adam Walker to TJ, August 20, 1787, *Papers,* XII, 47–49.

TO MARTHA JEFFERSON

Paris June 14. 1787.

I send you, my dear Patsy, the 15 livres you desired.[1] You propose this to me as an anticipation of five weeks allowance. But do you not see my dear how imprudent it is to lay out in one moment what should accomodate you for five weeks? That this is a departure from that rule which I wish to see you governed by, thro' your whole life, of never buying any thing which you have not money in your pocket to pay for? Be assured that it gives much more pain to the mind to be in debt, than to do without any article whatever which we may seem to want. The purchase you have made is one of those I am always ready to make for you, because it is my wish to see you dressed always cleanly and a little more than decently. But apply to me first for the money before you make a purchase, were it only to avoid breaking thro' your rule. Learn yourself the habit of adhering vigorously to the rules you lay down for yourself. I will come for you about eleven o'clock on Saturday. Hurry the making your gown, and also your reding-

come down to the carriage see exactly what oclock it is by the Convent clock that we may not be deceived as to the time. Adieu. Yours' affectionately,   TH: J.
Kisses to Polly. She will keep your supper for you till you return tomorrow night.

1. Second wife of Dominique-Louis Ethis de Corny, a *Commissaire des guerres* for the French army in America. On his return to France he married Marguerite Victoire de Palerne, a widow. The De Cornys became acquainted with Jefferson during his stay in France, and Madame de Corny corresponded with him for many years after his return to America.

According to the *Journal de Paris*, Martha attended *La Toison d'Or*, also known as *Médée à Colchis* (Medea in Colchis), which was performed in the Académie Royale de Musique.

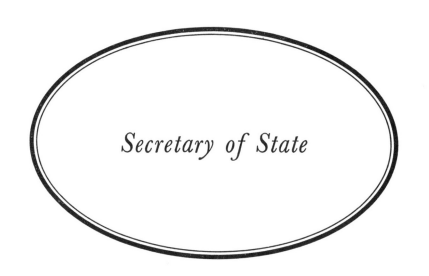

Secretary of State

MARRIAGE SETTLEMENT FOR MARTHA JEFFERSON

This indenture made on the 21st. day of Feb. in the year of our lord 1790. between Thos. Jefferson of the 1st. part, Martha Jefferson daughter of the said Thos. of the 2d. part Thos. Mann Randolph the elder of the 3d. part and Thos. Mann Randolph the younger, son of the said T. M. R. the elder of the 4th. part witnesseth that forasmuch as a marriage is shortly to be had between the said Thos. M. R. the younger and the said M. J. and the said T. M. R. the elder hath undertaken to convey in feesimple to the said T. M. the younger and did convey by deed indentured bearing date the 15th. day of this present month for his advancement a certain tract of land in the county of Henrico called Varina and containing 950. acres with 40. negroes then on and belonging to the same tract and the stocks and utensils thereto also belonging, now the said T. J. in consideration of the said undertaking and conveyance of the said T. M. the elder and also of the marriage so proposed to be had and of the natural love and affection which he the said Thos. bears to his daughter Martha, and for her advancement in life, and for the further sum of 5/ to him in hand paid by the said M. and another like sum of 5/ to him in hand paid by the said T. M. the elder, and yet another like sum of 5/ to him in hand paid by the said T. M. the younger, hath given granted bargained sold and appointed unto the said Martha and her heirs, and by these presents doth give grant bargain sell and according to powers in him legally vested doth appoint unto the said M. and her heirs a parcel of land in the county of Bedford containing 1000. as. be the same more or less, part of the tract of land called the Poplar Forest and at the Westernmost end thereof to be laid off and separated from the residue of the said tract by a line to begin at a red oak sapling expressed in the patent to be at the intersection of the two lines No. 21. W. 145. poles and N. 53½ E. 40. po. and to run thence across the said tract directly to the line expressed in the said patent to bear S. 60. E. 420. po. and to the point thereof which shall be 230. po. from a white oak expressed in the same patent to be at the Westernmost end of the

lately turned methodist, the former was married the evening I was there to a Mr. Turnbull[2] of Petersburg in Virginia. Of course you will see her there. I find it difficult to procure a tolerable house here. It seems it is a practice to let all the houses the 1st. of February, and to enter into them the 1st of May. Of course I was too late to engage one, at least in the Broadway, where all my business lies. I have taken an indifferent one nearly opposite Mrs. Elsworth's[3] which may give me time to look about me and provide a better before the arrival of my furniture. I am anxious to hear from you, of your health, your occupations, where you are etc. Do not neglect your music. It will be a companion which will sweeten many hours of life to you. I assure you mine here is triste enough. Having had yourself and dear Poll to live with me so long, to exercise my affections and chear me in the intervals of business, I feel heavily these separations from you. It is a circumstance of consolation to know that you are happier; and to see a prospect of it's continuance in the prudence and even temper both of Mr. Randolph and yourself. Your new condition will call for abundance of little sacrifices but they will be greatly overpaid by the measure of affection they will secure to you. The happiness of your life depends now on the continuing to please a single person. To this all other objects must be secondary; even your love to me, were it possible that that could ever be an obstacle. But this it can never be. Neither of you can ever have a more faithful friend than my self, nor one on whom you can count for more sacrifices. My own is become a secondary object to the happiness of you both. Cherish then for me, my dear child, the affection of your husband, and continue to love me as you have done, and to render my life a blessing by the prospect it may hold up to me of seeing you happy. Kiss Maria for me if she is with you, and present me cordially to Mr. Randolph: assuring yourself of the constant and unchangeable love of your's affectionately,

TH: JEFFERSON

1. Rachel Buchanan was a Philadelphia schoolmistress who resided on Cedar Street between Fifth and Sixth streets. James Hardee, *The Philadelphia Directory and Register* (Philadelphia, 1793).

2. The marriage was between Sarah Buchanan of Baltimore and Robert Turnbull of Prince George County, Virginia, and took place in March, 1791. Sarah being unable to consummate the marriage, Turnbull later sued for divorce. Reported in William Waller Hening, *The Statutes at Large; Being a Collection of All the Laws of Virginia* (Richmond, 1823), XIII, 301-2.

3. The house was located at 57 Maiden Lane. Mrs. Oliver Ellsworth was the wife of Chief Justice Oliver Ellsworth. Malone, *Jefferson and the Rights of Man*, 257.

please him in every *thing* and do consider all other objects as secondary to that *except* my love for you. I do not know where we are to spend the summer. Mr. Randolph has some thoughts of settling at Varina[3] for a little while till he can buy a part of Edgehill. I am much averse to it my self but shall certainly comply if he thinks it necessary. My health is perfectly good as also dear Polly's. I have recieved a letter from Mrs. Curson[4] who informs me that the Duke of Dorset and Lady Caroline[5] are both going to be married, the former to a Miss Cope.[6] Adieu My Dear Pappa. I am with the tenderest affection yours,

M RANDOLPH

1. Mary Randolph Fleming (Mrs. Tarlton) was Thomas Mann Randolph, Jr.'s aunt. Fleming owned land on both sides of the James River, his home Rockcastle being in Powhatan County opposite the present-day Rockcastle, Goochland County, site of the St. Emma Military School.

2. Possibly the Miss Holliday of TJ to Martha Jefferson Randolph, April 4, 1790.

3. A Randolph estate of 950 acres in Henrico County. Martha and Thomas Mann Randolph, Jr., resided there briefly in 1790.

4. Mrs. B. Carson; possibly the married name of a former classmate.

5. Lady Caroline Tufton was a particular friend of Martha's at school in Paris.

6. Arabella Diana Cope, daughter of Sir Charles Cope, married John Frederick Sackville, the third Duke of Dorset, British Ambassador-Extraordinary and Plenipotentiary to the Court of France from December 26, 1783, until August 8, 1790.

FROM MARY JEFFERSON

Richmond, April 25th. 1790.

MY DEAR PAPA

I am afraid you will be displeased in knowing where I am, but I hope you will not, as Mr. Randolph certainly had some good reason, though I do not know it. I have not been able to read in Don Quixote every day, as I have been traveling ever since I saw you last, and the dictionary is too large to go in the pocket of the chariot, nor have I yet had an opportunity of continuing my music. I am now reading Robertson's America.[1] I thank you for the advice you were so good as to give me, and will try to follow it. Adieu, my dear papa, I am your affectionate daughter,

MARY JEFFERSON

1. Probably Book I of William Robertson's *History of America*. The first edition was printed in London in 1777. This work, in all editions, contained a brief history of Virginia to 1652. Sowerby 468, 469.

his wife's adulterer "with the same shot" that wounded her. TJ to Thomas
Mann Randolph, Jr., April 18, 1790. *Papers*, XVI, 351.

3. *The Gazette of the United States*, a Federalist paper, edited by John
Fenno.

4. A very desirable tract of about 1,152½ acres in Albemarle County, on
the north side of the Rivanna River and adjacent to the Southwest Mountains,
a few miles east of Monticello. It had come into the Randolph family as part
of a grant of 2,400 acres to William Randolph, Thomas Mann Randolph,
Jr.'s grandfather. (The remainder of the tract was sold to John Harvie, Jr., on
January 1, 1792.) William Randolph devised this tract to his only son Thomas
Mann Randolph, Sr., by will probated March 18, 1745. Thomas Mann, Sr., then
by deed dated April 12, 1793, conveyed it with a general warranty to his son
in consideration of 2,000£. This deed, although executed in the presence of
three witnesses, was never proven by them and consequently was not entered
on the county records until August 10, 1822. For a complete record of these
proceedings, see "Abstract of Title to the Shadwell Properties," "Abstract
#II," drawn by Mr. Venable Minor, a distinguished member of the Albe-
marle bar. Copies may be seen in the Manuscripts Division at the Alderman
Library and at Monticello.

TJ was very anxious to have Martha and Thomas Mann settle in Albemarle
and so wrote to his son-in-law: "It . . . is essential to my happiness, our
living near together." (March 4, 1792. ViU.) He did not relinquish his efforts
until this wish had been realized. See also TJ to Thomas Mann Randolph, Jr.,
May 30, 1790. *Papers*, XVI, 449.

5. The Wayles debt was inherited through his wife, Martha Wayles Skelton.
For a comprehensive explanation, see *Papers*, XV, 642 ff., and Malone, *Jefferson the Virginian*, 441–46.

To Mary Jefferson

New York May 2. 1790.

My dear Maria

I wrote to you three weeks ago, and have not yet received an
answer. I hope however that one is on the way and that I shall
receive it by the first post. I think it very long to have been absent
from Virginia two months and not to have received a line either
from yourself, your sister or Mr. Randolph, and I am very uneasy
at it. As I write once a week to one of the other of you in turn,
if you would answer my letter the day or day after you receive it,
it would always come to my hands before I write the next to you.
We had two days of snow about the beginning of last week. Let me
know if it snowed where you are. I send you some prints of a new
kind for your amusement. I send several to enable you to be
generous to your friends. I want much to hear how you employ
yourself. Present my best affections to your uncle, aunt and cousins,
if you are with them, or Mr. Randolph and your sister, if with
them: be assured of my tender love to you, and continue yours to
your affectionate,   Th: Jefferson

and read in robertson's america. After I am done that I work till dinner and a little more after. It did not snow at all last month. My cousin Boling and myself made a pudding the other day. My aunt has given us a hen and chickens. Adieu my Dear papa. Believe me to be your ever dutiful and affetionate daughter,

MARIA JEFFERSON

1. David Meade Randolph was a cousin of TJ's who resided at Presqu'ile, in Chesterfield County.
2. John Bolling was married to TJ's sister Mary Jefferson, who was known in the family as Aunt Bolling. They resided at Chestnut Grove, also in Chesterfield County. For the Bolling family genealogy, see Robert A. Brock and Wyndham Robertson, *Pochontas, alias Matoaka, and Descendants* (Richmond, 1887).

To MARY JEFFERSON

New York May 23. 1790.

MY DEAR MARIA

I was glad to receive your letter of April 25. because I had been near two months without hearing from any of you. I hope you will now always write immediately on receiving a letter from me. Your last told me what you were not doing: that you were not reading Don Quixot, not applying to your music. I hope your next will tell me what you are doing. Tell your Uncle that the President after having been so ill as at one time to be thought dying, is now quite recovered. I have been these three weeks confined by a periodical headach. It has been the most moderate I ever had: but it has not yet left me. Present my best affections to your Uncle and aunt. Tell the latter I shall never have thanks enough for her kindness to you, and that you will repay her in love and duty. Adieu my dear Maria. Your's affectionately,

TH: JEFFERSON

To MARTHA JEFFERSON RANDOLPH

New York June 6. 1790.

MY DEAR DAUGHTER

Your favor of May 28. from Eppington came to me yesterday, with the welcome which accompanies ever the tidings I recieve from you. Your resolution to go to housekeeping is a good one, tho' I think it had better be postponed till the fall. You are not

and whip-poor-wills in Virginia? Take notice hereafter whether the whip-poor-wills always come with the strawberries and peas. Send me a copy of the maxims I gave you, also a list of the books I promised you. I have had a long touch of my periodical headach, but a very moderate one. It has not quite left me yet. Adieu, my dear, love your uncle, aunt and cousins, and me more than all. Your's affectionately,   TH: JEFFERSON

TO MARTHA JEFFERSON RANDOLPH

New York June 27. 1790.

MY DEAR MARTHA

My last news from you were conveyed in your letter of May 28. I ascribe this to your present ambulatory life. I hope when you are more in the way of the post, I shall receive letters regularly once a week from one or the other of you, as I write regularly once a week myself. In my letter of the last week to Mr. Randolph I mentioned the appearances of a war between England and Spain. We have nothing newer on that subject. There is a report indeed that there are three British frigates off our cost; but I know not on what it is founded. I think it probable that Congress will pass a bill for removing to Philadelphia for ten years, and then to Georgetown. The question will be brought on tomorrow and it's fate be determined probably in the course of the ensuing week. I shall not be able to decide the time of my coming to Virginia till Congress shall have adjourned. The moment I can fix it I will inform you of it. I inclosed you the last week a letter from some of your English acquaintance. I now inclose you an engraving of the President done by Wright [1] who drew the picture of him which I have at Paris. My tender affections attend you all. Adieu, my dear. Your's affectionately,   TH: JEFFERSON

1. Joseph Wright, the American portraitist, who worked in Philadelphia and New York City. TJ, in his draft copy of his "Catalogue of Paintings &c. at Monticello" (ViU), made this very interesting notation: "When Genl. Washington attended the meeting of the Cincinnati in Philadelphia May. 1784. then passing through that city on my way from Annapolis to Boston to embark for Europe I could only allow Wright time to finish the head and face, and sketch the outlines of the body. These and the drapery were afterwards finished at Paris by Trumbull." From a manuscript owned by Mrs. Page Kirk of Charlottesville, Virginia, now on loan to the University of Virginia.

The portrait is now in the Massachusetts Historical Society and is reproduced in *Papers*, VII, facing page 133, with a descriptive note on page xxvii.

cult in her dispositions, avoid what is rough, and attach her good qualities to you. Consider what are otherwise as a bad stop in your harpsichord. Do not touch on it, but make yourself happy with the good ones. Every human being, my dear, must thus be viewed according to what it is good for, for none of us, no not one, is perfect; and were we to love none who had imperfections, this world would be a desart for our love. All we can do is to make the best of our friends: love and cherish what is good in them, and keep out of the way of what is bad: but no more think of rejecting them for it than of throwing away a piece of music for a flat passage or two. Your situation will require peculiar attentions and respects to both parties. Let no proof be too much for either your patience or acquiescence. Be you my dear, the link of love, union, and peace for the whole family. The world will give you the more credit for it, in proportion to the difficulty of the task. And your own happiness will be the greater as you percieve that you promote that of others. Former acquaintance, and equality of age, will render it the easier for you to cultivate and gain the love of the lady. The mother too becomes a very necessary object of attentions. This marriage renders it doubtful with me whether it will be better to direct our overtures to Colo. R. or Mr. H. for a farm for Mr. Randolph. Mr. H. has a good tract of land on the other side Edgehill, and it may not be unadvisable to begin by buying out a dangerous neighbor. I wish Mr. Randolph could have him sounded to see if he will sell, and at what price; but sounded thro' such a channel as would excite no suspicion that it comes from Mr. Randolph or myself. Colo. Monroe would be a good and unsuspected hand as he once thought of buying the same lands. Adieu my dear child. Present my warm attachment to Mr. Randolph. Your's affectionately,   TH: JEFFERSON

1. Thomas Mann Randolph, Sr., married Gabriella Harvie, the daughter of John Harvie of Richmond. She was less than half his age. See Malone, *Jefferson the Virginian*, 428, and *Jefferson and the Rights of Man*, 320.

FROM MARY JEFFERSON

Eppington july 20, [1790]

DEAR PAPA

I hope you will excuse my not writing to you before tho I have none for myself. I am very sorry to hear that you have been sick but flatter myself that it is over. My aunt skipwith has been very

To Martha Jefferson Randolph

New York Aug. 8. 1790.

Congress being certainly to rise the day after tomorrow, I can now, my dear Patsy, be more certain of the time at which I can be at Monticello, and which I think will be from the 8th. to the 15th. of September: more likely to be sooner than later. I shall leave this about a fortnight hence, but must stay some days to have arrangements taken for my future residence in Philadelphia. I hope to be able to pass a month at least with you at Monticello. I am in hopes Mr. Randolph will take dear Poll in his pocket. Tell him I have sent him the model of the mould-board[1] by Mr. David Randolph who left this place yesterday. I must trouble you to give notice to Martin[2] to be at Monticello by the 1st. of September that he may have things prepared. If you know any thing of Bob,[3] I should be glad of the same notice to him, tho' I suppose him to be in the neighborhood of Fredericksbg, and in that case I will have him notified thro' Mr. Fitzhugh. I have written to Mr. Brown[4] for some necessaries to be sent to Monticello, and to send on some chairs which will go hence to the care of Mr. D. Randolph at the Hundred,[5] to be forwarded to Mr. Brown at Richmond. If Mr. Randolph can give a little attention to the forwarding these articles we shall be the more comfortable. Present me to him and Maria affectionately, and continue to love me as I do you, my dear, most sincerely,   Th: Jefferson

1. The exact date TJ fashioned his first mouldboard for a plough is not established. In the *Farm Book*, 47–49, Betts states it was not until after his return from Paris in 1789 that the idea was discussed with Thomas Mann Randolph, Jr. The model herein mentioned was completed sometime between that date and August, 1790, and sent on to his son-in-law. In recognition of his work on the mouldboard, TJ in 1810 was made a foreign associate of the French Society of Agriculture.

2. It was a practice when speaking of slaves, as Martin, to use their first names, which in most instances was the only one they had, several exceptions being the Hemingses and Joe Fosset. A white servant or employee was generally addressed as "Mr." or simply by his last name.

3. Robert Hemings (usually the "Bob" of these letters) was a member of the able slave family at Monticello who were extended many liberties and opportunities not available to others in bondage. Betty Hemings, a light-colored Negress, had twelve children, one of whom was Bob Hemings, by several individuals, at least one of whom was white. The name Hemings is believed to have come from an English sea captain, her father. The family came to Monticello as a part of Martha Jefferson's patrimony from her father John Wayles. For additional information on this family as well as on slaves in general at Monticello and other Jefferson farms, see the *Farm Book; Memoirs of a Monticello Slave;* Hamilton W. Pierson, *Jefferson at Monticello, The Private Life of Thomas Jefferson* (New York, 1862), this being chiefly the reminiscences of Edmund Bacon, the overseer at Monticello for twenty years

When we were in Cumberland[1] we went to Church and heard some singing Masters that sang very well. They are to come here to learn my cousins to sing and as I know you have no objections to my learning any thing I am to be a scholar and hope to give you the pleasure of hearing an anthem. We had pease the 14 of may and strawberries the 17 of the same month tho not in that abundance we are accustomed to in consequence of a frost this spring. As for the martins swallows and whippoorwills I was so taken up with my chickens that I never attended to them and therefore cannot tell you when they came tho I was so unfortunate as to lose half of them for my cousin Bolling and myself have raised but 13 between us. Adieu my Dear Papa.

Believe me to be your affectionate daughter,

MARY JEFFERSON

1. Mary was at Hors du Monde.

To Martha Jefferson Randolph

Philadelphia Dec. 1. 1790.

MY DEAR DAUGHTER

In my letter of last week to Mr. Randolph I mentioned that I should write every Wednesday to him, yourself and Polly alternately, and that my letters arriving at Monticello the Saturday and the answer being sent off on Sunday I should receive it the day before I should have to write again to the same person, so as that the correspondence with each would be exactly kept up. I hope you will do it on your part. I delivered the fan and note to your friend Mrs. Waters (Miss Rittenhouse that was)[1] she being now married to a Doctr. Waters. They live in the house with her father. She complained of the petit format of your letter, and Mrs. Trist of no letter. I inclose you the Magasin des Modes of July. My furniture is arrived from Paris: but it will be long before I can open the packages,[2] as my house will not be ready to recieve them for some weeks. As soon as they are the mattrasses &c. shall be sent on. News for Mr. Randolph. The letters from Paris inform that as yet all is safe there. They are emitting great sums of paper money. They rather believe there will be no war between Spain and England: but the letters from London count on a war, and it seems rather probable. A general peace is established in the North of Europe, except between Russia and Turkey. It is expected between them also. Wheat here is a French crown the

To Martha Jefferson Randolph

Philadelphia Dec. 23. 1790.

My dear daughter

This is a scolding letter for you all. I have not recieved a scrip of a pen from home since I left it which is now eleven weeks. I think it so easy for you to write me one letter every week, which will be but once in three weeks for each of you, when I write one every week who have not one moment's repose from business from the first to the last moment of the week. Perhaps you think you have nothing to say to me. It is a great deal to say you are all well, or that one has a cold, another a fever &c., besides that there is not a sprig of grass that shoots uninteresting to me, nor any thing that moves, from yourself down to Bergere or Grizzle.[1] Write then my dear daughter punctually on your day, and Mr. Randolph and Polly on theirs. I suspect you may have news to tell me of yourself of the most tender interest to me. Why silent then?

I am still without a house, and consequently without a place to open my furniture. This has prevented my sending you what I was to send for Monticello. In the mean time the river is frozen up so as that no vessel can get out, nor probably will these two months: so that you will be much longer without them than I had hoped. I know how inconvenient this will be and am distressed at it; but there is no help. I send a pamphlet for Mr. Randolph. My best affections to him, Polly and yourself. Adieu my dear,

Th: Jefferson

1. TJ's highly prized sheep dogs. Bergere was purchased in Le Havre October 7, 1789. The Account Book reads: "Pd. for a chienne bergere big with pup. 36ᴴ." For information regarding the actual purchase of this dog, see *Papers*, XV, 509n., and for a report on the dog population at Monticello several years later, consult Martha Jefferson Randolph to TJ, May 27, 1792.

To Mary Jefferson

Philadelphia Jan. 5. 1790 [1791][1]

I did not write to you, my dear Poll, the last week, because I was really angry at recieving no letter. I have now been near nine weeks from home, and have never had a scrip of a pen, when by the regularity of the post, I might recieve your letters as frequently and as exactly as if I were at Charlottesville. I ascribed it at first to indolence, but the affection must be weak which is so long overruled by that. Adieu.

Th: J.

1. Incorrectly dated 1790.

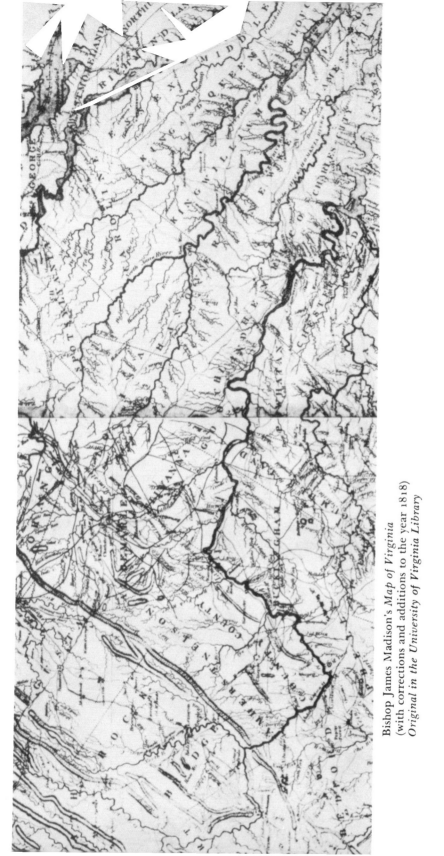

Bishop James Madison's *Map of Virginia*
(with corrections and additions to the year 1818)
Original in the University of Virginia Library

Thomas Jefferson. An engraving by St. Mémin after his life portrait done in 1804. This was a family favorite, especially with his daughters Martha and Mary. *Princeton University Library*

Martha Jefferson Carr. Wife of Dabney Carr and Jefferson's sister. In the family she was known as "Aunt Carr." *Thomas Jefferson Memorial Foundation*

Martha Jefferson Randolph. As a young lady of fifteen, when she was in France with her father. *Thomas Jefferson Memorial Foundation*

Francis Wayles Eppes. Grandson of Francis Eppes of Eppington and the only child of Mary Jefferson and John Wayles Eppes to survive infancy. Artist not known. *Thomas Jefferson Memorial Foundation*

into all these details because however trifling they would appear
to others, to you my Dear Papa I think they will be interesting.
I received a kind invitation from Aunt Eppes to spend the month
of February at Eppinton but Mrs. Fleming's being here at that
time will render it useless. The morning of the 13th. at 10 minutes past four we had an earth quake [2] which was severe enough
to awaken us all in the house and several of the servants in the
out houses. It was followed by a second shock very slight and an
aurora borealis. I am extremely obliged to you for the cypress
vine which with a bundle of seeds I found in rumaging up some
drawer in the chamber, written on the back cupressus Patula
and some others I intend to decorate my windows this spring.
You promised me a colection of garden seeds for a young Lady in
the west indies (*Bruni*)[3] for whom also I will send you a letter
to be forwarded to her with them. Adieu My Dearest Father. Mr.
Randolph and Polly join in love. Believe me ever your affectionate child,   M RANDOLPH

1. Mrs. Nicholas Lewis was the wife of Nicholas Lewis of The Farm, Albemarle County, under whose care Monticello came while TJ was in France.
2. This was not the first recorded earthquake at Monticello. TJ had noted
shocks on Februry 21 and 22, 1774. Account Book 1774.
3. Mme. Brunette de Châteaubrun, called "Bruni" or "Bruny," was a
schoolmate and close friend of Martha's.

To MARTHA JEFFERSON RANDOLPH

Philadelphia Jan. 20. 1791.

MY DEAR DAUGHTER

Mr. Short in a late letter says that your acquaintances in Panthemont complain excessively of your inattention to them and desired him to mention it. Matters there are going on well. The
sales of the church lands are successful beyond all calculation.
There has been a riot in Paris in which M. de Castrie's [1]
househould furniture was destroyed. I am opening my things from
Paris as fast as the workmen will make room for me. In a box
lately opened I find a copy of the octavo edition of the Encyclopedie, and a complete copy of Buffon's [2] works with Daubenton's
part which I had written for to present to Mr. Randolph. But I do
not know when I shall be able to send any thing forward, from
the slowness of workmen in making houseroom for me to open
my things and from the ice in the river. The cold of this place
has made me wish for some stockings of cotton and hair's fur

TO MARTHA JEFFERSON RANDOLPH

Philadelphia Feb. 2. 1791.

MY DEAR MARTHA

I have this moment recieved your's of January 16. and answer it by the first post. It is indeed and interesting letter to me as it gives me the details which I am sure will contribute to your happiness, my first wish. Nothing is so engaging as the little domestic cares into which you appear to be entering, and as to reading it is useful for only filling up the chinks of more useful and healthy occupations. I am sincerely sorry that the mattresses cannot yet be forwarded. But the state of the river here forbids it, and while it is incertain whether it will be found open or shut no vessels come here from Virginia. They shall go by the first possible opportunity. Whenever your letter to Bruny comes I will reccompany it with the seeds: but you must inform me at the sametime what kind of seeds to send her. Congress will certainly rise the 1st. of March, when you will again have Colo. Munroe[1] and Mrs. Monroe in your neighborhood. I write to you out of turn, and believe I must adopt the rule of only writing when I am written to, in hopes that may provoke more frequent letters. Mr. Randolph's letter of Dec. 27. and yours now acknowledged are all I have recieved from Monticello since I left it. Give my best affections to him and Poll, and be assured my dear daughter of the sincere love of your's affectionately,   TH: JEFFERSON

1. James Monroe.

TO MARTHA JEFFERSON RANDOLPH

Philadelphia Feb. 9. 1791.

MY DEAR MARTHA

Your two last letters are those which have given me the greatest pleasure of any I ever recieved from you. The one announced that you were become a notable housewife, the other a mother.[1] This last is undoubtedly the key-stone of the arch of matrimonial happiness, as the first is it's daily ailment. Accept my sincere congratulations for yourself and Mr. Randolph. I hope you are getting well, towards which great care of yourself is necessary: for however adviseable it is for those in health to expose themselves freely, it is not so for the sick. You will be out in time to begin your garden, and that will tempt you to be out a great deal, than which

Martha's copy is in the Alderman Library at the University of Virginia. TJ owned a 1779 edition (Sowerby 1354). This was a popular and widely read work on child care.

TO MARTHA JEFFERSON RANDOLPH

Philadelphia Mar. 2. [1791]

MY DEAR DAUGHTER

The present will serve just to tell you that I am well, and to keep up my plan of writing once a week whether I have any thing to say or not. Congress rises tomorrow. They have passed no laws remarkeable except the excise law [1] and one establishing a bank.[2] Mrs. Trist and Mrs. Waters always enquire after you and desire me to remember them to you. I hope you are by this time able to be about again and in good health as well as the little one.[3] Kiss it and Maria for me. I have recieved her letter and will answer it next week. I inclose a letter for M. de Rieux.[4] Present my esteem to Mr. Randolph. Yours affectionately,

TH: JEFFERSON

1. This law provided for the assessment and collection of internal revenue duties on distilled liquors and also additional duties on imported spirits.
2. The first Bank of the United States was chartered in 1791 for twenty years, with the parent bank in Philadelphia. Branches were established in principal seaports.
3. The reference is to Martha's daughter. The parents wanted TJ to name her, but as of this date, if their request had reached him, his reply had not been received.
4. The wife of Justin Pierre Plumard Derieux, a son-in-law of Philip Mazzei who resided at Colle, Mazzei's home in Albemarle County near Monticello.

FROM MARY JEFFERSON

march 6 [1791]

According to my dear Papa's request I now sit down to write. We were very uneasy for not having had a letter from you since six weeks till yesterday I received yours which I now answer. The marble Pedestal [1] and a dressing table are come. Jenny is gone down with Mrs. Fleming who came here to see sister while she was sick. I suppose you have not received the letter in which Mr. Randolph desires you to name the child. We hope you will come to see us this summer therefore you must not disapoint us and I expect you want to see my little neice as much as you do any of

in one month that it has taken [me almost] another to get the better of it. I have at last seriously [begun] writing to my European friends tho I fear it will be a difficult matter to forward my letters to you as the post has ceased to go. Doctor Gilmer's[1] eldest son is arrived from Scotland in a very deep consumption. His father and mother are gone down to Shirley[2] in all probability to take their last farewell of him if he is still alive which they almost dispaired of when they set off. A cousin of ours Randolph Lewis is lately married to Miss Lewis of the *bird* the bridegroom was 18 and she 15.[3] Young Mr. Monroe [and] a Miss Elizabeth Kerr daughter of old Jimmy Kerr have followed their example.[4] Polly and My self have planted the cypress vine in boxes in the window as also date seed and some other flowers. I hope you have not forgot the colection of garden seed you promised me for Bruni. I am under some obligation to her for several things which she has sent me and for which tho not yet come to hand I am not the less grateful. Flower seeds and fruit stones would no doubt be also very acceptable tho grain de jardinage was the expression she made use of. I will send you a letter to go with the seeds or be burnt if you can not get them. I should be extremely obliged to you My Dearest Papa for a green silk calash lined with green also, as a hat is by no means proper for such a climate as ours. The little girl grows astonishingly and has been uncommonly healthy. Adieu My dear Papa. I have read gregory and am happy to tell you it was precisely the plan who we had followed with her for her birth by Mrs. Lewis's advice.[5] We continue very great friends. She allways calls the child (who till you send her one will go by no other name) her grand daughter. Once more adieu My Dearest Papa. Your affectionate child,   M. RANDOLPH

1. Thomas Walker Gilmer, the eldest son of Dr. George Gilmer of Pen Park, Albemarle County, had been in Edinburgh studying medicine. He died in his twenty-second year; he is not to be confused with Governor Thomas Walker Gilmer.
2. Shirley, the Carter home in Charles City County.
3. Randolph Lewis was the son of Charles L. Lewis, Jr., and Lucy Jefferson, TJ's sister. Randolph Lewis was also a grandson of Charles L. Lewis, Sr., and Mary Randolph, a sister of Jane Randolph Jefferson, TJ's mother. His bride was Mary Lewis, a cousin, and daughter of Robert Lewis. See John Meriwether McAllister and Lura B. Tandy, editors, *Genealogies of the Lewis and Kindred Families* (Columbia, Missouri, 1906).
4. Joseph J. Monroe was the brother of James and Andrew Monroe.
5. Mrs. Nicholas Lewis.

FROM MARY JEFFERSON

march the 26 [1791]

It is three weeks my Dear Papa, since I have had a letter from you however as it is now my turn I shall not be ceremonious. We are all waiting with great impatience to know the name of the child. Mrs. Lewis was so kind as to give me a Calico habit. Adieu my Dear Papa. I am your affectionate daughter,

MARY JEFFERSON

TO MARY JEFFERSON

Philadelphia, March 31st, 1791.

MY DEAR MARIA

I am happy to have a letter of yours to answer. That of March 6th came to my hands on the 24th. By-the-by, you never acknowledged the receipt of my letters, nor tell me on what day they came to hand. I presume that by this time you have received the two dressing-tables with marble tops. I give one of them to your sister, and the other to you: mine is here with the top broken in two. Mr. Randolph's letter, referring to me the name of your niece, was very long on the road. I answered it as soon as I received it, and hope the answer got duly to hand. Lest it should have been delayed, I repeated last week to your sister the name of Anne,[1] which I had recommended as belonging to both families. I wrote you in my last that the frogs had begun their songs on the 7th; since that the blue-birds saluted us on the 17th; the weeping-willow began to leaf on the 18th; the lilac and gooseberry on the 25th; and the golden-willow on the 26th. I inclose for your sister three kinds of flowering beans, very beautiful and very rare. She must plant and nourish them with her own hand this year, in order to save enough seeds for herself and me. Tell Mr. Randolph I have sold my tobacco for five dollars per c., and the rise between this and September. Warehouse and shipping expenses in Virginia, freight and storage here, come to 2s.9d. a hundred, so that it is as if I had sold it in Richmond for 27s.3d. credit till September, or half per cent. per month discount for the ready money. If he chooses it, his Bedford tobacco may be included in the sale. Kiss every body for me. Yours affectionately,

TH: JEFFERSON

1. Anne Cary Randolph.

the piece I send you. Adieu, my dear papa. I am your affectionate
daughter,   MARIA JEFFERSON

1. Probably *The Life and Adventures of Lazarillo de Tormes* and Antonio
de Solis, *Historia de la Conquista de Mexico* . . . (Madrid, 1783–84) 2 volumes.
Sowerby 4119.

TO MARY JEFFERSON

Philadelphia Apr. 24. 1791.

I have received my dear Maria, your letter of Mar. 26. I find
I have counted too much on you as a Botanical and zoological
correspondent: for I undertook to affirm here that the fruit was
not killed in Virginia, because I had a young daughter there, who
was in that kind of correspondence with me, and who I was sure
would have mentioned it if it had been so. However I shall go on
communicating to you whatever may contribute to a comparative
estimate of the two climates, in hopes it will induce you to do the
same to me. Instead of waiting to send the two vails for your
sister and yourself round with the other things, I inclose them
with this letter. Observe that one of the strings is to be drawn
tight round the root of the crown of the hat; and the vail then
falling over the brim of the hat is drawn by the lower string as
tight or loose as you please round the neck. When the vail is not
chosen to be down, the lower string also is tied round the root of
the crown so as to give it the appearance of a puffed bandage for
the hat. I send also inclosed the green lining for the Calash. J.
Eppes[1] is arrived here. Present my affections to Mr. R. your sister
and niece.

April 5. Apricots in blossom.
          cherry leafing.
      9. Peach in blossom.
          Apple leafing.
     11. Cherry in blossom
              Your's with tender love,
                                    TH: JEFFERSON

1. John Wayles Eppes (or Jack, as TJ called him at this time) was the only
son of Elizabeth and Francis Eppes. He was in Philadelphia to further his
education, which was being done under TJ's supervision.

morrow however I will have the packages finished, and send them by any other conveyance which occurs. They will contain as follows.

6. mattrasses.

A package of James's[1] bedding from Paris. To be kept for him.

do.   Sally's   do.

The Encyclopedie.

Buffon.

Tacitus.   } for Mr. Randolph.

Journaux de physique

Magazin des modes.

Sacontalá.   } for yourself.

Calash

Anacharsis for Maria.

Herrera. 4. vols.

History of Florida. 2. vols.   } to be deposited in my library.

Acosta

A box containing 2. panes of glass for Mrs. Lewis.

Some Windsor chairs if the vessel can take them.

I am made happy by Petit's[2] determination to come to me. I had not been able to assume the name of a housekeeper for want of a real housekeeper. I did not look out for another, because I still hoped he would come. In fact he retired to Champaigne to live with his mother, and after a short time wrote to Mr. Short 'qu'il mouroit d'ennui.' and was willing to come. I shall acknowlege the receipt of Mr. Randolph's letter next week. Adieu, my dear, with affectionate esteem to you both. Your's,

TH: JEFFERSON

1. James Hemings, a slave, was taken to France for the express purpose of learning French cookery. Sally was his sister.

2. Adrien Petit was TJ's ablest and most trusted maître d'hôtel while in Paris. He came into TJ's service on May 22, 1785, and remained until after Jefferson's departure for America in 1789. He arrived in Philadelphia July 19, 1791, much to TJ's pleasure and remained until 1794, when he became homesick and returned to France. See Account Books 1785, 1791, and 1794.

TO MARY JEFFERSON

Philadelphia May 8. 1791.

MY DEAR MARIA

Your letter of Apr. 18. came to hand on the 30th. That of May 1. I recieved last night. By the stage which carries this letter I send you 12. yards of striped nankeen of the pattern inclosed. It is

the veils you sent us. I am with the tenderest love your affectionate child,   M. RANDOLPH

The largest of the beans you sent me is come up and very flourishing but none of the others have as yet made their appearance.

FROM MARY JEFFERSON

May 29 [1791]

MY DEAR PAPA

I am much obliged to you for the veil that you sent me and shall allways were it. I have began to learn botany and arithmetic with Mr. Randolph. The mare that he bought for me is come. She is very pretty and is sister to brimmer.[1] She can only trot and canter. The fruit was not killed as you thought. We have a great abundance of it here. Adieu Dear Papa. I am your affectionate daughter, MARY JEFFERSON. P.S. Little anna grows very fast an is very pretty.

1. TJ's horse, which he sold February 1, 1793, to Samuel Clarkson for $120. (Account Book 1793). This horse is not to be confused with Bremo, purchased from Gen. John Hartwell Cocke on April 20, 1814 (Account Book 1814), which Edmund Bacon, a long-time Monticello overseer, mistakenly identifies as Brimmer. See *Farm Book*, 105.

TO MARY JEFFERSON

[draft]
Lake George May 30. 91.

MY DEAR MARIA

I did not expect to write to you again till my return to Philada., but as I think always of you, so I avail myself of every moment to tell you so which a life of business will permit. Such a moment is now offered while passing this lake, and it's border, on which we have just landed, has furnished the means which the want of paper would otherwise have denied me. I write to you on the bark of the Paper birch, supposed to be the same used by the antients to write on before the art of making paper was invented, and which being called the Papyrus, gave the name of paper to the new invented substitute. I write to you merely to tell you that I am well, and to repeat what I have so often before repeated that I love you dearly, am always thinking of you and place much of the happiness of my life in seeing you improved in knowledge, learned in all the domestic arts, useful to your friends and good

any part of the world. Here they are locked up in ice and snow for 6. months. Spring and autumn which make a paradise of our country are rigorous winter with them, and a tropical summer breaks on them all at once. When we consider how much climate contributes to the happiness of our condn, by the fine sensation it excites, and the productions it is the parent of, we have reason to value highly the accident of birth in such a one as that of Virginia. From this distance I can have little domestic to write to you about. I must always repeat how much I love you. Kiss the little Anne for me. I hope she grows lustily, enjoys good health, and will make us all and long happy as the center of our common love. Adieu my dear. Yours affectionately,

TH: JEFFERSON

TO MARTHA JEFFERSON RANDOLPH

Philadelphia June 23. 1791.

MY DEAR DAUGHTER

I wrote to each of you once during my journey, from which I returned four days ago, having enjoyed thro' the whole of it very perfect health. I am in hopes the relaxation it gave me from business has freed me from the almost constant headach with which I had been persecuted thro the whole winter and spring. Having been entirely clear of it while travelling proves it to have been occasioned by the drudgery of business. I found here on my return your letter of May 23. with the pleasing information that you were all in good health. I wish I could say when I shall be able to join you: but that will depend on the movements of the President who is not yet returned to this place. In a letter written me by young Mr. Franklin,[1] who is in London, is the following paragraph. 'I meet here with many who ask kindly after you. Among these the D. of Dorset, who is very particular in his enquiries. He has mentioned to me that his niece[2] had wrote once or twice to your daughter since her return to America; but not recieving an answer had supposed she meant to drop her acquaintance, which his neice much regretted. I ventured to assure him that that was not likely, and that possibly the letters might have miscarried. You will take what notice of this you may think proper.' Fulwar Skipwith is on his return to the United States. Mrs. Trist and Mrs. Waters often ask after you. Mr. Lewis being very averse to writing, I must trouble Mr. Randolph to enquire of him rela-

be made of Mr. Lewis on the subject. But I received yesterday a letter from Mr. Lewis with full explanations, and another from Mr. Hylton informing me the tobo. was on it's way to this place. Therefore desire your sister to suppress that part of my letter and say nothing about it. Tell her from me how much I love her, kiss her and the little one for me and present my best affections to Mr. Randolph, assured of them also yourself from yours,

TH: J.

FROM MARY JEFFERSON

Monticello, July 10th, 1791.

MY DEAR PAPA

I have received both your letters, that from Lake George and of June the 26th. I am very much obliged to you for them, and think the bark that you wrote on prettier than paper. Mrs. Monroe[1] and Aunt Bolling are here. My aunt would have written to you, but she was unwell. She intends to go to the North Garden.[2] Mr. Monroe is gone to Williamsburg to stay two or three weeks, and has left his lady here. She is a charming woman. My sweet Anne grows prettier every day. I thank you for the pictures and nankeen that you sent me, which I think very pretty. Adieu, dear papa. I am your affectionate daughter,

MARIA JEFFERSON

1. Mrs. James Monroe; Mary Jefferson Bolling (Mrs. John).
2. A small community about sixteen miles southwest of Charlottesville on the road to Lynchburg.

TO MARTHA JEFFERSON RANDOLPH

Philadelphia July 10. 1791

MY DEAR DAUGHTER

I have no letter from Monticello later than Maria's of May 29. which is now six weeks old. This is long, when but one week is necessary for the conveyance. I cannot ascribe all the delay to the Charlottesville post. However to put that out of the way I am negotiating with the postmaster the establishment of a public post from Richmond to Staunton. In this case all the private riders will be prohibited from continuance, let their contracts be what they will, and the whole being brought into one hand, the public will be better served. I propose that the post shall pass by Tucka-

To Mary Jefferson

Philadelphia July 31. 1791.

The last letter I have from you, my dear Maria, was of the 29th. of May which is 9 weeks ago. Those which you ought to have written the 19th. of June and 10th. of July would have reached me before this if they had been written. I mentioned in my letter of the last week to your sister that I had sent off some stores to Richmond which I should be glad to have carried to Monticello in the course of the ensuing month of August. They are addressed to the care of Mr. Brown. You mentioned formerly that the two Commodes were arrived at Monticello. Were my two sets of ivory chessmen in the drawers? They have not been found in any of the packages which came here, and Petit seems quite sure they were packed up. How goes on the music, both with your sister and yourself? Adieu, my dear Maria; kiss and bless all the family for me. Your's affectionately,   Th: Jefferson

To Martha Jefferson Randolph

Philadelphia Aug. 14. 1791.

My dear daughter

Maria's letter of July 16. informs me you were all well then. However great my confidence is in the healthy air of Monticello, I am always happy to have my hopes confirmed by letter. The day of my departure is not yet fixed. I hope it will be earlier or later in the first week of September. I know not as yet how I am to get along, as one of my horses is in such a condition as to leave little hope of his life, and no possibility of his being in a condition to travel. I hope, before you recieve this, the articles sent by Capt. Stratton will be come to hand. The moment affording nothing new but what the gazettes will communicate, I have only to add my affections to Mr. Randolph and Maria, not forgetting the little one, and to yourself my dear Martha the warm love of your's affectionately,   Th: Jefferson

To Mary Jefferson

Philadelphia Aug. 21. 1791

My dear Maria

Your letter of July 10. is the last news I have from Monticello. The time of my setting out for that place is now fixed to some time

some of your friends among them. We expect hourly the arrival of capt. Stratton, by whom the clothes for the houseservants shall be sent. To forward them by any other vessel, is risking their miscarriage. Maria is fixed at Mrs. Pine's,[2] and perfectly at home. She has made young friends enough to keep herself in a bustle with them, and she has been honored with the visits of Mrs. Adams, Mrs. Randolph, Mrs. Rittenhouse, Sargeant, Waters, Davies &c. so that she is quite familiar with Philadelphia.[3] Present my sincere attachment to Mr. Randolph and kiss Anne for us. Adieu my dear, dear daughter. Your's affectionately,

TH: JEFFERSON

1. Benjamin Franklin Bache was a grandson of Benjamin Franklin and editor of the Philadelphia *Aurora*. Philip Freneau's paper was the *National Gazette*.
   2. Maria resided with her and attended a school she operated; TJ maintained a residence in the city of Philadelphia.
   3. Mesdames John Adams, Edmund Randolph, David Rittenhouse, Jonathan D. Sergeant, Nicholas Baker Waters, and Benjamin [?] Davies.

To Martha Jefferson Randolph

Philadelphia Dec. 4. 1791.

MY DEAR DAUGHTER

We are well here, tho' still without news from Mr. Randolph or yourself, tho' we have been eight weeks from Monticello. Maria was to have written to you to-day, but she has been so closely engaged in pasting paper together in the form of a pocket book that she has not been able. She has been constantly getting colds since she came here. I have just put on board Capt. Stratton a box with the following articles for your three house-maids.

      36. yds callimaneo
      13½ yds calico of different patterns
      25. yds linen
      9. yds muslin
      9. pr cotton stockings
      thread

I put into the same box for you la Cuisiniere Bourgeorsie [1] and the following books which Mr. Randolph wished to see. Ginanni del grano. Duhamel maniere de conserver le grain. Duhamel de l'insecte de l'Angoumois.[2] Mr. Randolph sees by the papers sent him what is the price of wheat here. Perhaps he might think it worth while to send his Varina wheat here. He could always have

To Martha Jefferson Randolph

Philadelphia Jan. 15. 1792

My dear Martha

Having no particular subject for a letter, I find none more soothing to my mind than to indulge itself in expressions of the love I bear you, and the delight with which I recall the various scenes thro which we have passed together, in our wanderings over the world. These reveries alleviate the toils and inquietudes of my present situation, and leave me always impressed with the desire of being at home once more, and of exchanging labour, envy, and malice for ease, domestic occupation, and domestic love and society, where I may once more be happy with you, with Mr. Randolph, and dear little Anne, with whom even Socrates might ride on a stick without being ridiculous. Indeed it is with difficulty that my resolution will bear me through what yet lies between the present day and that which, on mature consideration of all circumstances respecting myself and others, my mind has determined to be the proper one for relinquishing my office. Tho not very distant it is not near enough for my wishes. The ardor of these however would be abated if I thought that on coming home I should be left alone. On the contrary I hope that Mr. Randolph will find a convenience in making only leisurely preparations for a settlement, and that I shall be able to make you both happier than you have been at Monticello, and relieve you from *desagremens* to which I have been sensible you were exposed, without the power in myself to prevent it, but by my own presence. Remember me affectionately to Mr. Randolph and be assured of the tender love of Yours,   TH: JEFFERSON

To Martha Jefferson Randolph

Philadelphia Feb. 5. 92

My dear Martha

I was prevented writing to you last week by a bad cold attended with fever: and this week I have nothing to say but that I find myself nearly well, and to repeat the assurances of my love to you. Maria is well, and has come to a resolution to write to you no more. Whether this arises most from resentment or laziness I do not know. Mr. Randolph's last letter received was of Dec. 29. Yours of Nov. 29. In my last to him, knowing that Clarkson[1] could not write, I asked the favor of him to communicate to me

vious and more entertaining. I think she is also handsomer than she was and looks much better tho not as fat. Adieu my Dearest Papa. Tell me if we shall have the pleasure of seeing you this spring and believe me with tender and unchangeable love your affectionate child, M RANDOLPH

My best love to Dear Maria. Tell her I will certainly write to her next week.

1. Richard Randolph of Bizarre, Cumberland County.
2. Thomas Mann Randolph, Sr. The deed was dated April 12, 1793. For additional insight on this transaction, see Thomas Mann Randolph, Jr., to Peter Carr, June 26, 1793: "I shall send to you the deed for Edgehill, which I must beg the favor of you to present to Colo. Randolph, and to witness his acknowledgement of the signature. It is probable there may be some of our neighbours below at present, if there are any within call of you, demand of them in my name the same neighbourly duty. The names below affixed were taken thro. necessity: You will see they are persons whose attendance I cannot expect." (ViU.) See footnote 4 of TJ to Martha Jefferson Randolph, April 26, 1790.

To Martha Jefferson Randolph

Philadelphia Feb. 26. 92.

My dear Martha

We are in daily expectation of hearing of your safe return to Monticello, and all in good health. The season is now coming on when I shall envy your occupations in the feilds and garden while I am shut up drudging within four walls. Maria is well and lazy, therefore does not write. Your friends Mrs. Trist and Mrs. Waters are well also, and often enquire after you. We have nothing new or interesting from Europe for Mr. Randolph. He will preceive by the papers that the English are beaten off the ground by Tippoo Saib. The Leyden gazette assures that they were saved only by the unexpected arrival of the Mahrattas, who were suing to Tippoo Saib for peace for Ld. Cornwallis.[1] My best esteem to Mr. Randolph, I am my dear Martha your's affectionately,

TH: JEFFERSON

1. Reference is probably to conditions in the Indian province of Bengal. Tippoo Sahib was Sultan of Mysore and violently anti-British. The Mahrattas inhabited the district of Maharasthtra. Despite the report of the usually reliable Leyden *Gazette,* the British under Cornwallis won a victory near Seringapatam.

busy in your garden. Shackleford[2] promised me *on his honor* to cover it well with manure. Has he done it? If not, tell him I have written to enquire. Two or three straggling numbers of Fenno's gazette being found in my office, we presume they belong to Mr. Randolph's set, and therefore I send them. Present my best affections to him, and be assured of the cordial love of Your's,

TH: JEFFERSON

1. Benjamin Smith Barton was a physician and botanist of Lancaster, Pennsylvania. Mr. Randolph was an able botanist in his own right.
2. Tom Shackleford was a TJ slave.

TO MARTHA JEFFERSON RANDOLPH

Philadelphia Apr. 27. 1792.

MY DEAR DAUGHTER

I received yesterday your's and Mr. Randolph's of the 9th. which shews that the post somehow or other slips a week. Congress have determined to rise on the 5th. of May. Colo. Monroe and Mrs. Monroe will set out on the 7th. and making a short stay at Fredericksburg pass on to Albemarle. I have reason to expect that my visit to Virginia this year, instead of September as heretofore, will be about the last of July, and be somewhat longer than usual, as it is hoped Congress will meet later. Tell Mr. Randolph that Mr. Hylton informs me 43. hhds. of my tobacco, meaning of my mark, are arrived at the warehouse, and that he shall send them on by the first opportunity. As this cannot possibly be all mine, it must contain Mr. Randolph's, and therefore it is necessary he should enable Mr. Hylton to distinguish his, or it will all come round here. I am to have 5. dollars for mine, payable in September, from which will be deducted about half a dollar expences. Maria is well and joins me in affections to Mr. Randolph and yourself. Adieu my dear. Your's,

TH: JEFFERSON

FROM MARTHA JEFFERSON RANDOLPH

Monticello May 7, 1792

MY DEAREST PAPA

Mr. Randolph recieved your letter respecting the bonds 2 days before he set off for Richmond and carried them down with him. He has by Mr. Colquohoun's not appearing been cast in his suit

and the 2d. part of Payne's Rights of man[1] for Mr. Randolph.
Also, for yourself, my own copy of Lavater's aphorisms,[2] which
I fancy are not to be got here, and which I think you will sicken
of in a few pages. Mrs. Pine has determined to go to England, so
that I shall be obliged to send Maria to Mrs. Brodeau's,[3] a better
school, but much more distant from me. It will in fact cut off the
daily visits which she is able to make me from Mrs. Pine's. I do
not know whether I have before mentioned to you that the President will make his visit to Mount Vernon this year about the last
of July: consequently mine to Monticello will be earlier than
usual. Present my esteem to all my neighbors. My best affections
to Mr. Randolph and yourself, not forgetting little Anne, who I
suppose will be able to take a part in conversation by the time
we see her. Adieu my dear daughter. Your's,

TH: JEFFERSON.

1. Thomas Paine, *Rights of Man. Part the second* . . . (London, 1792).
Sowerby 2826.
2. Johann Kaspar Lavater, *Aphorisms on Man. Translated from the original
manuscript of* . . . *4th ed.* . . . . (Boston, 1790). This is probably the edition
mentioned, although there were others, a London and a Dublin edition, before
1791.
3. Mrs. Anne Brodeau, a Philadelphia schoolteacher, whose boarding school
was located at 2 Lodge Alley. The Account Book lists no payments to a Mrs.
Brodeau, and it is questionable if Mary ever attended her school.

TO MARTHA JEFFERSON RANDOLPH

Philadelphia May 27. 1792.

MY DEAR DAUGHTER

I was too much occupied to write by Friday's post and fear it
will occasion your recieving my letter a week later. Yours of the
7th. Inst. has come duly to hand. Colo. and Mrs. Monroe will
probably be with you by the time you recieve this. Mr. Madison
left us last Wednesday. I have promised, during his stay in Orange
to inclose to him Fenno's paper for his perusal, to be forwarded
on to Mr. Randolph, which will sometimes occasion his recieving
it later than he would have done. We expect the President tomorrow on his return from Mount-Vernon. To the news in the public
papers I may add the attempt to assassinate the K. of Sweden.
He was dangerously wounded. French affairs are going on pretty
well. Their assignats[1] begin to gain. The election in N. York will
be interesting to Colo. Monroe. Tell him it is generally thought
that Mr. Jay[2] has the most votes, but that one of the returns which

are burnt up for want of rain. The drouth has continued for upwards of 5 weeks and there is no appearance of its discontinuing
as yet. People are in great pain about their crops. Indeed they
have a wretched prospect before them and many of them are suffering for bread even at this time. Joseph Monroe has been
extreemely ill but he is perfectly recovered now. It is generally
supposed it was the gout. We are all in perfect health here myself
particularly. I do not recolect ever to have been so fat as I am at
present. Adieu my dearest father. Believe me ever yours most
affectionately,   M. RANDOLPH

    1. The son of Nicholas Lewis of The Farm. His lady was Mildred Hornsby,
daughter of Joseph Hornsby of Williamsburg.
    2. As early as 1769 TJ had cleared on the north side of Monticello mountain
a park of 1,850 yards' circumference in the vicinity of the North Spring near
the future location of the Fourth Roundabout. When the Marquis de Chastellux visited TJ in 1782 he reported a score of deer in the park. Howard C. Rice,
Jr., editor, *Travels in North America 1780, 1781 and 1782 by the Marquis de
Chastellux* (Chapel Hill, 1963), II, 394.

To MARY JEFFERSON

                           Wednesday morn. [ca. June 1, 1792]
TH: J. TO HIS DEAR MARIA.

    Ask, my dear, of Mrs. Pine, what would be the price of Mr.
Madison's picture,[1] and let me know when you come over to-day.

    1. TJ is referring to the Robert Edge Pine portrait of James Madison, which
at one time hung in the Monticello parlor. It is now lost. The date of the
letter is probably May 30 because on that day he sent Mrs. Pine an order on
the Bank of the United States, and on June 2 he paid her "for Mr. Madison's
picture 39.33." (Account Book 1792.) It is also to be noted that TJ, in a letter
to Thomas Mann Randolph, Jr., of June 1, 1792, stated: "Maria's mistress
is just now on her departure for England. She came home yesterday." (ViU.)

To MARTHA JEFFERSON RANDOLPH

                                Philadelphia June 8. 1792.
MY DEAR DAUGHTER

    The last news we have from Monticello is by your letter of May
7. I am in hopes tomorrow's post will bring us something, for
some how or other your letters (if you write by post to Richmond)
miss a post and are sometimes a week longer coming than they
ought to be. The news from the French West India islands is
more and more discouraging. Swarms of the inhabitants are quit-
ting them and coming here daily. I wonder that none of your
acquaintances write to you. Perhaps they may be in Martinique

before dinner prevented my writing last week tho Mr. Randolph did and sent his letter after him as far as fluvana courthouse before they could overtake him. So his iregularity is owing that which you complain of in the receipt of my letters. I am very sorry you can not fix the time of your departure. As it aproches my anxiety augments. All other thoughts give way to that of shortly seeing two people so infinitely dear to me. What I told you of my garden is really true indeed if you see it at a distance it looks very green but it does not bear close examination, the weeds having taken possession of much the greater part of it. Old George is so slow that by the time he has got to the end of his labour he has it all to do over again. 2 of the acasia's are come up and are flourishing. I have visited the two Mrs. Lewis's. The young lady appears to be a good little woman tho most intolerable weak. However she will be a near neighbor and of course worth cultivating. Dear little Anne has been in very bad health her illness having been occasioned by worms. Dr. Gilmer advised the tincture of sacre the effects of which were allmost imediate. She still looks badly but I imagine that may be partly owing to her cutting teeth. I must now trouble you with some little commissions of mine. The glass of one of those handsome engravings I brought in with me has by some accident got broke and not being able to suply the place of it in Richmond I should be extremely obliged to you to bring me one according to the measure and also a small frame with a glass to it for a picture of the size of the enclosed oval paper. Adieu my dear papa. The heat is incredible here. The thermometer has been at 96 in Richmond and even at this place we have not been able to sleep comfortably with every door and window open. I dont recolect ever to have suffered as much from heat as we have done this summer. Adieu my Dearest Father. Believe me with tender affection yours,

M. RANDOLPH

TO MARTHA JEFFERSON RANDOLPH

Philadelphia July 3. 1792.

MY DEAR MARTHA

I now inclose you Petit's statement of the stores sent round to Richmond to the care of Mr. Brown. They sailed from hence yesterday morning, and the winds have been and are so favorable that I dare say they will be in Chesapeak bay tomorrow, ready for the first Southernly breeze to carry them up the river. So that they

cello. Still should my former one desiring horses, have missed, this will be in time for them to meet me on the road, and relieve mine in the last and worst part of it.

I set out this afternoon, and can pretty certainly be with you early on Sunday sennight. My affections to Mr. Randolph. Adieu my dear,   TH: JEFFERSON

TO MARTHA JEFFERSON RANDOLPH

Philadelphia Oct. 26. 1792.

MY DEAR DAUGHTER

Having not received a letter by yesterday's post, and that of the former week from Mr. Randolph having announced dear Anne's indisposition, I am under much anxiety. In my last letter to Mr. Randolph I barely mentioned your being recovered, when somewhat younger than she is, by recurrence to a good breast of milk. Perhaps this might be worthy of proposing to the Doctor. In a case where weakness of the digesting organs enters into the causes of illness, a food of the most easy digestion might give time for getting the better of the other causes, whatever they may be. I [trust] it should however be some other than your own, if a breast of milk is to be tried. I hope you are perfectly well and the little one also, as well as Mr. Randolph to whom present my sincere regards. Adieu my dear. Your's affectionately,   TH: JEFFERSON

TO MARTHA JEFFERSON RANDOLPH

Philadelphia Nov. 12. 1792

MY DEAR MARTHA

The last post day for Monticello, which was the 9th. slipt by me without my recollecting it. However as you are perhaps in Cumberland, a letter of this day may get to you only three days the later. I have nothing indeed to tell you but that I love you dearly, and your dear connections, that I am well, as is Maria. I hope your little one has felt no inconvenience from the journey, that Anne is quite recovered, and Mr. Randolph's health good. Yours is so firm, that I am less apt to apprehend for you: Still, however, take care of your good health, and of your affection to me, which is the solace of my life. Remember me cordially to Mr. Randolph. Yours,   TH: JEFFERSON

To Martha Jefferson Randolph

Philadelphia Dec. 6. 92.

MY DEAR MARTHA

I have this day received yours of the 18th. Novembr. and sincerely sympathize with you on the state of dear Anne, if that can be called sympathy which proceeds from affection at first hand, for my affections had fastened on her for her own sake and not merely for yours. Still however experience (and that in your own case) has taught me that an infant is never desperate, let me beseech you not to destroy the powers of her stomach with medicine. Nature alone can re-establish infant-organs; only taking care that her efforts be not thwarted by any imprudencies of diet. I rejoice in the health of your other hope. Maria is well. Remember me affectionately to Mr. Randolph and be assured of my unceasing love for you both. Adieu my very dear Martha.   TH: JEFFERSON

To Martha Jefferson Randolph

Philadelphia Dec. 13. 1792.

MY DEAR MARTHA

By capt. Swaile, who sailed yesterday for Richmond I sent addressed to Mr. Randolph to the care of Mr. Brown a box containing the following articles for your three house maids.

2. peices of linen. 52. yards
9. pair cotton stockings (3 of them small)
13. yds. cotton in three patterns
36. yards Calimanco.
9. yards muslin.

Bob is to have a share of the linen. I had promised to send him a new suit of clothes. Instead of this I send a suit of superfine ratteen of my own, which I have scarcely ever worn. I forgot to get stockings for him: therefore must desire you to have him furnished with them from Colo. Bell's on my account. In the same box you will find 4. pair tongs and shovels which I observed the house to be in want of. I hope our dear Anne is got well and that all of you continue so. Maria is well. She begun a letter to you Sunday was sennight: but it is not finished. My affections to Mr. Randolph and your friends. Adieu, my dear, your's with all love,

TH: JEFFERSON

in a baloon. The security of the thing appeared so great that every body is wishing for a baloon to travel in. I wish for one sincerely, as instead of 10. days, I should be within 5 hours of home. Maria will probably give you the baloon details, as she writes to-day. Have you recieved the package with the servants clothes? My best attachments to Mr. Randolph. Adieu my dear. Your's affectionately,   TH: JEFFERSON

FROM MARTHA JEFFERSON RANDOLPH

Monticello January 16, 1793

With infinite pleasure I date once more from Monticello tho for the third time since my return. But from the negligence of the servant that carried the letters once and the great hurry of the post another time they never got farther than Charlottesville. Our dearest Anne has had an attack of a different nature from her former ones which the doctor imagines to proceed from her fatening too quickly. She is far from being well yet, tho considerably better. She is at present busily employed *yiting* to you, a thing she has never missed doing whenever her health has permitted her. Her memory is uncommonly good for a child of her age. She relates many circumstances that happened during her travels with great exactitude but in such broken language and with so many gestures as renders it highly diverting to hear her. Her spirits have as yet been proof against ill health so far as to recover them with the least intermission of it tho I much fear that will not long be the case if she does not mend speedily. The little boy continues well and is little inferior to his sister in point of size. He also begins to take a great deal of notice and bids fair to be as lively. I am afraid you will be quite tired of hearing so much about them but a fond Mother never knows where to stop when her children is the subject.

Mr. Randolph did not recieve the letter in which you mentioned the books and stalactite till after he had left Richmond with 4 or 5 other Letters of yours which had been detained by some accident. Peter [1] desires to be remembered to you and wishes to know if you have recieved one he wrote you from Richmond. Adieu dearest Papa. My Love to dear Maria. I will write to her by the next post. Believe me to [be] with tenderest affection Yours,

M RANDOLPH

1. Peter Carr, one of TJ's nephews and son of Martha and Dabney Carr.

bottom. But on this I shall write him particularly if I defer my departure. I have not received the letter which Mr. Carr wrote to me from Richmond nor any other from him since I left Monticello. My best affections to him, Mr. Randolph and your fireside and am with sincere love my dear Martha Yours,   TH: J.

1. A canal TJ was constructing on the south side of the Rivanna River. It was located about ¾ mile upstream from Milton and approximately six from Charlottesville. Its purpose was to carry water from the river to his Shadwell toll mill. See the *Farm Book*, 343–45 for additional details.
2. The individuals referred to were probably Manoah Clarkson, a Monticello overseer from 1792 to 1793, and "Big" George, a slave.

To Martha Jefferson Randolph

Philadelphia Feb 11. 1793

My Dear Martha

The hour of Post is come and a throng of business allows me only to inform you we are well, and to acknowledge the rect. of Mr. Randolph's letter of Jan. 24. with hopes that you are all so. Accept assurances [of] constant love to you all from Yours My Dear most affectionately,   Ths: Jefferson

To Martha Jefferson Randolph

Philadelphia Feb. 24. 1793.

My Dear Martha

We have no letter from Monticello since Mr. Randolph's of Jan. 30. to Maria. However we hope you are all well and that there are letters on the road which will tell us so. Maria writes to-day. Congress will rise on Saturday next, a term which is joyous to all as it affords some relaxation of business to all. We have had the mildest winter ever known, having had only two snows to cover the ground, and these remained but a short time. Heavy rains now falling will render the roads next to impassable for the members returning home. Colo. Monroe will stay some days after the rising of Congress. Bob was here lately, and as he proposed to return to Richmond and thence to Monticello I charged him with enquiring for the box with the servants clothes, should Mr. Randolph not yet have heard of it. It went from hence the 12th. of December by the Schooner Mary, Capt. Swaile, bound for Norfolk and

o'clock and the post goes off by day break. Once more adieu dear Father.

1. Martha's reference is to the breakdown in negotiations over the Edgehill property between Thomas Mann Randolph, Jr., and his father. Whatever this was, it may have accounted for the failure to have the deed recorded. It did not affect the Randolphs' ultimate possession and habitation at Edgehill. See notes for TJ to Martha Jefferson Randolph, April 26, 1790, and Martha to TJ of February 20, 1792.

2. Jane Barbara Carr Cary (Mrs. Wilson) and Lucy Carr Terrell (Mrs. Richard). Polly Carr was the daughter who remained with Aunt Carr.

To Martha Jefferson Randolph

Philadelphia Mar. 10. 1793.

MY DEAR DAUGHTER

Your letters of the 20th. and 27th. Feb. as well as Mr. Randolph's of the same dates, came to hand only yesterday. By this I percieve that your post must be under bad regulation indeed. I am sorry to learn that your garden is dismantled, and yourself thereby discoraged from attention to it. I beg that Mr. Randolph will employ the whole force, he has been so kind as to direct, in repairing the inclosure in preference to every other work I had proposed. Nothing can be placed in competition with the loss of the produce of the garden during the season, either for health or comfort, and my own are less dear and desirable to me than the health and comfort of yourself, Mr. Randolph and the little ones. I had hoped that from the same resources your supplies of wood in the winter would not have failed. I again repeat it that I wish every other object to be considered as secondary in my mind to your accomodation and insist that Mr. Randolph make the freest use of the people under his direction for his and your convenience in the first place. When I shall see you I cannot say: but my heart and thoughts are all with you till I do. I have given up my house here, and taken a small one [1] in the country on the banks of the Schuylkill to serve me while I stay. We are packing all our superfluous furniture and shall be sending it by water to Richmond when the season becomes favorable. My books too, except a very few, will be packed and go with the other things, so that I shall put it out of my own power to return to the city again to keep house, and it would be impossible to carry on business in the winter at a country residence. Tho' this points out an ultimate term of stay here, yet my mind is looking to a much shorter one if the circumstances will permit it which broke in on my first resolution. In-

posed with little fevers, nausea, want of appetite, and is become weak. The Doctor thinks it proceeds from a weakness of the stomach, and that it will soon be removed. I learn from the head of Elk that a person of the name of Boulding set out from thence some days ago, to view my lands with an intention to become a tenant. He carried a letter from Mr. Hollingsworth,[1] whom I had desired to procure tenants for me; not addressed I beleive to any particular person. I am in hopes he will apply to Mr. Randolph. The lands I should first lease would be the upper tract joining Key: but if enough of them would join to take the whole lands on that side of the river, they might divide them as they pleased. I have never heard yet whether you got the servants' clothes which were sent by water. I have got all my superfluous furniture packed and on board a vessel bound to Richmond, to which place she will clear out to-day. I have written to Mr. Brown to hire a Warehouse or rather Ware-room for it, there being 1300. cubical feet of it, which would fill a moderate room. Some packages containing looking glass will have to remain there till next winter I presume, as they can only be trusted by water. Indeed I do not know how the rest will be got up. However, on this subject I will write to Mr. Randolph the next week. War is certainly declared between France, England and Holland. This we learn by a packet the dispatches of which came to hand yesterday. J. Eppes sets out for Virginia to-day, to go and finish his course of study at Wm. and Mary. Tell Mr. Carr his letter is just now received, and shall be answered the next week, as I am now in the throng of my removal into the country. Remember me affectionately to him, to Mr. Randolph and kiss the little ones for me. Adieu my dear. Your's most affectionately,   TH: JEFFERSON

1. Jacob Hollingsworth of Elkton, Maryland, who had found tenants for some of TJ's lands, among them Eli Alexander and Nicholas Biddle.

To Martha Jefferson Randolph

Philadelphia Apr. 28. 1793.

My dear Martha

I am now very long without a letter from Monticello, which is always a circumstance of anxiety to me. I wish I could say that Maria was quite well. I think her better for this week past, having for that time been free from the little fevers which had harrassed her nightly. A paper which I some time ago saw in the Richmond gazette under the signature R. R. proved to me the existence of

at Richmond till they can be carried up by water, as to put them into a waggon would be a certain sacrifice of them. They are the Nos. 2. 5. 10. 18. 19. 22. 23. 25. 26. 27. 28. Such of the others as contain any thing that you think would be convenient immediately, you may perhaps find means of having brought up. As to the rest they may lie till I can have waggons of my own or find some other oeconomical means of getting them up. In any way it will be expensive, many of the boxes being enormously large. I got a person to write to Scotland for a mason and house-joiner for me. I learn that they were engaged and only waited for a ship. They will be delivered at Richmond to the address of Mr. Brown. A person who is come here, and knows them personally, says they are fine characters, will be very useful to have on a farm; it is material therefore that they do not remain 24. hours in Richmond to be spoiled. I shall write to Mr. Brown to send them off instantly and shall be obliged to Mr. Randolph to have an eye to the same object. How to employ them will be the subject of consideration It will be puzzling till my return. It is one of the great inconveniences I experience by having been persuaded by my friends to defer carrying into execution my determination to retire. However when I see you, it will be never to part again. In the mean time my affairs must be a burthen to Mr. Randolph. You have never informed me whether the box containing the servant's clothes, which were sent in December last, have been received. I am anxious to hear, because if it has not, I will prosecute the captain. Maria's brain is hard at work to squeeze out a letter for Mr. Randolph. She has been scribbling and rubbing out these three hours, and this moment exclaimed 'I do not think I shall get a letter made out to-day.' We shall see how her labours will end. She wonders you do not write to her. So do I. Present me most affectionately to Mr. Randolph and be assured of my unceasing love to yourself. Kiss the dear little ones for me. Yours,

TH: JEFFERSON

FROM MARTHA JEFFERSON RANDOLPH

Monticello May 16 1793

DEAR PAPA

I recieved your kind letter of April the 28 a week ago and should have answered it imediately but that the house was full of company at the time. The subject of it has been one of infinite anx-

up and even the Leaves of the trees. Adieu my dear Papa. We are all impatient to see you. My love to Dear Maria and believe me ever yours,   M. RANDOLPH

TO MARTHA JEFFERSON RANDOLPH

Philadelphia May 26. 1793.

MY DEAR MARTHA

Your and Mr. Randolph's welcome favors of the 16th. came to hand yesterday, by which I perceive that your post-day for writing is the Thursday. Maria is here and, tho not in flourishing health, is well. I will endeavor to prevail on her to write, and perhaps may succeed, as the day is too wet to admit her saunters on the banks of the Schuylkill, where she passes every Sunday with me. We are in sight of both Bartram's and Grey's gardens, but have the river between them and us. We have two blind stories here. The one that Dumourier[1] is gone over to the Austrians. The authority for this is an English paper. No confidence in DuMourier's virtue opposes it, for he has none: but the high reputation he has acquired is a pledge to the world, which we do not see that these were any motives on this occasion to induce him to forfeit. The other story is that he has cut off 10,000 Prussians, and among them the K. of Prussia and D. of Brunswick. The latter we know is out of command, and the former not in DuMourier's way. Therefore we concluded the story fabricated merely to set off against the other. It has now come thro' another channel and in a more possible form to wit that Custine has cut off 10,000 Prussians without naming the King or Duke. Still we give little ear to it. You had at your Convent so many —courts (as terminations of names) that I wish the following paragraph of a newspaper may involve none of them. 'A few days ago several rich and respectable inhabitants were butchered at Guadaloupe. The following are the names of the unfortunate victims. Madame Vermont and Madame Meyercourt. Monsr. Gondrecourt, three daughters just arrived from France from 11. to 18. years of age. Messrs. Vaudrecourt &c.' Maria thinks the Gondrecourts were at the convent.[2] The French minister Genet told me yesterday that matters appeared now to be tolerably well settled in St. Domingo. That the Patriotic party had taken possession of 600 aristocrats and monocrats, had sent 200 of them to France, and were sending 400. here: and that a coalition had taken place among the other inhabitants. I wish we could distribute our 400 among the Indians, who would teach them lessons

weeks, indeed Their negligence is intolerable. We have just heard
of some of Mr. Randolph's Letters to you that have gone on to
Lexington in kentucke. Those that we do get, come so irregularly
with out any regard to Their dates that it is impossible to follow
your directions with any degree of punctuality. Mr. Randolph
thinks it would be adviseable to have all your furniture brought
by water as it is not only much more oeconomical but also safer. I
have a terible account to give you of your cyder. Of 140 bottles that
were put away you will hardly find 12. It flew in such a manner
as to render it dangerous going near them. Those that were care-
lessly corked forced their corks, the rest burst the bottles amongst
which the havoc is incredible. The servants cloaths are not arrived nor have we been able to hear any thing about them. I am
going on with such spirit in the garden that I think I shall conquer
my *oponent* the *insect* yet, tho hither to they have been as in-
difatigable in cutting up as I have been in planting. I have added
to your accasia which is at Least 2 feet high 2 lemmon trees and
have the promise of an egg plant from Mr. Derieux. My dear little
Anne [grows] daily more and more entertaining. She is very observing and very talkative and of course charming in the eyes of
a mother. The dear Little boy tho not in perfect health is very
well for one that is cutting teeth. *You* will easily concieve how
great the satisfaction is I derive from the company of my sweet
Little babes tho none but those who have experienced it can. I
have allways forgot to mention Petit in any of my Letters. My
negligence hurt his feelings I know, as it is not my Design to do
so. You would oblige me infinitely by delivering some message to
him *de ma part*. Adieu my Dear Papa. Believe me with tender
affections yours,   M RANDOLPH

To MARTHA JEFFERSON RANDOLPH

Philadelphia July 7. 1793.

MY DEAR DAUGHTER

My head has been so full of farming since I have found it necessary to prepare a plan for my manager, that I could not resist
the addressing my last weekly letters to Mr. Randolph and boring
him with my plans. Maria writes to you to-day. She is getting into
tolerable health, tho' not good. She passes two or three days in
the week with me, under the trees, for I never go into the house
but at the hour of bed. I never before knew the full value of trees.
My house is entirely embosomed in high plane trees, with good

will have ready to send by him. He proposes to set out for Monticello in 8. or 10. days. Present my best respects to Mrs. Randolph [2] and my regrets at my absence during the favor of her visit. I hope to be more fortunate another time. We have had a remarkeable death here which I will mention for example sake. Mrs. Lear,[3] wife of the gentleman who is secretary to the President, by eating green plumbs and apples brought on a mortification of the bowels which carried her off in six days. She was 23. years old, and of as fine healthy a constitution as I ever knew. Tell Anne this story, and kiss her for me, in presenting one of the inclosed caricatures. I put up several as Mrs. Randolph may have some of her family to whom they may give a moment's pleasure. My best affections are with Mr. Randolph and yourself. Adieu my dear.

1. For selected Monticello recipes that include certain of Petit's, consult Marie Kimball, *Thomas Jefferson's Cookbook* (Richmond, 1949).
2. Probably Mrs. Beverley Randolph. See TJ to Martha Jefferson Randolph, September 8, 1793.
3. Mrs. Tobias Lear. *The Pennsylvania Journal and Weekly Advertiser,* July 31, 1793, has her obituary notice.

TO MARTHA JEFFERSON RANDOLPH

Philadelphia Aug. 18. 93.

MY DEAR MARTHA

Maria and I are scoring off the weeks which separate us from you. They wear off slowly, but time is sure tho' slow. Mr. D. Randolph left us three days ago. He went by the way of Presquisle and consequently will not enrapture Mrs. Randolph till the latter end of the month. I wrote to Mr. Randolph sometime ago to desire he would send off Tom Shackleford or Jupiter [1] or any body else on the 1st. of September with the horse he has been so kind as to procure for me to meet at Georgetown (at Shuter's tavern). A servant whom I shall send from hence on the same day with Tarquin, to exchange them, Tarquin [2] to go to Monticello and the other come here to aid me in my journey. The messenger to ride a mule and lead the horse. I mention these things now, lest my letter should have miscarried. I received information yesterday of 500 bottles of wine arrived for me at Baltimore. I desired them to be sent to Richmond to Colo. Gamble [3] to be forwarded to Monticello. They will be followed the next week with some things from hence. Should any waggons of the neighborhood be going down they might enquire for them. With the things sent from hence will go clothes for the servants to replace those sent last

To Martha Jefferson Randolph

Germantown Nov. 10. 1793.

I wrote, my dear Martha, by last week's post to Mr. Randolph. Yesterday I received his of Oct. 31. The fever [1] in Philadelphia has almost entirely disappeared. The Physicians say they have no new infections since the great rains which have fallen. Some previous ones are still to die or recover, and so close this tragedy. I think however the Executive will remain here till the meeting of Congress, merely to furnish a rally point to them. The refugee inhabitants are very generally returning into the city. Mr. T. Shippen and his lady are here. He is very slowly getting better. Still confined to the house. She is well and very burly. I told her of her sister's pretensions to the fever and ague at Blenheim. [2] She complained of receiving no letter. Tell this to Mrs. Carter, making it the subject of a visit express, which will be an act of good neighborhood. The affairs of France are at present gloomy. Toulon has surrendered to England and Spain. So has Grand Anse and the country round about in St. Domingo. The English however have received a check before Dunkirk, probably a smart one, tho the particulars are not yet certainly known. [3] I send Freneau's papers. He has discontinued them, but promises to resume again. I fear this cannot be till he has collected his arrearages. My best regards to Mr. Randolph, accept my warmest love for yourself and Maria, compliments to miss Jane, kisses to the children, friendly affections to all. Adieu. Yours,   TH: J.

1. The yellow fever epidemic of 1793 began about the last of August, and by September hundreds had been stricken and nearly seventy had died. As mid-September approached, its intensity increased, causing a considerable number of the populace to flee the city. TJ remained at his desk until September 17, long after the other Cabinet members and the President had departed. He arrived at Monticello on September the 25. See Malone, *Jefferson and the Ordeal of Liberty*, 140–42, for an account of TJ and the epidemic; J. H. Powell, *Bring Out Your Dead: The Great Plague of Yellow Fever in Philadelphia in 1793* (Philadelphia, 1949), for broader aspects of it.

2. Jane Wood Shippen (Mrs. Thomas Lee) was a sister of Lucy Wood Carter (Mrs. Edward) of Blenheim, a Carter estate eight miles south of Monticello on the North Fork of the Hardware River.

3. The Duke of York was driven from there in September, 1793. By December Bonaparte had regained Toulon from the English, but TJ had no way of knowing this.

town and means to take a small house and 3. or 4. boarders. Mr. Randolph, the Atty Genl. having removed to German town during the fever, proposes not to return again to live in the city. Mrs. Washington is not yet returned. So much for small news. As to great, we can only perceive in general that the French are triumphing in every quarter. They suffered a check as is said by the D. of Brunswick, losing about 2000. men, but this is nothing to their numerous victories. The account of the recapture of Toulon comes so many ways that we think it may now be believed. St. Domingo has expelled all it's whites, has given freedom to all it's blacks, has established a regular government of the blacks and coloured people, and seems now to have taken it's ultimate form, and that to which all of the West India islands must come. The English have possession of two ports in the island, but acting professedly as the patrons of the whites, there is no danger of their gaining ground. Freneau's and Fenno's papers are both put down for ever. My best affection to Mr. Randolph, Maria and friends. Kisses to the little ones. Adieu affectionately,   TH: J.

To Mary Jefferson

Philadelphia, Dec. 15, 1793

MY DEAR MARIA

I should have written to you the last Sunday in turn, but business required my allotting your turn to Mr. Randolph, and putting off writing to you till this day. I have now received your and your sister's letters of Nov. 27 and 28. I agree that Watson shall make the writing desk for you. I called the other day on Mrs. Fullarton,[1] and there saw your friend Sally Cropper. She went up to Trenton the morning after she left us and staid there till lately. The maid servant who waited on her and you at our house caught the fever on her return to town and died. In my letter of last week I desired Mr. Randolph to send horses for me to be at Fredericksburg on the 12th. of January. Lest that letter shoud miss carry I repeat it here and wish you to mention it to him. I also informed him that a person of the name of Eli Alexander[2] would set out this day from Elkton to take charge of the plantation under Byrd Rogers[3] and praying him to have his accommodations at the place got ready as far as should be necessary before my arrival. I hope to be with you all about the 15th. of January no more to leave you. My blessings to your Dear Sister and little

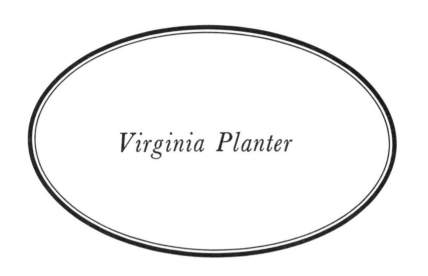

Virginia Planter

Varina Jan. 15 1795

We intended writing to my Dearest Father from Richmond, but that care devolving upon me on account of Mr. Randolph's business it was as is often the case with me put off till the hurry of packing obliged me to neglect it entirely. Col. Blackden[1] and W. C. Nicholas[2] had both left Richmond before we arrived there. The letter for the former was put in the post office imediately. That to Mr. Nicholas Mr. Randolph thought better to keep untill a direct opportunity offered, of sending it as the post does not pass near Warren. I have the paper you desired me to get, ready to send. It is not handsome but their was no choice their being only three pieces in Richmond that I could hear of except complete hangings for a room which they would not break in upon, borders were not to be had at any price.

I saw Bob[3] frequently while in Richmond. He expressed great uneasiness at having quitted you in the manner he did and repeatedly declared that he would never have left *you* to live with any person but his wife. He appeared to be so much affected at having deserved your anger that I could not refuse my intercession when so warmly solicited towards obtaining your forgiveness. The poor creature seems so deeply impressed with a sense of his ingratitude as to be rendered quite unhappy by it but he could not prevail upon himself to give up his wife and child. We found every thing here in such a ruinous condition that it is impossible to say what stay we shall be forced to make here. The monstrous crops of wheat which was represented to be 3000. bushels has dwindled away to 800 Most of the corn out still at the mercy of thieves hogs birds &c. and in short every thing in such disorder that Mr. Randolph has been obliged to discharge the overseer and take the management of the plantation in his own hands. We were quite happy at your having made use of the waggon as we were in no hurry at all for the horses indeed we did not leave Rock castle in several days after their arrival and then loitered away much of our time on the road. If you had any idea My dear Papa of the

high as the thawing point, 32°. So much the better for our wheat, and for the destruction of the weavil. But you are impatient to hear something of the children. They are both well, and have never had even a finger-ach since you left us. Jefferson is very robust. His hands are constantly like lumps of ice, yet he will not warm them. He has not worn his shoes an hour this winter. If put on him, he takes them off immediately and uses one to carry his nuts etc. in. Within these two days we have put both him and Anne into mockaseens, which being made of soft leather, fitting well and lacing up, they have never been able to take them off. So that I believe we may consider that as the only effectual shoe which can be made for them. They are inseparable in their sports. Anne's temper begins to develope itself advantageously. His tempests give her opportunities of shewing and exercising a placid disposition: and there is no doubt but that a little time will abate of his impatience as it has done hers. I called her in to ask what I should write for her to yourself and her papa. She says I must tell you that she loves you, and that you must come home. In both these sentiments we all join her. Maria gives all her love to you. We are alone at present; but are in hopes soon of a visit from my sister Anne. I shall address the next week's letter to Mr. Randolph. In the mean while present me to him affectionately, and continue to love me yourself as I do you most tenderly. Adieu; come home as soon as you can, and make us happy in seeing you here, and Mr. Randolph in better health.

1. This exchange reflects the freeing of Robert Hemings who was manumitted December 24, 1794. "Executed a deed of emancipation for Bob. by the name of Robert Hemmings. He has been valued at £ 60. which Stras [Dr. George Frederick Strauss, of Richmond] is to advance." (Account Book, December 24, 1794.) Hemings later worked for Dr. Strauss and married one of his slaves. On January 8, 1795, TJ remitted ". . . 51 $\frac{D}{-}$ 67 the balance of Stras's money to Mussie [Joseph Mussie] of Philadelphia." (Account Book.) He thus rid himself of an obligation to Mussie. The indenture freeing Hemings is at the MHi. See Malone, *Jefferson and the Ordeal of Liberty*, 208, and *Memoirs of a Monticello Slave* (1955), 10.

2. John Watson, a Milton resident.

3. Possibly William Snelson, Jr., a one-time resident of Hanover and Louisa counties. TJ had varied business dealings with a "Mr. Snelson." See Account Books 1795 and 1796, entries from June, 1795, to December, 1796.

4. TJ slave who often drove him in his light four-wheeled vehicle drawn by a pair of horses.

5. Probably Mrs. Lucy Wood, with whom TJ had business dealings. It is to be noted that there were nineteen Woods paying a property tax in Fredericksville Parish and six in Saint Anne's in 1795. Albemarle County Personal Property Book 1795, Virginia State Library, Richmond, Virginia.

6. Mother of Hastings Marks, TJ's brother-in-law.

has been occupied. J. Eppes has been for some time gone to
Champe Carter's[4] and that neighborhood with P. Carr. Mrs.
Dunbar is just gone there also. Our weather has been very sea-
sonable. But I hear an unfavorable account of a field of corn of
Mr. Randolph's on the road, as being yellow and ill-looking, sup-
posed to be too thick planted. We are very anxious to hear what
effect the springs have on his health. My best esteem to him. Adieu.
Yours affectionately,   TH: JEFFERSON

1. These watering places or spas were located in the western counties of
Bath and Greenbrier. The latter is now in West Virginia.
2. Dr. James Currie of Richmond.
3. She did not come to Monticello.
4. William Champe Carter was a son of Edward Carter of Blenheim, Albemarle County. In 1790 he purchased Viewmont from Edmund Randolph and
resided there until he sold it to his brother Edward Hill Carter on August 3,
1801. In December he purchased from Robert Beverley 1,904¼ acres in the
northwest section of Culpeper County, near the present village of Brandy.
See George S. Wallace, *The Carters of Blenheim* (Richmond, 1955), 64.

From Martha Jefferson Randolph

Dunginess[1] Jan 1st 1796

Mr. Randolph having determined to spend some months at
Varina I am under the necessity of troubling you my dearest
Father with a memorandum of the articles we shall want from
Monticello. We have spent hollidays and indeed every day in such
a perpetual round of visiting and recieving visits that I have not
had a moment to my self since I came down and we shall leave
this on our way to Richmond next sunday where I hope to recieve
a letter from you. Give my love to Maria and the children and
believe me dearest Father with unchangeable affection your's in
great haste.   M RANDOLPH
The waggon will be at Monticello the 5th or 6th of the month.

1. Dungeness, the home of Isham Randolph in Goochland County, Virginia.

To Martha Jefferson Randolph

Jan. 25. 1796.
MY DEAR MARTHA

After the departure of my last letter to Mr. Randolph I found
the details I had given him respecting the waggon were erroneous.
The rise of the river had cut off our communications for several
days. I presume it arrived at Varina as soon as my letter.

my dear Martha; kisses to Anne, and my best salutations to Mr. Randolph.

1. Monticello is actually two houses, the present, or second, having evolved from the first. The earlier was begun about 1769 and had a central mass of two stories with octagonal projections. (See James A. Bear, Jr., *Old Pictures of Monticello, An Essay in Historical Iconography* [Charlottesville, 1957], 5-7.) This was the house that Mrs. Jefferson knew, the one that was nearing completion or had been completed when she died in September, 1782. This sad event caused the suspension of all future plans and construction, and the house stood in this condition until several years after TJ's return from France, where he undoubtedly began to contemplate remodeling. Such plans were formulated by 1793 and were mentioned in a letter of March 3, 1793 (DLC), to the carpenter, Stephen Willis. Active demolitions did not begin until February, 1796, and consisted chiefly of "taking down the upper story . . . and building it on the ground, so as to spread all my rooms on one floor." (To Benjamin Hawkins, March 22, 1796, DLC.) TJ envisaged a job of several years, but it was not completed (if indeed it ever was) until 1809. For a step-by-step account of the remodeling of the house, consult the "Construction File" at Monticello. This is a chronologically arranged file of extracts, chiefly from Jefferson, and family correspondence pertaining to all phases of construction and remodeling.

2. Samuel Swann and Caleb Lownes. Consult Account Books for numerous references to Lownes and the *Virginia Gazette and Richmond Chronicle*, May 20, 1794, p. 3, for a Swann advertisement.

To Martha Jefferson Randolph

Monticello Mar. 6. 96.

Our neighborhood my dear daughter furnishes us with not one word of news to you, and I am so fatigued with writing for this post that I can only inform you we are all well, Jefferson robust as a beef, and all our desires alive to see you. My kisses to dear Anne, and best affections to Mr. Randolph and yourself. Adieu my dear and love me as I do you.   TH: J.

To Martha Jefferson Randolph

Chester-town Maryland Feb. 28. 1797.

I have got so far, my dear Martha, on my way to Philadelphia which place I shall not reach till the day after tomorrow. I have lost one day at Georgetown by the failure of the stages, and three days by having suffered myself to be persuaded at Baltimore to cross the bay and come by this route as quicker and pleasanter. After being forced back on the bay by bad weather in a first attempt to cross it, the second brought me over after a very rough passage, too late for the stage. So far I am well, tho' much fatigued.

*Vice-President of the
United States of America*

To Mary Jefferson

Philadelphia Mar. 11. 97.

My dear Maria

I recieved with great pleasure your letter from Varina, and though I never had a moment's doubt of your love for me, yet it gave me infinite delight to read the expressions of it. Indeed I had often and always read it in your affectionate and attentive conduct towards me. On my part, my love to your sister and yourself knows no bounds, and as I scarcely see any other object in life, so would I quit it with desire whenever my continuance in it shall become useless to you. I heard, as I passed thro' Wilmington, that your acquaintance Miss Geddis was well, and not yet married. I have here met with another who was at Mrs. Pine's with you, Miss McKain, who sings better than any body I have heard in America, and is otherwise well accomplished. I recieved a letter yesterday from Bruni,[1] praying a seat *in my carriage* to some place in Virginia where she could get a passage by water which would shorten that to Varina. I am sincerely sorry not only that I have not my own carriage to offer her a seat, but that I had engaged with a party to take the whole of the mail stage back, so that there was not a place left to offer her. I am obliged to apologize to her on this ground, but people under misfortune are suspicious, and I fear these little accidental checks may make her think them intentional. I leave this the day after tomorrow, and shall be at home on the 19th. or 20th. but my dear, do not let my return hasten yours. I would rather you should stay where you are till it becomes disagreeable to you, because I think it better for you to go more into society than the neighborhood of Monticello admits. My first letter from Monticello shall be to your sister. Present her my warmest love and be assured of it yourself. Adieu my dear daughter.

1. Mme. Brunette de Châteaubrun.

141

FROM MARTHA JEFFERSON RANDOLPH

Varina March 31st 1797

MY DEAREST FATHER

The first certain account we had of your arrival were conveyed by your letter to Mr. Randolph which would as you suposed have met on his way up had we not previously determined upon having the children innoculated. But every circumstance of season health &c. conspiring to make the present opportunity favorable Mr. Randolph thought no interest of his could excuse his letting it slip. I have often experienced that a mother's heart was of all things in nature the least subject to reason but never more fully than at present. The idea of exposing my children to such a disorder with out being able to accompany them alltho I have the certainty of their finding in their Father as tender and an infinitely more skillfull nurse than my self, makes me perfectly miserable. I never look at them but my eyes fill with tears to think how soon we shall part and *perhaps* for ever. The anxiety I feel on their account my Dear Father does not prevent my feeling most sensibly for the solitude and gloom of your present situation. I never take a view of your solitary fire side but my heart swells. However as nothing detains us now but the children I hope soon [to] be restored to your paternal embraces and dispel by the presence of your children the cloud which obscures the beauties of spring, no where so enchanting as at Monticello. My sister joins me in the tenderest love. As the boys are waiting I am obliged to conclude with Dearest Father yours most affectionate,

M. RANDOLPH

TO MARTHA JEFFERSON RANDOLPH

Monticello Apr. 9. 97.

I recieved yours, my dear Martha, of Mar. 31. four days ago. The inoculation at Richmond having stopped that post I send this by way of Fredsbg. I entirely approve of your resolution to have the children inoculated. I had before been so much convinced of the expediency of the measure that I had taken it for granted before your letter informed me of it. I am called to Philadelphia to a meeting of Congress the 15th. of May and shall leave Monticello on the 3d. or 4th. of that month, as Mr. Randolph informs me you would have quitted Varina and come up the beginning of this month but for the inoculations, would it not be best for you as soon as the children are quite recovered, from the dis-

slowly indeed; being only able to walk a little stronger.[1] I see by the newspapers that Mr. and Mrs. Church and their family are arrived at New York. I have not heard from them, and therefore am unable to say any thing about your friend Kitty, or whether she be still Miss Kitty.[2] The condition of England is so unsafe that every prudent person who can quit it, is right in doing so. James[3] is returned to this place, and is not given up to drink as I had before been informed. He tells me his next trip will be to Spain. I am afraid his journeys will end in the moon. I have endeavored to persuade him to stay where he is, and lay up money. We are not able yet to judge when Congress will rise. Opinions differ from two to six weeks. A few days will probably enable us to judge. I am anxious to hear that Mr. Randolph and the children have got home in good health; I wish also to hear that your sister and yourself continue in health; it is a circumstance on which the happiness of my life depends. I feel the desire of never separating from you grow daily stronger, for nothing can compensate with me the want of your society. My warmest affections to you both. Adieu, and continue to love me as I do you. Yours affectionately,

TH: JEFFERSON

1. This attack does not appear to have been severe, since he failed to mention it in his letter of the 12th to Martha or in any following. These spells on occasion were very painful and sometimes rendered him almost immobile. Consult the "Medical Chronology" under appropriate dates.

2. Mrs. and Mrs. John Baker Church. He was an Englishman who married Angelica Schuyler, daughter of General Philip Schuyler of New York. Catherine (Kitty) Church was their daughter. She was a schoolmate of Martha and Mary at Panthemont in Paris and a close friend of Mary.

3. James Hemings was taken to France by TJ in 1784 for the purpose of learning the art of French cookery. He was freed by indenture February 5, 1796 (original at MHi), but not until he had instructed another member of the Monticello household staff in French cuisine. On February 26 (Account Book 1797) TJ gave him $30 for the trip to Philadelphia, where he presumably was to take up residence. An examination, however, of Philadelphia directories fails to list him as a resident. His later whereabouts is unknown.

To MARTHA JEFFERSON RANDOLPH

Philadelphia June 8. 1797.

MY DEAR MARTHA

Yours of May 20 came to hand the 1st. inst. I imagine I recieved mine of May 18. about six days after the date of yours. It was written the first post day after my arrival here. The commission you inclosed for Maria is executed, and the things are in the care of Mr. Boyce of Richmond, who is returning from hence

dent to get me along earlier, or him later, we might meet on the road. Not yet informed that Mr. Randolph is returned I have thought it safest to commit this article to my letter to you. The news of the day I shall write to him. My warmest love to yourself and Maria. Adieu affectionately.   TH: JEFFERSON

1. Probably Charles Johnston of Charles Johnston & Co., a Richmond mercantile house with which TJ often transacted business.

2. The engagement of Mary and John Wayles Eppes delighted TJ, for he was very kindly disposed toward the Eppington household and especially toward "Jack," as he had addressed him since childhood. After the wedding on October 13, 1797, he altered this form of address to a more dignified "Mr. Eppes."

3. For his daughter's dowry TJ, on October 12, 1797, deeded to "Mary and her heirs" 819¼ acres of land "on the north east side of the Rivanna River and adjacent thereto called Pantops." Included were slaves, cattle, and farm equipment; unfortunately, there was no dwelling house, which certainly influenced "Mr. Eppes's" decision not to settle near Monticello where his possessive father-in-law strongly desired them. Albemarle County Deed Book 12, 363–64.

For Mary's sole heir's inheritance, see footnote 1 to TJ to Francis Wayles Eppes, May 6, 1824.

4. A light one-horse-drawn vehicle, that is, a chaise or gig.

5. Noel's, an Orange County inn. TJ often breakfasted here when traveling north.

FROM MARY JEFFERSON

Monticello June 12th 1797

DEAR PAPA

Your letters to my sister and myself did not arrive here till the 9th. They were stopt in Fredericksburg by the sickness of the post boy, and were at last sent round by Richmond. We learnt with sorrow indeed that you had again been tormented by your rheumatism. The consolation of seeing you when you are ill is the only one I know. I never feel the distress of separation as much as then. I have at last written to Sally Cropper and inclose the letter to you to direct to her in Acomac county, and if she will answer it [I] will try for the future to keep up a more regular correspondence with her. Mr. Randolph and the children arriv'd here last Tuesday all in perfect health. Ann and Jefferson grown so much as to amaze us, Ann seems to promise more every day of resembling her mother. Her disposition is the same allready. She will no doubt be worthy of her. We are alone at present. Mr. Hylton[1] and Mr. Lawrence with whom he is travelling left us today after a visit of ten days. We have seen no one else, I hope we shall not for some time, solitude after such company as his is by no means unpleasant. I am not able to tell you whether Mr. Richardson[2] is going on well. They today, began to raise the walls of the hall, the other rooms

with the utmost impatience day after day drawn out here in useless debate, and rhetorical declams. Take care of your health my
dear child for my happiness as well as your own and that of all
those who love you. And all the world will love you if you continue
good good humored, prudent and attentive to every body, as I
am sure you will do from temper as well as reflection. I embrace
you my dear in all the warmth of my love, and bid you affectionately adieu.

To Mary Jefferson Eppes

Monticello Dec. 2. 97.

My dear Maria

You will be surprised at recieving a letter from me dated here
at this time but a series of bad weather having suspended our
works many days, has caused my detention. I have for sometime
had my trunk packed and issued my last orders, and been only
waiting for it to cease raining. But it still rains. I have a bad
prospect of wars and work before me. Your sister moved to Belmont about three days ago. The weather ever since has kept us
entirely asunder. If tomorrow permits my departure I shall be in
Philadelphia in a week from this time. You shall hear from me
there, should it be only to provoke answers to my letters assuring
me of your health, of Mr. Eppes's and the good family of Eppington. I received his letter from Mrs. Payne's which gave us great
comfort; but we have apprehended much that you did not get to
Eppington before the bad weather set in. Tell Mr. Eppes that
I have orders for a sufficient force to begin and finish his house [1]
during the winter after the Christmas holidays; so that his people
may come safely after New year's day. The overseer at Shadwell
will furnish them provisions. Present my affections to him, and
the family, and continue to love me as you are tenderly beloved
by Your's affectionately,   Th: Jefferson

1. TJ was referring to the Pantops property. See Dumas Malone, "Polly Jefferson and Her Father," *The Virginia Quarterly Review*, VII, No. 1 (1931), 90.

From Mary Jefferson Eppes

Chestnut grove December the 8th 1797

Dear Papa

The fortnight that I spent at Eppington was so taken up in
recieving and returning visits, that it was out of my power while

who stay at home, enjoying the society of their friendly neighbors, blessed with their firesides, and employed in doing something every day which looks useful to futurity. I expect you will of course charge me before my departure with procuring you such articles of convenience here as you can get best here. I shall be sending some things for my self in the spring. Tell Mr. Randolph I shall be glad from time to time to exchange meteorological diaries with him, that we may have a comparative view of the climates of this place and ours.[1] I received a letter from Maria last week. She had got quite well of her sprain and was then at the Chestnut grove. However I suppose you hear from one another more directly than through me. Let me also hear from you, as your welfare, Mr. Randolph's and the little ones are the things nearest my heart. Do not let them forget me. Adieu my dear Martha. Affectionately,

1. TJ made these observations from 1766 until 1820. They appear in three manuscript volumes: 1776–1820, 1785–1786, and 1802–1815 (MHi). He also made similar notations in certain of his account books. The exchange with Thomas Mann Randolph, Jr., was first made in New York City in 1790.

To Mary Jefferson Eppes

Philadelphia Jan. 7.98.

I acknowledge, my dear Maria, the reciept of yours in a letter I wrote to Mr. Eppes. It gave me the welcome news that your sprain was well. But you are not to suppose it entirely so. The joint will remain weak for a considerable time and give you occasional pains much longer. The state of things at Chestnut grove is truly distressing. Mr. B's habitual intoxication will destroy himself, his fortune and family. Of all calamities this is the greatest. I wish my sister could bear his misconduct with more patience. It might lessen his attachment to the bottle, and at any rate would make her own time more tolerable. When we see ourselves in a situation which must be endured and gone through, it is best to make up our minds to it. Meet it with firmness and accomodate every thing to it in the best way practicable. This lessens the evil, while fretting and fuming only serves to increase our own torment. The errors and misfortunes of others should be a school for our own instruction. Harmony in the marriage state is the very first object to be aimed at. Nothing can preserve affections uninterrupted but a firm resolution never to differ in will and a determination in each to consider the love of the other as of more value than any object whatever on which a wish has been fixed. How

circle of my acquaintance, are most in the dispositions which will make you happy. Cultivate their affections, my dear, with assiduity. Think every sacrifice a gain which shall tend to attach them to you. My only object in life is to see yourself and your sister, and those deservedly dear to you, not only happy, but in no danger of becoming unhappy. I have lately recieved a letter from your friend Kitty Church. I inclose it to you. I think the affectionate expressions relative to yourself and the advance she has made will require a letter from you to her. It will be impossible to get a chrystal here to fit your watch without the watch itself. If you should know of any one coming to Philadelphia, send it to me, and I will get you a stock of chrystals. The river being frozen up, I shall not be able to send your things till it opens, which will probably be some time in February. I inclose to Mr. Eppes some pamphlets. Present me affectionately to all the family, and be assured of my tenderest love to yourself. Adieu,   TH: JEFFERSON

FROM MARTHA JEFFERSON RANDOLPH

Bellmont Jan. 22, 1798

Jupiter had given us so terrible an account of your sufferings from the ice on the potowmac that we began to be seriously alarmed about you before the arrival of your letters, which came both to gether; it was with infinite pleasure that we learned you had got the better of your cold and were at least comfortably if not agreably fixed for the winter. It is much more than we can boast of, for the extreme dampness of the situation and an absolute want of offices of every kind to shelter the servants whilst in the performance of their duties, have occasioned more sickness than I ever saw in a family in my life. Pleurisies, rhumatism and every disorder proceeding from cold have been so frequent that we have scarcely had at any one time *well* enough to tend the sick. Our intercourse with Monticello has been allmost *daily*. They have been generally well there except Tom and Goliah who are both *about* again and poor little Harriot[1] who died a few days after you left us. I shall joyfully accept the offer you made of executing my commissions in Philadelphia. Mr. Randolph has some money remaining in Barnes's hands[2] which I should be extremely obliged to you to lay out in plate, table spoons tea spoons, &c. as far as it will go. I imagine there is enough of it for that purpose and as

funeral. We shall stay sometime there to comfort the poor children and most of all poor Betsy whose sufferings for her mothers
situation have but too much allready affected her health. We left
Richmond a few days ago and I should have written to you there,
but I had not time. We saw Mr. W. Hylton there, who inform'd
us that his son, with Mr. Lawrence, had rented Richneck[2] of him
for 1000 pounds a year, in consequence of which he goes to live
in Berkely[3] where he has bought land of a gentleman who is engaged to Mrs. Campbell his daughter and will be married to her
this spring. This piece of news I thought would not be disagreable to you as he has given over all thoughts of settling in our
neighbourhood. I will write to Kitty Church soon and enclose
my letter in one to you. Adieu dear Papa. I am your affectionate
daughter,   M E

1. Anne Wayles Skipwith (Mrs. Henry).
2. Richneck was an estate of 4,000 acres in Warwick County owned by
Wilson Miles Cary. Jane Carr Cary lived there after her husband's (Wilson
Cary, son of Miles) death until financial conditions forced a sale. Daniel Hylton informed TJ on May 24, 1793 (Carr Cary Papers, ViU), "that in con-
junction with Mr. Miles King Doctor Wm. Foushee and brother Mr. Wm.
Hylton we have made a purchase of Mr. Wilson Miles Cary for his plantation
call'd Richneck situated on the Warwick River to carry on the lumber business in its various branches."
    An excellent map for locating Richneck, Ceeleys, Rock Castle, Eppington,
and other Virginia and Maryland estates, and particularly churches, of the
17th and 18th centuries is Leonard Leland, *Map of the Chesapeake Bay Country . . . Featuring more Particularly Tidewater Virginia* (n.p., MCMXXXIX),
original in the College of William and Mary Library. Photocopies at ViU and
Monticello.
3. Probably Berkeley County (now West Virginia), which at this time was
attracting a number of eastern Virginians.

To Martha Jefferson Randolph

Philadelphia Feb. 8. 98.

I ought oftener, my dear Martha, to recieve your letters, for the
very great pleasure they give me, and especially when they express
your affections for me. For though I cannot doubt them, yet they
are among those truths which tho' not doubted we love to hear
repeated. Here too they serve like gleams of light, to chear a
dreary scene where envy, hatred, malice, revenge, and all the worse
passions of men are marshalled to make one another as miserable
as possible. I turn from this with pleasure to contrast it with your
fire side, where the single evening I passed at it was worth more
than ages here. Indeed I feel myself detaching very fast, perhaps

in the next month. I still count on joining you at Eppington on my return. I recieve from home very discouraging accounts of Davenport's[1] doing nothing towards covering the house. I have written to him strongly on the subject, expressing my expectations to find the roof finished at my return. But I fear it will not pro-duce the effect desired. We are sure however of the Outchamber for you, and the Study for myself, and will not be long in getting a cover over some room for your sister. My last letter from Belmont was of Feb. 12. when they were all well. They have found the house there unhealthy, and their situation in general not pleasant. I pressed them to go to Monticello where they would be relieved from the inconvenience if just of a cellar full of water under them. I have not heard from them since. Mr. Trist is gone on to purchase Mr. Lewis's place.[2] They will not remove there till the fall. He is to be married to a Miss Brown of this place, an amiable girl, and who I hope will be of value to you as a neighbor. Having no news for Mr. Eppes but what he will find in a paper inclosed herewith, I do not write to him. My salutations to him, Mr. and Mrs. Eppes and the family at Eppington. To yourself my tenderest love,

TH: JEFFERSON

1. William Davenport was a sawyer and carpenter at Monticello.
2. Hore Browse Trist, son of Eliza House Trist (Mrs. Nicholas), purchased property in Albemarle County, Virginia, from James Lewis. The present estate of Birdwood was part of the original Trist purchase. Trist married Mary Brown of Philadelphia.

FROM MARY JEFFERSON EPPES

Eppington March 20th 1798

DEAR PAPA

We have been to Cumberland since I wrote to you last and saw while there the last melancholy rites paid to my Aunt Skipwith; I was never more affected, and never so sensible of the cruelty of requiring the presence of those who are most deeply afflicted at the ceremony. We came down immediately after it and brought poor Betsy for whom the scene had been too much with us, as her father fear'd her relapsing into her former state of melancholy if left alone so soon after it. We had a dreadful journey down and thought ourselves fortunate in escaping with one oversetting only, in which except the fright, none of us suffer'd, for the roads were as bad as they could possibly be. I am sorry to hear that my sisters situation at Belmont is not as agreeable as she expected,

Eppington, still, tell Mr. Eppes, I will make a visit from Monticello, rather than lose the colonnade and octagon.¹ So he will not get off from his purposes by that excuse. My last letter from Belmont was of the 19th. but Mr. Trist came from there since and reports that all were well. He is about sending off his furniture He has taken the house in Charlottesville that was George Nicholas's,² and will be living there before mid summer. My affectionate salutations to Mrs. Eppes, the gentlemen, and young ones, and kisses and everlasting love yourself. Adieu.

Mar. 16. The 1st. shad here.

28. The weeping willow begins to shew green leaves.

1. TJ did offer suggestions for the alteration of Eppington. A colonnade and octagonal projection were constructed. They are not visible today nor are they shown on a delineation of the front of the house that is included on a survey of the property made in 1865. This survey is now hanging in Eppington.

2. Wilson Cary Nicholas' brother. It was he who moved in the legislature for an investigation of TJ as war governor. He later removed to Kentucky.

To Martha Jefferson Randolph

Philadelphia. Apr. 5. 98.

Mr. Randolph's letter of Mar. 26. informs me you are all well at Belmont. My last news from Eppington was of Mar. 20. when all were well there. I have myself had remarkeably good health through the winter, since the cold which I took on my way here. The advance of the season makes me long to get home. The first shad we had here was Mar. 16. and Mar. 28. was the first day we could observe a greenish hue on the weeping willow from it's young leaves. Not the smallest symptom of blossoming yet on any species of fruit tree. All this proves that we have near two months in the year of vegetable life, and of animal happiness so far as they are connected, more in our canton than here. The issue of a debate now before the H. of Representatives will enable us to judge of the time of adjournment. But it will be some days before the issue is known. In the mean time they talk of the last of this month. Letters by a late arrival from France give reason to believe they do not mean to declare war against us; but that they mean to destroy British commerce with all nations, neutral as well as belligerent. To this the Swedes and Danes submit, and so must we unless we prefer war. A letter from Mr. Short informs me of the death of the old Dutchess Danville. He talks of coming in this spring or summer. I have purchased an excellent harpsichord¹ for Maria,

Father's house a few weeks since. We have been all well but Jefferson who had declined rapidly for some time from a disorder which had baffled every attention and change of diet, the only remedy we ventured to try, but Mr. Sneed⁴ opening school and Jeffy⁵ being hurried out of bed every morning at sunrise and obliged after a breakfast of bread and milk to walk 2 miles to school: his spirits returned his complexion cleared up and I am in hopes that his disorder has left him entirely. He is much mended in appearance strength and spirits, which had been low to an alarming degree. Anne just begins to read and little Ellen points at grand Papa's picture⁶ over the chimney when ever she is asked where he is. Adieu my Dearest Father. Blest as I am in my family you are still wanting to compleat my happiness. Monticello will be interesting indeed when with the prospect of it the loved idea of yourself and Dear Maria will be so intimately blended as they will in a few weeks I hope. Once more adieu and believe me with every sentiment of affection yours,   MRANDOLPH

1. A slave.
2. Mary Randolph Fleming (Mrs. Tarlton).
3. Martha Bolling Archer (Mrs. Field), a Jefferson niece.
4. Possibly Benjamin Snead.
5. Thomas Jefferson Randolph.
6. Probably the Mather Brown original of Jefferson, which was lost at sea in 1823 while in transit from Monticello to Boston with other possessions of Ellen Wayles Coolidge (Mrs. Joseph). See Alfred L. Bush, *The Life Portraits of Thomas Jefferson* (Charlottesville, 1962), [14]–16. This is the latest and most authoritative study of Jefferson's iconography.

TO MARTHA JEFFERSON RANDOLPH

Philadelphia May 17. 98.

MY DEAR MARTHA

Having nothing of business to write on to Mr. Randolph this week I with pleasure take up my pen to express all my love to you, and my wishes once more to find myself in the only scene where, for me, the sweeter affections of life have any exercise. But when I shall be with you seems still uncertain. We have been so long looking forward from 3. weeks to 3. weeks, and always with disappointment, that I know not now what to expect. I shall immediately write to Maria and recommend to Mr. Eppes and her to go up to Monticello as soon as my stores, which went from here a week ago, shall be sent on from Richmond; because our groceries &c. were pretty well exhausted when I left home. These may well arrive at Richmond by about the 20th. instant, so that time your journey so as to find them there. All other necessaries, either in the house or for me, have [administered] to you as if I were there. I have given notice to them at home that you will come and I shall have the pleasure of finding you there as soon as I can get from here, and in the mean time brood over the pain of being uselessly kept from among the society and scenes for which alone I would wish to prolong life one moment. For here it is worse than nothing. You will find your harpsichord arrived at Monticello, and without injury as Mr. Randolph informs me. I shall go of necessity by the shortest route to Monticello, and of course must deny myself the pleasure of taking Eppington in my way this time. Present my friendly salutations to Mr. and Mrs. Eppes; as also to our Mr. Eppes and the family. To yourself my tenderest love and Adieu.   TH: JEFFERSON

1. George Jefferson was a partner in the Richmond firm of Gibson and Jefferson and also TJ's cousin.

FROM MARY JEFFERSON EPPES

Eppington May 27th 98
DEAR PAPA

In hopes every day of recieving the long wish'd for and long expected summons to meet you at Monticello, I have delayed answering your last letter which you laughing and reproved me so justly for my negligence and inattention in writing. From your last to Mr. Eppes he does not expect that you will come in till near the 20th of next month, till which time unless your return should be sooner we shall stay down, as he is obliged to be here at that time. I have been to Petersburg lately with the girls, Bolling, and Tabby Walker,[1] one of her cousins, to take the small-pox which they have had most favourably; and from there we went to Shirley with my mother who is an old acquaintance and was recieved with much pleasure. We there met with Mr. John Walker and his lady, the latter seem'd pleas'd to see me and press'd me to visit her at her house, but I was not sorry that her husband did not think proper to invite me, for it would have been disagreeable to be forced to invent excuses where there was one so evident and so insurmountable.[2] I suppose you have not heard of Polly Archers death, render'd more afflicting to Aunt Bolling from her just suspicions that she hasten'd it by her intemperance in eating. She died of a bilious fever, a fort-night after her child was born, which is now alive and well and seems allready to afford

Volney[2] and a ship load of others of his nation will sail from hence on Sunday. Another ship load will go in about 3. weeks. A bill is now brought in to suspend all communication with France and her dominions: and we expect another to declare our treaty with her void. Mr. Randolph will percieve that this certainty of war must decide the objects of our husbandry to be such as will keep to the end of it. I am sorry to hear of Jefferson's indisposition, but glad you do not physic him. This leaves nature free and unembarrassed in her own tendencies to repair what is wrong. I hope to hear or to find that he is recovered. Kiss them all for me. Remember me affectionately to Mr. Randolph and be assured yourself of my constant and tenderest love. Adieu,

TH: JEFFERSON

P.S. It would be well that Davenport should be immediately informed that I am coming home. Since writing this I have recieved a letter from Mr. Eppes, informing me that all are well there. He and Maria will set out for Monticello June 20th.

TH: JEFFERSON

1. Charles Cotesworth Pinckney, John Marshall, and Elbridge Gerry had been sent to France to secure a treaty of amity and commerce. Their contemptuous treatment by and the attitude of the French government thoroughly aroused public opinion in America. Congress, fearing war, attempted to consolidate the national defense by passing twenty acts between March 27 and July, 1798, aimed at improving our military posture. On June 13 a bill suspending commercial intercourse with France was enacted. Other bills of May and July authorized the seizure of armed French ships but not of merchantmen, and on July 7 Congress declared the treaty with France void.

2. Count Constantin François Volney was a French philosopher and a friend of TJ's then residing in Philadelphia.

To Mary Jefferson Eppes

Philadelphia [June. 6. 98.]

MY DEAR MARIA

I wrote you last on the 18th. of May since which [I have received Mr. Eppes's] letter of May 20. and yours of May 27. I have deter[mined to set out from this] place on the 20th. inst. and shall, in my letters of tomo[rrow, order] my horses to meet me at Fredericksburg on the 24th. and may therefore be at home on the 26th. or 27th. where I shall hope to have the happiness of meeting you. I can supply the information you want as to your harpsichord. Your sister writes me it is arrived in perfect safety except the lock and a bit of moulding broke off. She played on it and pronounces it a very fine one, though without some of the advan-

was that of the carriage which was once more to bring us together. It was not till yesterday I learnt by the reciept of Mr. Eppes's letter of June 30th. that you had been sick, and were only on the recovery at that date. A preceding letter of his, referred to in that of the 30th. must have miscarried. We are now infinitely more anxious, not so much for your arrival here as your firm establishment in health, and that you may not be thrown back by your journey. Much therefore, my dear, as I wish to see you, I beg you not to attempt the journey till you are quite strong enough, and then only by short day's journies. A relapse will only keep us the longer asunder and is much more formidable than a first attack. Your sister and family are with me. I would have gone to you instantly on the reciept of Mr. Eppes's letter, had that not assured me you were well enough to take the bark. It would also have stopped my workmen here, who cannot proceed an hour without me, and I am anxious to provide a cover which may enable me to have my family and friends about me. Nurse yourself therefore with all possible care for your own sake, for mine, and that of all those who love you, and do not attempt to move sooner or quicker than your health admits. Present me affectionately to Mr. Eppes father and son, to Mrs. Eppes and all the family, and be assured that my impatience to see you can only be moderated by the stronger desire that your health may be safely and firmly re-established. Adieu affectionately,   Th: J.

To Mary Jefferson Eppes

Monticello July 14. 1798

I arrived here, my dear Maria, on the 3d. inst. and was in the daily hope of recieving you, when Mr. Eppes's letter of June 30. by the post of day before yesterday, gave us the first notice of your being sick.[1] Some preceding letter we infer had explained the nature of your indisposition, but it has never come to hand. We are therefore still uninformed of it. Your sister and myself wrote yesterday to you by post, but I have concluded to-day to send express that we may learn your situation of a certainty, and in a shorter time. I hope the bearer will find you so advanced in recovery as to be able ere long to set out for this place. Yet anxiously as we wish to see you, I must insist on your not undertaking the journey till you are quite strong enough, and then only by very short stages. To attempt it too soon will endanger a relapse which will keep us longer apart, and is always more tedious than the

To Mary Jefferson Eppes

Monticello Dec. 8. 98.

My dear Maria

I wrote to Mr. Eppes three weeks ago. Immediately after the date of that letter Lucy increased her family. She is doing well except as to her breasts. The one so much out of order when you went away, still continues in the same state, and the other threatens to rise also, which would entirely prevent her giving suck. She could not be moved in their present condition. I expect to set out for Philadelphia within ten days, within which time I hope to see the two Mr. Eppes's here. Mr. Randolph is not yet returned from Richmond, tho' now expected in a day or two. His family is here and all well. Ellen continues as much so as a weak digestion will permit. Our house I hope will all be covered in in the course of three or four weeks more so as to be out of the way of suffering, but Buck's[1] leaving us, without laying any more floors has prevented our getting the use of any other room. We shall hear from you I hope by Mr. Eppes and learn that you are well, and all the good family at Eppington. Present me to them affectionately and tell [remainder torn away]

1. John H. Buck, a Monticello workman.

To Martha Jefferson Randolph

Philadelphia Dec. 27. 98.

My dear Martha

I reached Fredericksburg the day after I left you, and this place on Christmas day, having (thanks to my pelisse[1]) felt no more sensation of cold on the road than if I had been in a warm bed. Nevertheless I got a small cold which brought on an inflammation in the eyes, head ach &c., so that I kept within doors yesterday and only took my seat in Senate to-day. I have as yet had little opportunity of hearing news; I only observe in general that the republican gentlemen whom I have seen consider the state of the public mind to be fast advancing in their favor. Whether their opponents will push for war or not is not yet developed. No business is as yet brought into the Senate, and very little into the other house: so that I was here in good time. I shall be at a loss how to direct to you hereafter, uncertain as I am whether you will leave home and where you will be. On this subject you must inform

and son, and all the family. Remember how pleasing your letters will be to me, and be assured of my constant and tender love. Adieu, my ever dear Maria. Your's affectionately,

TH: JEFFERSON

1. John Wayles Eppes and Mary removed from Eppington and resided here, a few miles from Petersburg, during the first months of their marriage.

FROM MARY JEFFERSON EPPES

Eppington January 21st 99

I was writing to you My Dear Papa and apologizing for my silence which has for sometime past had been occasion'd by a slight indisposition when I recieved your last letter. How much does your kindness affect me my dear Papa? A kindness which I so little merit and surely, if the most grateful sense of it, if the tenderest love could in any degree entitle me to it, I should not be undeserving of it. Suffer me dear Papa to tell you, how much above all others you are dear to me. That I feel more if possible every day how necessary your presence is to my happiness, and while blest with that and your affection I can never be otherwise. But the time is not far-distant I hope that will again reunite us all. With what pleasure do I look forward to it, to see you once more settled at home and to be after so long an absence allways within a mile or two of you and my dear sister. An if you are indeed with us whose happiness can be compared with our! Mr. Eppes is now at the Hundred. He had turn'd off his overseer and finds his presence there indispensable. I shall join him as soon as it is in my power which will be in a week or two at the farthest. We shall remain there till he gets another. We shall then remove to Mont Blanco, and there I hope it will not be long before we shall see you. Let me remind you of your promise my dear Papa if not too inconvenient for you to perform, and tell you what delight I feel at the hope of seeing you there. Adieu my dear Papa, excuse this hasty scrawl for it is very late. Believe me your affectionate daughter,   M E

P S Mr. Eppes desired me to tell you that his father expects to recieve the next Cumberland court 30 pound more for you and wishes to know into whose hands he must commit it. The family here all join in love to you.

morning from this place. My letters hitherto have been written for Thursday morning, so that you will have recieved them a week later. Tell Mr. Randolph that the day on which I wrote to him, but after I had sealed my letter, a bill was brought in to raise 30. regiments of infantry, cavalry and artillery, on the event of an invasion or in case of imminent danger of invasion in the opinion of the President. Regiments are now proposed to be about 1000. Our land army will then be the *existing* army 5000. The additional army *9000*, this *eventual* army 30,000. (instead of the Provisional one of 10,000 the act for which is expired) and the *volunteer* army, which is now to be formed into brigades and divisions and to be exercised. We have no particular information as to the price of tobo. but generally that that as well as all other produce is higher in England than ever known. The immense quantities of paper which their circumstances have forced them to create are now sensibly felt in the enlivening effect which always takes place in the first moment in the delusive shape of prosperity. They are accordingly now singing Hosannas for the unparalleled rise of their finances, and manufactures. We shall catch a little of the benefit in the beginning as their paper money price for tobo. will be hard money to us. But it will soon be fetched up as their paper money price for manufactures will be a hard money price to us. We ought to prepare against being involved in their embarassments by setting in by times to domestic manufacture. Jupiter with my horse must be at Fredericksburg on Tuesday evening the 5th. of March. I shall leave this place on the 1st. or 2d. You will recieve this the 14th. inst. I am already lighthearted at the approach of my departure. Kiss my dear children for me. Inexpressible love to yourself and the sincerest affection to Mr. Randolph. Adieu.

TO MARY JEFFERSON EPPES

Philadelphia Feb. 7. 99.

Your letter, my dear Maria, of Jan. 21. was recieved two days ago. It was, as Ossian[1] says, or would say, like the bright beams of the moon on the desolate heath. Environed here in scenes of constant torment, malice and obloquy, worn down in a station where no effort to render service can aver any thing, I feel not that existence is a blessing but when something recalls my mind to my family or farm. This was the effect of your letter, and it's affectionate expressions kindled up all those feelings of love for you and our dear connections which now constitute the only real

and the newspapers have informed you of the loss the friends of Liberty have sustained in the death of young Thomson[4] of Petersburg; which is the only event of any consequence that has taken place since you left us. For the rest, every thing stands as you left it, even your house. Davenport has I am afraid sold the plank he engaged to furnish for it, at least McGehee[5] told Mr. Randolph so, and he has certainly agreed to furnish some one in Milton with plank immediately. Mr. Randolph has some thoughts of employing a young man who has engaged to work for him (an acquaintance and recommended by McGehee) to do it if Davenport delays any longer. The children all join in tender love to you, from Virginia to *Annin Zoon*[6] who speaks much of you, and as a constant resource against *ill treatment* from her Papa and my self, whom she frequently threatens with going to *Phildelphy*. She sends her love to you and begs you will bring her a *cake*. I must beg the favor of you to bring for Jefferson the *newest* edition of Sandford and Merton.[7] The old edition consisting of two volumes are to be had in Richmond but as we have heard there is a third and perhaps fourth volume come out which are not to be met with there, I must apply to you to acquit my word with him. Since I began to write we have been informed that Davenport has this very day set about your work. Mr. Randolph finds it impossible to write by this post but bids me tell you the tobacco is just prized (13 hogsheads in all) and by the next post he will give you the details of the other operations of the farm. Adieu Dearest Father. I write in the midst of the noise of the children and particularly your little *seet heart*[8] who has interrupted me so often that I have scarcely been able to connect one sentence with another. Believe me with tenderest reverence and affection yours unchangeably,

M. RANDOLPH

1. Martha Walker Divers (Mrs. George), who resided at Farmington.
2. Probably Richard H. Allen, who in 1799 paid taxes on 328 acres in Fredericksville Parish, where Belmont was located. There were no Allens residing in Saint Anne's Parish. Albemarle County Land Book 1799, Albemarle County Courthouse.
3. Possibly Mrs. George Jefferson of Richmond or Mrs. Randolph Jefferson, TJ's sister-in-law.
4. John Lewis Thomson was author of *The Letters of Curtius*.
5. William McGehee.
6. Virginia (Jenny) Randolph was then living at Monticello and probably Anne Cary, a TJ granddaughter.
7. Thomas Day, *The History of Sandford and Merton* (London, 1783–1789), 3 volumes. A work intended for the use of children. Martha was referring probably to the 7th edition, of 1795. There was also a French edition [1798] and others.
8. Ellen Wayles Randolph.

Mr. Eppes's affairs will permit. We are not without hopes he will take a trip up soon to see about his affairs here, of which I yet know nothing. I hope you are enjoying good health, and that it will not be long before we shall be again united in some way or other. Continue to love me, my dear, as I do you most tenderly. Present me affectionately to Mr. Eppes and be assured of my constant and warmest love. Adieu my ever dear Maria.

TH: JEFFERSON

To MARY JEFFERSON EPPES

Monticello Apr. 13. 99.

Your letter, my dear Maria, of Mar. 13. came safely to hand and gave us the information, always subject of anxiety, and therefore always welcome, that yourself and Mr. Eppes were well. It would yet have been better that we could all have been well together, as the health we enjoy separately would be more enjoyed together. Whether we can visit you is still uncertain, my presence here is so constantly called for when all our works are going on. However I have not altogether abandoned the idea. Still let it not retard your movements towards us. Let us all pray the fish to get into motion soon that Mr. Eppes may be done with them. His affairs here are going on well. Page [1] has made a noble clearing of about 80. thousand of the richest tobo. land and is in good forwardness with it. I have provided the place with corn till harvest. Our spring has been remarkeably backward. I presume we shall have asparagus tomorrow for the first time. The Peach trees blossomed about a week ago, the cherries are just now (this day) blossoming. I suppose you have heard before that Peter Carr had a son and Sam a daughter. Sam and his wife are daily expected from Maryland.[2] Dr. Bache is now with us at Monticello. His furniture is arrived at Richmond. He goes back to Philadelphia to bring on Mrs. Bache.[3] I expect he will buy James Key's land;[4] but what he will do for a house this summer is uncertain. Champe Carter is endeavoring to move into our neighborhood, and we expect Dupont de Nemours (my old friend) every day to settle here also. Baynham[5] is not quite decided. Ellen gives her love to you. She always counts you as the object of affection after her mama and uckin Juba.[6] All else join in love to you and Mr. Eppes. Add mine to the family at Eppington, and continue me your most tender

not take it, as he has had several applications from gentlemen well able to purchase it. I anticipate the time with real pleasure, had I no other reasons, regard for my health would make it desirable for the sallow complexions of my neighbours and their own complaints even at this season are sufficient proofs of the unhealthiness of the country. But I have been desir'd by Mr. Eppes's father to assure you that would you try the air of this place you would find it as healthy as any situation below the mountains. It is indeed uncommon for any one to be sick here. Adieu dear Papa. This is the last letter I hope that I shall write to you this year. The 15th or 16th I shall again behold dear Monticello and with it all that is most dear to me in the world and in that idea I allready feel a degree of happiness which makes me more sensible of that which I shall experience when that moment arrives, that heartfelt happiness which I only feel with you and my dear Sister. Adieu once more my dear Papa. Believe me your affectionate daughter,   M E

To Mary Jefferson Eppes

Philadelphia Jan. 17. 1800

My dear Maria

I recieved at Monticello two letters from you, and meant to have answered them a little before my departure for this place; but business so crowded on me at that moment that it was not in my power. I left home on the 21st. and arrived here on the 28th. of Dec. after a pleasant journey of fine weather and good roads, and without having experienced any inconvenience. The Senate had not yet entered into business, and I may say they have not yet entered into it: for we have not occupation for half an hour a day. Indeed it is so apparent that we have nothing to do but to raise money to fill the deficit of 5. millions of Dollars, that it is proposed we shall rise about the middle of March; and as the proposition comes from the Eastern members who have always been for setting permanently, while the Southern are constantly for early adjournment, I presume we shall rise then. In the mean while they are about to renew the bill suspending intercourse with France, which is in fact a bill to prohibit the exportation of tobacco and to reduce the tobacco states to passive obedience by poverty. J. Randolph has entered into debate with great splendor and approbation. He used an unguarded word in his first speech,

dear, of my most tender and constant love. Adieu. Your's affectionately and forever,   TH: JEFFERSON

1. Randolph was speaking to a resolution offered by John Nicholas of
Virginia leading to a reduction of the regular army. Captain James McKnight
and Lieutenant Michael Reynolds, Marine Corps officers, were the individuals
who jostled him. The matter of Randolph's intemperate language finally
came to President Adams' attention and hence to a congressional debate. The
sum of the affair appears only to have enhanced Randolph's public reputation. See William Cabell Bruce, *John Randolph of Roanoke 1773–1833* (New
York, 1922), I, 156–65 for a full account.
2. Dr. Frank Carr was a son of Garland Carr and nephew of Martha Jefferson and Dabney Carr.

To MARTHA JEFFERSON RANDOLPH

Philadelphia Jan. 21. 1800.
MY DEAR MARTHA

I wrote on the 13th. inst. to Mr. Randolph. I now inclose you
a letter from your friend Mde. Salimben. It came under cover to
me. And without looking at the second cover, or suspecting it not
for me, I broke the seal. A few words in the beginning shewed me
it was not, and on looking at the back I found it was addressed
to you. M. Bureau Pusy, the companion of la Fayette, with his
family and Mde. Dupont arrived at N. York some time ago.
Dupont, with his son (late consul) and family arrived there a few
days ago. I have a letter from La Fayette in which he says he should
sail for America in July, but as he also expressed a wish to see the
event of our negociation I suppose he will not come till reconcilia-
tion is established by that. J. Randolph's affair is not over. A
rancorous report was made to the H. of R. yesterday by a com-
mittee. It would seem as if the army themselves were to hew down
whoever shall propose to reduce them. The non-intercourse law
is to be renewed, but whether only for the tobacco states; or for
all, is a question. Were it not for the prospect of it's expiring by
the effect of a treaty, our state would do better to drop the culture
of tobo. altogether. I am made happy by a letter from Mr. Eppes,
recd two or three days ago and informing me that Maria was become a mother and was well.[1] It was written the day after the
event. These circumstances are balm to the painful sensations of
this place. I look forward with hope to the moment when we are
all to be reunited again. It is proposed that we shall adjourn about
the middle of March; and as the proposition comes from the
Eastern members it will probably prevail. There is really nothing
to do but to authorise them to make up their deficit of 5. millions

languished nine days but was never heard to speak from the first of his being seized to the moment of his death. Ursula [2] is I fear going in the same manner with her husband and son, a constant puking, shortness of breath and swelling first in the legs but now extending it self. The doctor I understand had also given her means as they term it and upon Jupiter's death has absconded. I should think his murders sufficiently manifest to come under the cognizance of the law. Mr. Trist had left Charlottesville before I recieved your letters but should Mr. Randolph be able to procure any other conveyance he will send them. As he is not at home at present I have of course answered those parts of his letter which required an immediate one. Adieu my dearest Father. I have written this with the messenger who is to carry it at my elbow impatiently waiting. I will write by the next post more deliberately. We are all well. Ellen sends her love to dear *seet* grand papa. Believe me with tenderest affection yours,   M RANDOLPH

1. Randolph Jefferson.
2. The Georges, "Little" and "Great," were slaves; Ursula was their mother and wife, respectively. "Little" George died in June of 1799 and his father on November 2 of this same year. See *Memoirs of a Monticello Slave* (1955), 66, and the *Farm Book*.

To MARTHA JEFFERSON RANDOLPH

Philadelphia Feb. 11. 1800.

MY DEAR MARTHA

I wrote to Mr. Randolph on the 2d. inst. acknoleging the receipt of his letter of the 18th. Jan. I had one also at the same time from Mr. Richardson giving me the details from Monticello. The death of Jupiter obliges me to ask of Mr. Randolph or yourself to give orders at the proper time in March for the bottling my cyder. I forgot to bring with me a morsel cut from one of our sheets, as a sample to guide Mr. Barnes in providing some sheeting for me. Being entirely ignorant of it myself I must ask the favor of you to inclose me a bit in a letter by the return of post. I suppose our French sheets to be of the proper fineness and quality. A person here has invented the prettiest improvement in the Forte piano I have ever seen. It has tempted me to engage one for Monticello, partly for it's excellence and convenience, partly to assist a very ingenious, modest and poor young man, who ought to make a fortune by his invention. His strings are perpendicular, so that the instrument is only 3.f. 4.I. wide, 15.I. deep, and 3.f. 6.I. high.

FEBRUARY 12, 1800   185

To Mary Jefferson Eppes

Philadelphia February 12. 1800.
My dear Maria

Mr. Eppes's letter of Jan. 17. had filled me with anxiety for your little one, and that of the 25th. announced what I had feared. How deeply I feel it in all it's bearings, I shall not say, nor attempt consolation where I know that time and silence are the only medecines. I shall only observe as a source of hope to us all that you are young and will not fail to possess enough of these dear pledges which bind us to one another and to life itself. I am almost hopeless in writing to you, from observing that at the date of Mr. Eppes's letter of Jan. 25. three which I had written to him and one to you had not been recieved. That to you was Jan. 17. and to him Dec. 21. Jan. 22. and one which only covered some pamphlets. That of Dec. 21. was on the subject of Powell and would of course give occasion for an answer. I have always directed to Petersburg. Perhaps Mr. Eppes does not have enquiries made at the post office there. His of Jan. 1. 12. 17. and 25. have come safely tho' tardily. One from the Hundred never came. I will inclose this to the care of Mr. Jefferson.

The Representatives have proposed to the Senate to adjourn on the 7th. of April, and as the motion comes from the Eastern quarter and the members from thence are anxious, for political reasons, to separate, I expect we shall adjourn about that time. I fully propose, if nothing intervenes to prevent it, to take Chesterfield in my way home. I [am] not without hopes you will be ready to go on with me; but at any rate that you will soon follow. I know no happiness but when we are all together. You have perhaps heard of the loss of Jupiter. With all his defects, he leaves a void in my domestic arrangements which cannot be filled.

Mr. Eppes's last letter informed me how much you had suffered from your breasts: but that they had then suppurated, and the inflammation and consequent fever abated. I am anxious to hear again from you, and hope the next letter will announce your reestablishment. It is necessary for my tranquility that I should hear from you often: for I feel inexpressibly whatever affects either your health or happiness. My attachments to the world and whatever it can offer are daily wearing off, but you are one of the links which hold to my existence, and can only break off with that. You have never by a word or a deed given me one moment's uneasiness; on the contrary I have felt perpetual gratitude to heaven for having given me, in you, a source of so much pure and unmixed

slow in getting to you that he will see every thing first in the news-papers. Assure him of my sincere affections, and present the same to the family of Eppington if you are together. Cherish your own health for the sake of so many to whom you are dear, and espe-cially for one who loves you with unspeakable tenderness. Adieu my dearest Maria.

TO MARTHA JEFFERSON RANDOLPH

Philadelphia Apr. 22. 1800.

MY DEAR MARTHA

It is very long since I wrote to you, because I have been uncer-tain whether you would not have left Eppington before the arrival of my letters there and the rather as I found them very long getting there. Mr. Randolph's letter of the 12th. informs me you had then returned to Edgehill. In a letter of Mar. 24. which is the last I have recieved from Eppington, Mr. Eppes informed me Maria was so near well that they expected in a few days to go to Mont-blanco. Your departure gives me a hope her case was at length established. A long and a painful case it has been, and not the most so to herself or those about her. My anxieties have been excessive. I shall go by Mont-blanco to take her home with me, which Mr. Eppes expressed to be their desire. I wrote last week to Mr. Richardson to send off my horses to Mont Blanco on the 9th. of May. But both houses having agreed to rise on the 2d Monday (12th. of May) I shall write to him by this post, not to send them off till Friday the 16th. of May; as I shall be 7. or 8 days from the 12th. getting to Mont Blanco, and near a week after-wards getting home. I long once more to get all together again: and still hope, notwithstanding your present establishment, you will pass a great deal of the summer with us. I would wish to urge it just so far as not to break in on your and Mr. Randolph's de-sires and convenience. Our scenes here can never be pleasant. But they have been less stormy, less painful than during the XYZ. paroxysms. Our opponents perceive the decay of their power. Still they are pressing it, and trying to pass laws to keep themselves in power. Mr. Cooper[1] was found guilty two days ago, under the Sedition law, and will be fined and imprisoned. Duane[2] has 16. or 17 suits and indictments against him. The sheriff and justices who got the letters of Mr. Liston[3] which Sweeny the horse thief abandoned, are indicted. This is all the news I have for Mr. Ran-dolph. Of foreign news we know nothing but what he will see in

have overtaken you also. Dr. and Mrs. Bache have been with us till the day before yesterday. Mrs. Monroe is now in our neighborhood to continue during the sickly months. Our Forte-piano arrived a day or two after you left us. It had been exposed to a great deal of rain, but being well covered was only much untuned. I have given it a poor tuning. It is the delight of the family, and all pronounce what your choice will be. Your sister does not hesitate to prefer it to any harpsichord she ever saw *except her own.* And it is easy to see it is only the celestini which retains that preference. It is as easily tuned as a spinette, and will not need it half as often. Our harvest has been a very fine one. I finish to day. It is the heaviest crop of wheat I ever had. A murder in our neighborhood is the theme of it's present conversation. George Carter shot Birch [1] of Charlottesville, in his own door, and on very slight provocation. He died in a very few minutes. The examining court meets tomorrow. As your harvest must be over as soon as ours, we hope soon to see Mr. Eppes and himself. I say nothing of his affairs lest he should be less impatient to come to see them. All are well here except Ellen, who is rather drooping than sick; and all are impatient to see you. No one so much as him whose happiness is wrapped up in yours. My affections to Mr. Eppes and tenderest love to yourself. Hasten to us. Adieu.

TH: JEFFERSON

1. Samuel Birch. Peter Carr gives an account of this affair in a letter to Mary Carr of July 24, 1800. Carr-Cary Papers, ViU.

FROM MARY JEFFERSON EPPES

Bermuda Hundred Dec. 28. 1800.

I feel very anxious to hear from you My Dear Papa. It is a long time since you left us, and it appears still longer from not having heard from you, opportunitys from Eppington to Petersburg so seldom occur that I could not write to you while there, here I hope we shall recieve your letters more regularly. By directing them to City Point [1] which Mr. Eppes thinks will be the best, we can get them the same day they arrive there and in the expectation of hearing from you a little oftener I shall feel much happier. We have had the finest spell of weather ever known allmost for the season here, fires were uncomfortable till within a day or two past, and it still continues very mild and pleasant. It happen'd fortunately for us, as the house was not in a very comfortable state and every thing was to be moved from Mount Blanco here. We have

would compensate to me a separation from yourself and your sister. But the distance is so moderate that I should hope a journey to this place would be scarcely more inconvenient than one to Monticello. But of this we will talk when we meet there, which will be to me a joyful moment. Remember me affectionately to Mr. Eppes: and accept yourself the effusions of my tenderest love. Adieu my dearest Maria.

1. Betty Washington Lewis (Mrs. Fielding), sister of George Washington.
2. Aaron Burr.

To Martha Jefferson Randolph

Washington Jan. 16, 1801.

My dear Martha

I wrote to Mr. Randolph on the 9th. and 10th. inst. and yesterday recieved his letter of the 10th. It gave me great joy to learn that Lilly[1] had got a recruit of hands from Mr. Allen,[2] tho' still I would not have that prevent the taking all from the nailery[3] who are able to cut, as I desired in mine of the 9th. as I wish Craven's ground[4] to be got ready for him without any delay. Mr. Randolph writes me you are about to wean Cornelia. This must be right and proper. I long to be in the midst of the children, and have more pleasure in their little follies than in the wisdom of the wise. Here too there is such a mixture of the bad passions of the heart that one feels themselves in an enemy's country. It is an unpleasant circumstance, if I am destined to stay here, that the great proportion of those of the place who figure are federalists, and most of them of the violent kind. Some have been so personally bitter that they can never forgive me, tho' I do them with sincerity. Perhaps in time they will get tamed. Our prospect as to the election has been alarming: as a strong disposition exists to prevent an election, and that case not being provided for by the constitution, a dissolution of the government seemed possible. At present there is a prospect that some tho' federalists, will prefer yielding to the wishes of the people rather than have no government. If I am fixed here, it will be but three easy days journey from you: so that I should hope you and the family could pay an annual visit here at least; which with mine to Monticello of the spring and fall, might enable us to be together 4. or 5. months of the year. On this subject however we may hereafter converse, lest we should be counting chickens before they are hatched. I inclose for Anne a story, too long to be got by heart, but worth reading. Kiss them all for me: and keep

in the family. He was 6 or seven weeks in constant and familiar intercourse with us before we suspected what was the matter with him, the moment it was discovered that the other little boy had it, we were no longer at a loss to account for Jefferson's irruption which had been attributed all along to his covering too warm at night. I am delighted that your return will happen at a season when we shall be able to enjoy your company with out interuption. I was at Monticello last spring 1 day before the arrival of any one, and one day more of interval between the departure of one family and the arrival of another, after which time I never had the pleasure of passing one sociable moment with you. Allways in a crowd, taken from every useful and pleasing duty to be worried with a multiplicity of disagreable ones which the entertaining of such crowds of company subjects one to in the country. I suffered more in seeing you allways at a distance than if you had still been in Philadelphia, for then at least I should have enjoyed in anticipation those pleasures which we were deprived of by the concourse of strangers which continually crowded the house when you were with us. I find my self every day becoming more averse to company. I have lost my relish for what is usually deemed pleasures and duties incompatible with it have surplanted all other enjoyments in my breast. The education of my children to which I have long devoted every moment that I could command, but which is attended with more anxiety now as they increase in age without making those acquirements which other children do. My 2 eldest are uncommonly backward in every thing much more so than many others, who have not had half the pains taken with them. Ellen is wonderfully apt. I shall have no trouble with her, but the two others excite serious anxiety with regard to their intellect. Of Jefferson my hopes were so little sanguine that I discovered with some surprise and pleasure that he was quicker than I had ever thought it possible for him to be, but he has lost so much time and will necessarily lose so much more before he can be placed at a good school that I am very unhappy about him. Anne does not want memory but she does not improve. She appears to me to learn absolutely without profit. Adieu my Dear Father. We all are painfully anxious to see you. Ellen counts the weeks and continues storing up complaints against Cornelia whom she is perpetually threatning with *your* displeasure. Long is the list of misdemeanors which is to be communicated to you, amongst which the stealing of 2 potatoes carefully preserved 2 whole days for you but at last stolen by Cornelia forms a weighty article.

much afflicted to learn that your health is not good, and the particular derangement of your stomach. This last is the parent of many ills, and if any degree of abstinence will relieve you from them it ought to be practiced. Perhaps in time it may be brought to by beginning with a single one of the hostile articles, taking a very little of it at first, and more and more as the stomach habituates itself to it. In this way the catalogue may perhaps be enlarged by article after article. I have formed a different judgment of both Anne and Jefferson from what you do; of Anne positively, of Jefferson possibly. I think her apt, intelligent, good humored and of soft and affectionate dispositions and that she will make a pleasant, amiable and respectable woman. Of Jefferson's disposition I [have] formed a good opinion, and have not suffered myself to form any other good or bad of his genius. It is not every heavy-seeming boy which makes a man of judgment, but I never yet saw a man of judgment who had not been a heavy seeming boy, nor knew a boy of what are called sprightly parts become a man of judgment. But I set much less store by talents than good dispositions: and shall be perfectly happy to see Jefferson a good man, industrious farmer, and kind and beloved among all his neighbors. By cultivating those dispositions in him, and they may be immensely strengthened by culture, we may ensure his and our happiness: and genius itself can propose no other object. Nobody can ever have felt so severely as myself the prostration of family society from the circumstance you mention. Worn down here with pursuits in which I take no delight, surrounded by enemies and spies, catching and perverting every word which falls from my lips or flows from my pen, and inventing where facts fail them, I pant for that society where all is peace and harmony, where we love and are loved by every object we see. And to have that intercourse of soft affections hushed and supported by the eternal presence of strangers goes very hard indeed, and the harder as we see that the candle of life burning out, so that the pleasures we lose are lost forever. But there is no remedy. The present manners and usages of our country are laws we cannot repeal. They are altering by degrees, and you will live to see the hospitality of the country reduced to the visiting hours of the day, and the family left to tranquility in the evening. It is wise therefore under the necessity of our present situation to view the pleasing side of the medal and to consider that these visits are evidences of the general esteem which we have been able all our lives trying to merit. The character of those we recieve is very different from the loungers who infest

to the moment when we can all be settled together, no more to separate. I feel no impulse from personal ambition to the office now proposed to me, but on account of yourself and your sister, and those dear to you. I feel a sincere wish indeed to see our government brought back to it's republican principles, to see that kind of government firmly fixed, to which my whole life has been devoted. I hope we shall now see it so established, as that when I retire, it may be under full security that we are to continue free and happy. As soon as the fate of the election is over, I will drop a line to Mr. Eppes. I hope one of you will always write the moment you recieve a letter from me. Continue to love me my dear as you ever have done, and ever have been and will be your's affectionately,   TH: JEFFERSON

1. The balloting in the Electoral College ended in a tie between TJ and Burr; each received 73 votes. This threw the election into the House of Representatives, where another deadlock occurred. The Federalists in caucus decided to support Burr; Alexander Hamilton, however, backed TJ as the lesser of two evils, and on the 36th ballot on February 17 TJ was named President.

President of the
United States of America

To Mary Jefferson Eppes

Monticello Apr. 11. 1801.

MY DEAR MARIA

I wrote to Mr. Eppes on the 8th. instant by post, to inform him I should on the 12th. send off a messenger to the Hundred for the horses he may have bought for me. Davy Bowles[1] will accordingly set out tomorrow, and will be the bearer of this. He leaves us all well, and wanting nothing but your's and Mr. Eppes's company to make us compleatly happy. Let me know by his return when you expect to be here, that I may accomodate to that my orders as to executing the interior work of the different parts of the house. John[2] being at work under Lilly, Goliah is our gardener, and with his veteran aids, will be directed to make what preparation he can for you. It is probable I shall come home myself about the last week of July or first of August to stay two months, and then be absent again at least six months. In fact I expect only to ma[ke a sh]ort visit to this place of a fortnight or three weeks in April and two months during the sickly season in autumn every year. These terms I shall hope to pass with you here, and that either in spring or fall you will be able to pass some time with me in Washington. Had it been possible, I would have made a tour now on my return to see you, but I am tied to a day for my return to Washington to assemble our new administration, and begin our work systematically. I hope, when you come up, you will make very short stages, drive slow and safely, which may well be done if you do not permit yourselves to be hurried. Surely the sooner you come the better. The servants will be here under your commands and such supplies as the house affords. Before that time our bacon will be here from Bedford. Continue to love me, my dear Maria, as affectionately as I do you. I have no object so near my heart as your's and your sister's happiness. Present me affectionately to Mr. Eppes and be assured yourself of my unchangeable and tenderest attachment to you.   TH: JEFFERSON

1. A trusted slave.
2. John Hemings.

ent construction of our family. I inclose for Anne some trifles cut out of the newspapers.[2] Tell Ellen I will send her a pretty story as soon as she can read it. Kiss them all for me; my affectionate esteem to Mr. Randolph and warmest love to yourself.

TH: JEFFERSON

1. Meriwether Lewis.

2. This was a TJ practice that he carried on with the older Randolph grand-children, particularly Ellen. Unfortunately, none of these scrapbooks have sur-vived; however, TJ's own volume "The Jefferson Scrapbook" is in the Alder-man Library at the University of Virginia. This contains a great variety of material, including several poetical works sent to his grandchildren for their scrapbooks. For a discussion of the contents of Jefferson's, consult John W. Wayland, "The Poetical Tastes of Thomas Jefferson," *Sewanee Review*, XVIII, 283–99, and William H. Peden, "Thomas Jefferson: Book Collector," an un-published dissertation at the University of Virginia (1942), 61–63.

TO MARY JEFFERSON EPPES

Washington May 28. 1801.

An immense accumulation of business, my dear Maria, has pre-vented my writing to you since my arrival at this place. But it has [not] prevented my having you in my mind daily and hourly, and feeling much anxiety to hear from you, and to know that Mr. Eppes and yourself are in good health. I am in hopes you will not stay longer than harvest where you are, as the unhealthy sea-son advances rapidly after that. Mr. and Mrs. Madison staid with me about three weeks till they could get ready a house to recieve them. This has given me an opportunity of making some acquaint-ance with the ladies here. We shall certainly have a very agreeable and worthy society. It would make them as well as myself very happy could I always have yourself or your sister here but this desire, however deeply felt by me, must give way to the private concerns of Mr. Eppes. I count that in autumn both yourself and sister, with Mr. Eppes and Mr. Randolph will pass some time with me but this shall be arranged at Monticello where I shall be about the end of July or beginning of August. Ask the favor of Mr. Eppes, to inform me as soon as he can learn himself the age, and blood of the several horses he was so kind as to purchase for me. Present him my affectionate attachment, as also to the family at Eppington when you have an opportunity. Remember that our letters are to be answered immediately on their reciept, by which means we shall mutually hear from each other about every three weeks. Accept assurances of my constant and tender love.

TH: JEFFERSON

of those we most love once more at Monticello and as the time approaches the spirits of the family proportionably increase. You have suffered a little from the last tremendous hail storm, from the [circumstance?] of 2 of the sky lights being uncovered. *They* were totally demolished and I believe it is owing to the accident of the storm's raging with so much more fury in the valley than on the mountains that you escaped so much better than your neighbours. The damage was immense in Charlottesville and Milton, allmost every window broken in some houses; we also suffered considerably and the more so as we have not been able to replace in either of the above mentioned places the glasses which has occasioned us to the violence of every succeeding rain in a degree that renders the house scarcely tenantable.

Your stockings are at last disposed of, but not to my satisfaction because I am sure they will not be so to yours. Aunt Carr after many ineffectual efforts to put them *out* acceded at last to the united and importunate entreaties of Mrs. Randolph[1] and Mrs. Lilburn Lewis[2] to let them knit them for you; and Aunt Lewis dining with me a few days after and hearing of the failure of the means upon which I had counted in accomplishing my part of the under taking, insisted in a manner [baffled?] resistance upon my letting her and her Daughters take them home and do them. It is a disagreable piece of business, but one not to have been fore seen in the first instance and not to be avoided afterwards with out hurting the feelings and perhaps giving offence to those without hurting the feelings and perhaps giving offence to those ladies. Inclosed are samples Fontrice[3] was to have carried, of the cotton one is too fine, the other too coarse. A size between the two would answer better than either. The sheeting is also I think rather coarse but not much so. Adieu dearest Father. The children are all confusing me with messages of various descriptions but the post hour is past and I am afraid my letter will scarcely be in time. Believe me with ardent affection yours,   M. RANDOLPH

1. Possibly Jane Cary Randolph Randolph (Mrs. Thomas Eston).
2. Lucy Jefferson Lewis (Mrs. Charles Lilburn, Jr.) was TJ's sister; she had five daughters.
3. Valentine Fontress was an Albemarle County resident who hauled for the Monticello family.

pected my large panes of glass would have broken easily. I inclose
a little story for Anne as I have sometimes done before. Tell Ellen
as soon as she can read them, I will select some beautiful ones for
her. They shall be black, red, yellow, green and of all sorts of
colours. I suppose you have had cucumbers and raspberries long
ago. Neither are yet at market here, tho some private gardens have
furnished them. Present me affectionately to Mr. Randolph who
I suppose is now busy in his harvest. I rejoice at the prospect of
price for wheat, and hope he will be able to take the benefit of
the early market. If his own threshing machine is not ready, he
is free to send for mine, which is in order and may expedite his
getting out. Kiss the little ones for me and be assured of my constant and tenderest love.   TH: JEFFERSON

TO MARTHA JEFFERSON RANDOLPH

Washington July 16. 1801.

MY DEAR MARTHA

I recieved yesterday Mr. Randolph's letter of the 11th. and at
the same time one from Mr. Eppes. He had just carried Maria to
Eppington with the loss of a horse on the road. They are to
leave Eppington tomorrow at farthest for Monticello, so that by
the time you recieve this they will be with you. From what Mr.
Randolph writes I should think you had better go over at once
with your sister to Monticello and take up your quarters there. I
shall join you in the first seven days of August. In the mean time
the inclosed letter to Mr. Craven (which I pray you to send him)
will secure you all the resources for the house which he can supply.
Liquors have been sent on and I learn are arrived, tho' with some
loss. Lilly has before recieved orders to furnish what he can as if
I were there. I wish you would notify him to be collecting geese
and ducks and to provide new flour. Of lambs I presume he has
plenty. I have had groceries waiting here some time for a conveyance. Would it not be well for you to send at once for Mrs. Marks?[1]
Remus[2] and my chair are at Monticello, and Phill[3] as usual can
go for her. I this day inclose to Dr. Wardlaw[4] some publications
on the kine pox, with a request to make himself acquainted with
them. I shall probably be able to carry on some infectious matter
with a view of trying whether we cannot introduce it there. The
first essay here has proved unsuccessful but some matter recieved
6. days ago and immediately used, will prove this day whether it

FROM MARTHA JEFFERSON RANDOLPH

Edgehill July 25 1801

Your letters found us all *together* at Edgehill. Maria does not look well but considering all things she seems to be in as good health as can be expected. My own has been uncommonly so, since my return from Monticello. With your request of going over immediately it is utterably impossible to comply; Mrs. Bache's family being with us at present, and to remain untill, the Doctor's return. Maria stays with *us* untill you join us and from what she says will not I hope require *my* attentions until I am *able* to bestow them entirely upon her. We have not sent for Aunt Marks because of the present size of our family which would render it, (with the expected addition) impossible to accomodate her. She might feel hurt at the idea of being at Monticello. Your other commissions shall be faithfully executed with regard to Lilly and altho it will not be in my power to be with you as soon as I could wish yet the idea of being so near you and the pleasure of seeing you sometimes will enliven a time otherwise dreary and monotonous. Adieu ever dear Father. Believe me with unchangeable affections yours,

M. RANDOLPH

TO MARTHA JEFFERSON RANDOLPH

Washington Oct. 19. 1801.

I am in hopes, my dear Martha, that I shall hear by the arrival of tomorrow morning's post that you are all well. In the mean while the arrangement is such that my letter must go hence this evening. My last letter was from Mr. Eppes of Oct. 3. when all were well. I inclose a Crazy Jane[1] for Anne, and a sweetheart[2] for Ellen. The latter instead of the many coloured stories which she cannot yet read. From the resolution you had taken I imagine you are now at Edgehill surrounded by the cares and the comforts of your family. I wish they may be less interrupted than at Monticello. I set down this as a year of life lost to myself, having been crowded out of the enjoiment of the family during the only recess I can take in the year. I believe I must hereafter not let it be known when I intend to be at home, and make my visits by stealth. There is real disappointment felt here at neither of you coming with me. I promise them on your faith for the ensuing spring. I wish however that may be found as convenient a season of absence

me affectionately to Mr. Eppes, Mr. Randolph and my dear
Martha, and be assured yourself of my tenderest love.

TH: JEFFERSON

1. Possibly Mrs. James Suddarth, a midwife. TJ was suggesting that she
assist Mary in recovering from any aftereffects of the birth of her son Francis
Wayles Eppes, who was born September 20 at Monticello.

FROM MARY JEFFERSON EPPES

Monticello November the 6th [1801]

I did not write to you last week My dear Papa, I had discover'd
my little Francis had the hooping cough and my apprehensions
about him were so great that I could not at that time write. He
has now struggled with it eleven days and tho he coughs most
violently so as to become perfectly black with it in the face he is
so little affected by it otherwise that my hopes are great that he
will go through with it. He has as yet lost no flesh and has had
only one fever. We shall endeavour to travel with him the last
of next week if he is not worse. I have borrow'd Crita[1] as a nurse
for this winter. Betsy's ill health was such that I could not depend
on her as one and we shall return with Crita in the spring to meet
you. The children at Edgehill stand the disorder very well,
Cornelia suffers most with it but she still looks very well (Mr.
Eppes says who saw her yesterday). Ellen next to her is most unwell, the other three are better, Virginia[2] particularly. I have not
seen my sister since her return to Edgehill. She remain'd here four
weeks after you left us during which time except a few days we
were entirely alone. How much we did wish for you then, My
dear Papa, but I am afraid that except in the spring we shall never
enjoy the happiness of being alone with you. Nothing would give
me greater pleasure could Mr. Eppes so arrange it as to spend the
next summer here. The hope of a flying visit sometimes from you,
would alone make it most desirable independent of every thing
else. Adieu dear Papa. Believe me most tenderly yours,

M EPPES

1. Crita was a slave daughter of Betty Hemings.
2. Virginia Jefferson Randolph was born August 22, 1801, at Monticello.

FROM ELLEN WAYLES RANDOLPH

recd Nov. 10. [1801]

How do you do my dear Grand papa. I thank you for the picture you sent me. All my sisters have got the hooping cough. Vir-

pected, but in a very precarious state of being. He is (altho healthy except for the whooping cough) the most delicate creature I ever beheld. Mine are doing well, all but poor Ellen, who looks wretchedly is much reduced and weakened by the cough which still continues upon her with extreme violence. Little Virginia is recovering, still distressing us at times but the crisis seems to be over with all of them. It was a terrible moment. Ellen and Cornelia were particularly ill both delirious one singing and laughing the other (Ellen) gloomy and terrified equally unconscious of the objects around them. My God what moment for a Parent. The agonies of Mr. Randolph's mind seemed to call forth every energy of mine. I had to act in the double capacity of nurse to my children and comforter to their Father. It is of service perhaps to be obliged to exert one self upon those occasions. Certainly the mind acquires strength by it to bear up against evils that in other circumstances would totally overcome it. I am recovering from the fatigue which attended the illness of my children and I am at this moment in more perfect health than I have been for years. Adieu beloved Father. You would write oftener if you knew how much pleasure your letters give. There is not a child in the house that does not run at the return of the messenger to know if there is a letter from Grand Papa. Stewart[1] your white smith is returned. The plaistering at Monticello goes on, not as well as the first room which was elegantly done but better than the 3d and fourth, the two I think you would have been most anxious about, being below stairs. Moran[2] goes on slowly. Every one the children with the whoping cough excepted is well and they are none of them bad but every thing upon the land (at Monticello) has it. Once more Adieu. Believe me with ardent affection yours. To tell you that it is past one o'clock will appologize for a great deal of incorectness in this scrawl and the hurried way in [which] I generally work will account for the rest.   M. Randolph

1. William Stewart the very able Monticello blacksmith fashioned much of the ironwork used in Monticello.
2. Joseph Moran was a Monticello workman, a stonemason.

To Ellen Wayles Randolph

Washington Nov. 27. 1801.

My dear Ellen

I have recieved your letter and am very happy to find you have made such rapid progress in learning. When I left Monticello you

when our campaign will begin and will probably continue to April. I hope I shall continue to hear from you often, and always that the children are doing well. My affections and contemplations are all with you, where indeed all my happiness centers. My cordial esteem to Mr. Randolph, kisses to the little ones, and tenderest love to yourself.   TH: JEFFERSON

1. John Perry, a Monticello carpenter.

TO MARY JEFFERSON EPPES

Washington Dec. 14. 1801.

MY DEAR MARIA

I recieved in due time yours and Mr. Eppes's letters of Nov. 6. and his of Nov. 26. This last informed me you would stay in Eppington 2. or 3. weeks. Having had occasion to write during that time to Mr. F. Eppes without knowing at the moment that you were there, you would of course know I was well. This with the unceasing press of business has prevented my writing to you. Presuming this will still find you at Eppington, I direct it to Colesville.[1] Mr. Eppes's letter having informed me that little Francis was still in the height of his whooping cough, and that you had had a sore breast, I am very anxious to hear from you. The family at Edgehill have got out of all danger. Ellen and Cornelia have been in the most imminent danger. I hear of no death at Monticello except old Tom Shackelford. My stonemasons have done scarcely anything there. Congress is just setting in on business. We have a very commanding majority in the house of Representatives and a safe majority in the Senate. I believe therefore all things will go on smoothly, except a little ill-temper to be expected from the minority, who are bitterly mortified. I hope there is a letter on the road informing how you all are. I percieve that it will be merely accidental when I can steal a moment to write to you, however that is of no consequence; my health being always so firm as to leave you without doubt on that subject. But it is not so with yourself and little one. I shall not be easy therefore if either yourself or Mr. Eppes do not once a week or fortnight write the three words 'all are well.' That you may be so now and so continue is the subject of my perpetual anxiety, as my affections are constantly brooding over you. Heaven bless you my dear daughter. Present me affectionately to Mr. Eppes and my friends at Eppington if you are there.   TH: JEFFERSON

P. S. After signing my name, I was called to receive Doctr. Walker[2]

closely[1] employ'd with work which during that time had greatly
accumulated that without intending it it has been postponed 'till
now. I have only thought the more of you My Dear Papa, of that
I hope you need never be assured, that you are of all most dear
to my heart and most constantly in my thoughts. With how much
regret have I look'd back on the last two months that I was with
you, more as I fear it will allways be the case now in your summer
visits to have a crowd, and in the spring I am afraid it not be
in my power to go up. It would make me most happy to go to
Washington to see you but I have been so little accustom'd to be
in as much company as I should be in there to recieve the civilitys
and attentions which as your daughter I should meet with and
return, that I am sensible it is best for me to remain where I am. I
have not heard from Edgehill since I left it. Mr. Eppes wrote once
to my sister when I was unable to do it. But I must bid you adieu
My dear Papa. Could I be as certain of the continuance of your
good health as you may now be of mine I should endeavour to be
satisfied in not hearing from you oftener, but while you are devoting your days and nights to the business of your country I must
feel anxious and fearful that your health will suffer by it. Adieu
once more my dear Papa. I shall write to you once more from here.
My little son is getting much better tho' he still engrosses so much
of my time that it is scarcely in my power to do any thing else. He
is cutting teeth now which makes him more fretful than usual.
Adieu. Yours with the most tender affection,   M EPPES

1. The nature of Maria's ailment is not known.

FROM ANNE CARY RANDOLPH

                                        Edgehill Feb. 26. 1802

DEAR GRAND PAPA

   I am very glad that I can write to you. I hope you are well. We
are all perfectly recovered from our whooping cough. I thank you
for the book you sent me. I am translating Justin's ancient history.[1]
I want to see you very much believe me. Cornelia sends her love
to you and has been trying to write to you. Adieu my Dear Grand
Papa. Believe me your affectionate Grand Daughter.

                                        ANNE CARY RANDOLPH

1. Marcus Junianus Justinus [De historiis Philippicis et totius Mundi
originibus . . .]. TJ owned the London 1701 edition, and it may be presumed
this is what the eleven-year-old Anne Cary was translating. Sowerby 36.

could have come together on a visit here. I observe your reluctance at the idea of that visit, but for your own happiness must advise you to get the better of it. I think I discover in you a willingness to withdraw from society more than is prudent. I am convinced our own happiness requires that we should continue to mix with the world, and to keep pace with it as it goes; and that every person who retires from free communication with it is severely punished afterwards by the state of mind into which they get, and which can only be prevented by feeding our sociable principles. I can speak from experience on this subject. From 1793. to 1797. I remained closely at home, saw none but those who came there, and at length became very sensible of the ill effect it had upon my own mind, and of it's direct and irresistible tendency to render me unfit for society, and uneasy when necessarily engaged in it. I felt enough of the effect of withdrawing from the world then, to see that it led to an antisocial and misanthropic state of mind, which severely punishes him who gives in to it: and it will be a lesson I never shall forget as to myself. I am certain you would be pleased with the state of society here, and that after the first moments you would feel happy in having made the experiment. I take for granted your sister will come immediately after my spring visit to Monticello, and I should have thought it agreeable to both that your first visit should be made together. In that case your best way would be to come direct from the Hundred by Newcastle, and Todd's bridge to Portroyal where I could send a light Coach to meet you, and crossing Patomac at Boyd's hole you would come up by Sam Carr's to this place. I suppose it 60. miles from Portroyal to this place by that route, whereas it would be 86. to come from Portroyal up the other side of the river by Fredericksburg and Alexandria. However if the spring visit cannot be effected then I shall not relinquish your promise to come in the fall: of course, at our meeting at Monticello in that season we can arrange it. In the mean time should the settlement take place which I expect between Mr. Wayles's and Mr. Skelton's executors, and Eppington be the place, I shall rely on passing some time with you there. But in what month I know not. Probably towards mid summer. I hardly think Congress will rise till late in April. My trip to Monticello will be about a fortnight. I am anxious to hear from you, as during the period of your being a nurse, I am always afraid of your continuing in health. I hope Mr. Eppes and yourself will soon make your calculations as to leave the Hundred by the beginning of July at least. You should never trust yourselves in

when I shall be going on to Monticello for the months of Aug. and Sep. I cannot help hoping that while your sister is here you will take a run, if it be but for a short time to come and see us. I have enquired further into the best rout for you, and it is certainly by Portroyal,[2] and to cross over from Boyd's hole,[3] or somewhere near it to Nangemy. You by this means save 30. miles, and have the whole of the way the finest road imaginable, whereas that from Fredericksburg by Dumfries and Alexandria is the worst in the world. Will Mr. Eppes not have the curiosity to go up to his plantation in Albemarle the 1st. or 2d. week of May? There we could settle every thing, and he will hear more of the Georgia expedition. I inclose you two medals,[4] one for yourself, the other with my best affections for Mrs. Eppes. They are taken from Houdon's bust. Present me affectionately to Mr. Eppes and be assured of my tenderest love.   TH: JEFFERSON

1. Thomas Mann Randolph, Jr., never went to the Mississippi Territory or to the state of Georgia.

2. A small Caroline County landing on the south side of the Rappahannock River, about 23 miles below Fredericksburg.

3. Boyd's Hole is in King William County, on the western side of the Potomac River.

4. These were by John Reich, and the delineation is found on the 1801 Indian Peace Medal.

TO MARTHA JEFFERSON RANDOLPH

Washington Apr. 3. 1802.

MY DEAR MARTHA

I recieved Anne's letter by the last post, in which she forgot to mention the health of the family, but I presume it good. I inclose you a medal executed by an artist lately from Europe and who appears to be equal to any in the world. It is taken from Houdon's bust, for he never saw me. It sells the more readily as the prints which have been offered the public are such miserable caracatures.[1] Congress will probably rise within three weeks and I shall be on in a week or ten days afterwards. My last to Mr. Randolph explained my expectations as to your motions during his journey. I wrote lately to Maria, encouraging her to pay us a flying visit at least while you are here, and proposing to Mr. Eppes so to time his next plantation visit in Albemarle as to meet me there in the beginning of May. My last information from the Hundred stated them all well, little Francis particularly healthy. Anne writes me that Ellen will be through all her books before I come. She may

are indebted to your letter expressing your surprise at her having in so short a time learned to read and write; she began with it her self, and by continually spelling out lines and putting them together and then reading them to who ever would listen to her, she convinced me of the practicability of carrying on reading and spelling together before in the regular course of the business she had got into two syllables. The writing she attempted also but the trouble was so much greater than any end to be answered by teaching her at so early a period that very reluctantly I prevailed upon her to defer that part of her education to a more distant one. So much for my hopes and fears with regard to those objects in which they center. The former preponderate upon the whole, yet my anxiety about them frequently makes me unreasonably apprehensive. Unreasonably I think for surely if they turn out well with regard to morals I *ought* to be satisfied, tho I *feel* that I never can sit down quietly under the idea of their being blockheads. Adieu Dear adored Father. We look forward with transport to the time at which we shall all meet at Monticello tho not on my side unmixed with pain when I think it will be the precursor of a return to the world from which I have been so long been secluded and for which my habits render me every way unfit, tho the pleasure of seeing you every day is a good that will render every other evil light. Once more adieu. The children are clamorous to be remembered to you and believe your self *first* and unrivaled in the heart of your devoted child.   M. RANDOLPH

1. Possibly the Reverend Mr. Matthew Maury, son of the Reverend James, who succeeded his father in his classical school as well as in the Rectory of Fredericksville Parish.

TO ANNE CARY RANDOLPH

Apr. 18. 1802.

TH: JEFFERSON TO HIS VERY DEAR GRANDAUGHTER
ANNE C. RANDOLPH

I send you, my dear Anne, more poems for our 1st. volume.[1] Congress will rise about the last day of the month, and it will not be many days after that before I shall be in the midst of you. In the mean time all is well here, and I have not time to say more, except that you must kiss all the little ones for me and deliver my affections to your papa and mama. Health and tender love to you all.

1. A scrapbook.

your visit to this place. Against this I must remonstrate. Every principle respecting them, and every consideration interesting to yourself, Mr. Randolph or myself, is in favor of their coming here. If Virginia owes a visit to Dungeoness (as S. Carr says) the winter season will be more safe and convenient for that. Knowing that Mr. Randolph's resources must all be put to the stretch on his visit to Georgia, I insist that they not be touched by any wants which the visit of the family to this place might produce; but that all that shall be mine. As to the article of dress particularly, it can be better furnished here, and I shall intreat that it be so without limitation, as it will not be felt by me. Let there be no preparation of that kind therefore but merely to come here. Congress will rise in a few days. I think I can now fix the 5th. or 6th. of May for my departure and the 8th. or 9th. for my being with you. Mr. and Mrs. Madison go about the same time: that of their return is unknown to me, but cannot be much later than mine. I think it will be for your ease and convenience to arrive after Mrs. Madison's return, and consequently that this will give time for me after I get back here to send a carriage to meet you on a day to be fixed between us. Some groceries, intended for use while we are at Monticello, were sent from here a week or 10. days ago. I hope they will arrive in time, and with their arrival at Milton to be attended to. Mr. Milledge will dine with me to-day, and be able perhaps to tell me on what day he will be with you. A Mr. Clarke,[1] son of Genl. Clarke of Georgia, and a very sensible young man goes with him. I think they will be at Edgehill a day or two after you recieve this. Present me affectionately to Mr. Randolph and the family, and be assured of my tenderest love.

TH: JEFFERSON

P.S. On further enquiry I doubt if Congress will rise before the last day of the month. This will retard Mr. Milledge's[2] departure, but not mine.

1. John Clarke was the son of General Elijah Clarke of Georgia.
2. John Milledge was a congressman from the same state.

To Mary Jefferson Eppes

Washington May 1. 1802.

MY DEAR MARIA

I recieved yesterday your's of April 21. bringing me the welcome news that you are all well. I wrote 2. or 3. days ago to Mr. Eppes to inform him that Congress would rise the day after tomorrow,

the driver will not be acquainted with the road, and it is a difficult one to find. It is generally a good and a safe one except the last day's journey which is very hilly, and will require you to get out of the carriage in several places on the Alexandria road between Fairfax court house and Colo. Wren's which is 8. miles, and once after you pass Wren's. I am not without fear that the measles may have got into your family, and delay the pleasure of seeing you here: but I expect to hear from you by the post which arrives tomorrow morning. My affectionate attachment to Mr. Randolph, kisses to the children, and tenderest love to yourself.

TH: JEFFERSON

1. An inn and stopping place eleven miles north of Stevensburg, Culpeper County, on a route often used by TJ traveling to and from Washington. It was eighty-three miles southwest of Washington.
2. John (Jack) Shorter was a Washington servant.

From Edgehill

To Gordon's 18. miles.	A good tavern, but cold victuals on the road will be better than any thing which any of the country taverns will give you.
Lodge at Gordon's go to	Orange courthouse 10. miles to breakfast. A good tavern. On leaving Orange courthouse be very attentive to the roads, as they begin to be difficult to find.
Adam's mill 7. miles.	Here you enter the flat country which continues 46. miles on your road.
Downey's ford 2.	Here you ford the Rapidan. The road leads along the bank 4 miles further, but in one place, a little below Downey's, it turns off at a right angle from the river to go round a cut. At this turn, if not very attentive, you will go strait forward, as there is a strait forward road still along the bank, which soon descends it and enters the river. If you get into this, the space on the bank is so narrow you cannot turn. You will know the turn I speak of, by the left hand road (the one you are to take) leading up directly towards some

Thomas Jefferson Randolph. The eldest son of Martha Jefferson and Thomas Mann Randolph, Jr. The silhouette was probably made at Monticello and shows him in his sixteenth year. *Thomas Jefferson Memorial Foundation*

Elizabeth Wayles Eppes. "Aunt Eppes" was the wife of Francis Eppes of Eppington and a half sister of Mrs. Thomas Jefferson. *Thomas Jefferson Memorial Foundation*

Anne Cary Randolph. The eldest of the twelve Jefferson grandchildren. She was the wife of Charles Lewis Bankhead and the first grandchild to leave Monticello. *Thomas Jefferson Memorial Foundation*

Francis Eppes. Father of John Wayles Eppes, called "Uncle" and "Father" Eppes. *Thomas Jefferson Memorial Foundation*

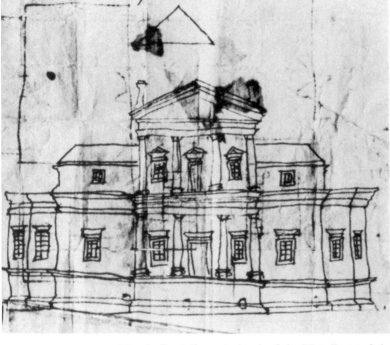

Monticello. Jefferson's sketch of the West Front of the house as it appeared in 1782. This is the house that Martha Wayles Jefferson lived in. *Thomas Jefferson Memorial Foundation*

ing when I came away the measles were in the neighborhood. I saw it was but too possible your visit here would be delayed. As it is, we must agree to the fall visit; and as Maria will be at Monticello, I trust she will come on with you. I believe we shall conclude here to leave this place the last week of July; probably I shall be with you by the 24th. say 5. weeks from this time, and I shall endeavor that Mr. Eppes and Maria be there also by that time. I hope Peter Hemings [1] will get the better of his complaint, or I know not what we should do, as it is next to impossible to send Ursula [2] and her child home and bring them back again. The servants here have felt great disappointment at your not coming. The coachman is particularly chagrined. I suppose he wishes to have an opportunity of shewing himself on his box; which with me he has never had. Mr. and Mrs. Trist are to set out in a few days for Albemarle, and I believe the two young ladies go with them. He, I fancy will proceed immediately to the Missisipi. Present my best esteem to Mr. Randolph, abundance of soft things to the children, and warmest affections yourself.   TH: JEFFERSON

1. Peter Hemings was the ninth son of Betty Hemings.
2. A slave, but not to be confused with Ursula, the wife of "Great" George who died in 1799. Her child was born in March, 1802. It is interesting to note that as a servant in the President's House she received a salary of $2 a month. Consult *Memoirs of a Monticello Slave* (1955), 66, the *Farm Book*, and Account Book 1802.

FROM MARY JEFFERSON EPPES

Eppington June 21st [1802]

My little son and Myself have both been very sick since I wrote to you last My Dear Papa. We are now however getting better tho' he is still very far from being well. His indisposition proceeded from mine I believe and cutting teeth together, which occasion'd constant fevers and have reduced him extremely, and perhaps nursing him in my weak state of health made me worse for I had only slight tho constant fevers on me and my stomach at last so weak that nothing that I took remained on it. Change of air and bark tho' have been allready of great service to me, for my dear mother hearing of my sickness went down, and continued with us tho to her extremely inconvenient at that time till I was able to bear the journey up with her. I have kept Crity with me in consequence of it my Dear Papa. She should have gone up otherwise in may but I was not well enough to undertake changeing his nurse. I am very much in hopes now that he will mend daily as we have

Dabney seems to have effected this. Peter and his wife are expected here daily on their way to Baltimore.[1] From this sketch you may judge of the state of our neighborhood when we shall meet there it will be infinitely joyful to me to be with you there, after the l[ong se]paration we have had for years. I count from one meeting to another as we do between port and port at sea: and I long for the moment with the same earnestness. Present me affectionately to Mr. Eppes and let me hear from you immediately. Be assured yourself of my tender and unchangeable affections.

TH: JEFFERSON

1. Another son of Martha Jefferson Carr (Mrs. Dabney), who married Elizabeth (Betsy) Overton Carr, daughter of his uncle Overton Carr. Samuel Carr had previously married another of Overton Carr's daughters, Eleanor (Nelly) Carr. Dunlora was a Carr farm a few miles north of Charlottesville. Peter was another nephew of TJ.

To MARTHA JEFFERSON RANDOLPH

Washington July 2. 1802.

MY DEAR MARTHA

I yesterday recieved letters from Mr. Eppes and Maria. She has been for a considerable time very unwell, with low but constant fevers, and the child very unwell also. Mrs. Eppes had gone there and staid with her till she was well enough to be removed to Eppington, where the air and the bark had already produced a fa vorable effect. She wishes to proceed to Monticello as soon as she is strong enough, but is in dreadful apprehensions from the measles. Not having heard from you she was uninformed whether it was in your family. I have this day informed her it is there, and advised her when she goes, to pass directly on to Monticello; and that I would ask the favor of Mr. Randolph and yourself to take measures for having the mountain clear of it by the 15th. of this month, by which time she may possibly arrive there, or by the 20th. at farthest. After that date should any one on the mountain have it they must remove. Squire's house[1] would be a good place for the nail boys, should they have it, and Betty Hemings's for Bet's or Sally's children. There are no other children on the mountain. I shall be at home from the 25th. to the 28th. My affectionate esteem to Mr. Randolph and tenderest love to yourself.

TH: JEFFERSON

1. Squire, a slave; the location of his house is not known. Betty Hemings' house was on the Third Roundabout Road several hundred yards southeast of the east portico of Monticello. Bett and Sally were her children.

FROM MARTHA JEFFERSON RANDOLPH

Edgehill July 10th 1802

My children have escaped the measles most wonderfully and unaccountably for so strongly were we all prepossessed with the idea of it's being impossible that from the moment of it's appearing upon the plantation I rather courted than avoided the infection and the children have been on a regimen for 4 or 5 weeks in the constant expectation of breaking out. Anne has been twice declared full of it by Doctor Bache and another time by the whole family but it went in as sudenly as it came out and has left much uneasiness upon my mind for fear of her being subject to something like Mrs. Kingkade's. I think the smoothness of her skin is affected by it and it shews, upon her heating herself immediately. Cornelia has been very low. The sickness which I mentioned to you in my last was but the beginning of a very long and teasing complaint of which however she is getting the better. She is still very pale and much emaciated but has recovered her appetite and spirits and I hope will be perfectly well before you return. We are entirely free from the measles here now. Those of our people who had it have recovered and Mr. Watson's family[1] living on the same plantation every individual of which had it are all recovered. The intercourse between them and us thro the servants was daily yet it has stopped and there is not at this moment one instance of it here. At Monticello the last time I heard from there 3 of the nail boys had it and others were complaining but whether with the measles or not I could not learn. I will send over to Lilly immediately to let him know your orders upon the subject. I regret extremely my children have missed it. The season was so favorable and it was so mild generally that no time or circumstance for the future can ever be as favorable again, besides having had the anxiety for nothing. I delayed writing to Maria untill I could give her a favorable account, for I know she has had great apprehensions on that score for a long time. Adieu my dear Papa. I do not know if I gave you a list of the things most wanting in the house. I do not exactly recollect what they were but sheets towels counterpanes and tea china were I think foremost on the list. Your linen has not arrived or it would have been made up before your return. The children all join in love and anxious prayer that nothing may retard your wished for return and believe me with tenderest affection yours.   MRANDOLPH.

Peter Hemmings is entirely well.

1. Possibly either David or John Watson.

FROM MARY JEFFERSON EPPES

Eppington July 17th [1802]

Mr. Eppes thinks we had best remain here My Dear Papa till we hear further from you about the measles, I must therefore beg you will write as soon as you can conveniently after arriving at Monticello. You know not how anxious I am to see you, after having so long look'd forward to this period with so much pleasure. To be disappointed at the very moment which was to reunite us after so long an absence requires a greater degree of fortitude then I have to bear it, and your stay at home will be so short that it makes me doubly anxious to be with you. If my little sons health was not in the precarious state it is I should not fear the disorder so much on his account but he suffers so much and is so ill with every tooth that comes out that I should dread any additional complaint.

We had proposed going by the green springs[1] as we went up but the danger of finding the measles there has made us give up that journey. Your last letter to Mr. Eppes my dear Papa must be deferr'd answering till the happy moment which brings us together, yet suffer me to tell you how much I feel it. Your kindness knows no bounds nor is it the first time that it has gone so far as to pain the heart entirely yours. You have allready disfurnish'd yourself too much for us Dearest Papa. Suffer me to remind you of it and do not take it amiss if with grateful hearts we should not accept this present offer. It will I hope have this good effect on Mr. Eppes as to make him exert himself to begin a building of some sort at Pantops. He knows I should be satisfied with any for a while and would chearfully agree to any rules of economy when there that would enable him to continue independent and clear of debt. It must before long take place certainly. He is himself becoming very sensible of the many inconveniences attending the life we lead and which are increasing on us the longer we continue it. Adieu My dear Papa. This day week I expected to have met you and to have forgotten in the delight of meeting you the pain I have felt in being so long separated from you for I experience more at each separation. How little the heart can ever become accustom'd to them. Adieu. Believe me yours with tenderest love,

M EPPES

1. Possibly a Carr dwelling in Louisa County and located in the Green Springs area several miles east of Gordonsville. See Joseph Martin, *Comprehensive Gazetteer of Virginia and District of Columbia* (Charlottesville, 1835), 217.

the three first days journey, can encounter the 4th. which is hilly beyond any thing you have ever seen. I shall expect to learn from you soon, the day of your departure, that I may take proper arrangements. Present me affectionately to Mr. Eppes, and accept yourself my tenderest love.   TH: JEFFERSON

P. S. Mr. Eppes's bridle is delivered to Davy Bowles.

TO MARTHA JEFFERSON RANDOLPH

Washington Oct. 18. 1802.

MY DEAR MARTHA

I have been expecting by every post to learn from you when I might send on to meet you. I will expect it daily. In the mean time I enclose you 100 Dol for the expences of yourself, Maria and all your party. Mr. Randolph would do well to exchange the bills for gold and silver which will be more readily used on the road. The indisposition I mentioned in my letter by Bowles[1] turned out to be rheumatic. It confined me to the house some days, but is now nearly gone off so that I ride out daily. The hour of the post obliges me to conclude here with my affectionate attachment to Mr. Randolph and tender love to yourself and the children.

TH: JEFFERSON

1. Davy Bowles.

TO MARY JEFFERSON EPPES

Washington Oct. 18. 1802.

MY DEAR MARIA

I have been expecting by every post to learn from yourself or your sister when I might send to meet you. I still expect it daily. In the mean time I have sent to Mr. Randolph, who I understand is to be your conductor money for the expences of the road, so that that may occasion no delay. The indisposition mentd in my letter by Davy Bowles turned out to be rheumatic. It confined me to the house some days, but is now nearly gone off. I have been able to ride out daily for a week past. The hour of the post leaves me time to add only assurances of my constant and tender love to you; and to pray you to tender my best affections to Mr. Eppes when he returns.   TH: JEFFERSON

they are a great luxury to me. Deliver to my dear Maria my love, and my rebukes that she should not once have written to me. Kiss the little ones, and be assured yourself of my unceasing affections.

TH: JEFFERSON

1. David Higginbotham was a Milton merchant.

FROM MARY JEFFERSON EPPES

November 5th [1802]

Mr. Randolph has been summon'd to Richmond My Dear Papa about the time we were to set off, which will prevent his going with us and obliges us to request Mr. Lewis to meet us at Strodes on Tuesday week. Mr. Eppes will go that far with us but says he cannot possibly go farther. I lament sincerely that it has not been possible for us to go sooner, as the visit will be scarcely worth making for so short a time and should prefer waiting till the spring and returning there with you as we could then remain with you some time but my sister will not agree to put it off any longer. On Tuesday week then if Mr. Lewis can meet us at Strodes we shall be there. Adieu dearest Papa. I am afraid the post will be gone and must conclude this scrawl, excuse it and believe me with the tenderest love yours,   M EPPES

P. S. I send the lock of hair which is to be the colour of the wigs.

FROM MARTHA JEFFERSON RANDOLPH

November 9th [1802]

DEAR PAPA

It will be more convenient to us to leave this on wednesday than monday. It will occasion a delay of 2 days only, as this is a flying visit only to shew that we are in earnest with regard to Washington. I have determined to leave the children all but Jefferson considering the lateness of the season and the bad weather we may reasonably expect in december. The short time [I] shall have to spend with you it is better to part with them for a time than risk such a journey with a carriage full of small children. Next spring I hope I shall have it in my power to return with you and carry them all: Maria thinks it would be better to send a carriage with the horses as Mr. Eppes['s] in which we shall go is much out of repair and ours absolutely not in travelling condition. Adieu Dearest Father. Yours most truly affections,   M R

TO MARY JEFFERSON EPPES

Washington, Jan. 18. 1803.

MY DEAR MARIA

Your's by John came safely to hand, and informed me of your ultimate arrival at Edgehill. Mr. Randolph's letter from Gordon's,[1] recieved the night before gave me the first certain intelligence I had recieved since your departure. A rumor had come here of your having been stopped two or three days at Ball run,[2] and in a miserable hovel; so that I had passed ten days in anxious uncertainty about you. Your apologies my dear Maria on the article of expense, are quite without necessity. You did not here indulge yourselves as much as I wished, and nothing prevented my supplying your backwardness but my total ignorance in articles which might suit you. Mr. Eppes's election[3] will I am in hopes secure me your company next winter and perhaps you may find it convenient to accompany your sister in the spring. Mr. Giles's[4] aid indeed in Congress, in support of our administration, considering his long knoledge of the affairs of the Union, his talents, and the high ground on which he stands through the United States had rendered his continuance here an object of anxious desire to those who compose the administration: but every information we recieve states that prospect to be desperate from his ill health, and will relieve me from the imputation of being willing to lose to the public so strong a supporter, for the personal gratification of having yourself and Mr. Eppes with me. I inclose you Lemaire's reciepts.[5] The orthography will be puzzling and amusing: but the reciepts are valuable. Present my tender love to your sister, kisses to the young ones, and my affections to Mr. Randolph and Mr. Eppes whom I suppose you will see soon. Be assured of my unceasing and anxious love for yourself.   TH: JEFFERSON

1. N. Gordon operated an Orange County inn about fifteen miles from Monticello, on the road to Orange Court House.
2. A small tributary of the Appomattox River in Powhatan County.
3. He was elected to Congress in 1802 while residing at Eppington and served until March 3, 1811, when defeated by John Randolph of Roanoke; re-elected from Buckingham County in 1812 and again defeated by Randolph in 1814. Chosen a senator in 1816, John W. Eppes served until ill health caused his resignation in 1819.
4. William Branch Giles, a Virginia congressman.
5. Etienne Lemaire, TJ's maître d'hôtel while in the President's House.

roads will be so deep that I can not flatter myself with catching
Ellen in bed. Tell her that Mrs. Harrison Smith desires her compliments to her. Your mamma has probably heard of the death of
Mrs. Burrows. Mrs. Brent is not far from it. Present my affections
to your papa, mamma, and the young ones, and be assured of
them yourself.   TH: JEFFERSON

FROM THOMAS JEFFERSON RANDOLPH

[Edgehill] Recd. Feb. 24. 1803.

DEAR GRAND PAPA

We have been expecting the measles but have escaped it as yet.
Virginia has learnt to speak very well. Ellen is learning french.
Cornelia sends her love to you. I would be very much obliged to
you if you would bring me a book of geography. Adieu Dear Grand
Papa. Your affectionate Grand son,   THOMAS JEFFERSON R

TO ANNE CARY RANDOLPH

Washington Feb. 26. 1803.

MY DEAR ANNE

Davy Bowles is to call on me this morning, and if he can carry
your dictionary I will deliver it to him, having recieved it yesterday from Mr. Duane. If he cannot, I will endeavour to carry it
when I go. In the last case you will recieve it about the 9th or
10th of March, or as soon after health, the weather and roads will
permit. Tell Jefferson that there is not a book of geography to be
had here, but I will give him one I have at Monticello. Tell Ellen,
Cornelia and Virginia how d'ye. [. . .]¹ Give my affectionate
esteem to your Papa and to your Mama. My constant love for
yourself. I deliver numberless kisses on this letter which you are
to take from it. I hope in a few days we shall all be happy together
at Monticello.   TH: JEFFERSON

1. Word following *d'ye* is illegible in original.

TO MARTHA JEFFERSON RANDOLPH

Washington Apr. 23.1803.

MY DEAR MARTHA

A promise made to a friend some years ago, but executed only
lately, has placed my religious creed on paper. I have thought it

To Mary Jefferson Eppes

Washington Apr. 25. 1803.

My dear Maria

A promise made to a friend some years ago, but executed only lately, has placed my religious creed on paper. I have thought it just that my family, by possessing this, should be enabled to estimate the libels published against me on this, as on every other possible subject. I have written to Philadelphia for Dr. Priestley's history of the corruptions of Christianity, which I will send to you, and recommend to an attentive perusal, because it establishes the ground work of my view of this subject.

In a letter from Mr. Eppes dated at the Hundred Apr. 14. he informed me Francis had got well through his measles; but he does not say what your movements are to be. My chief anxiety is that you should be back to Monticello by the end of June. I shall advise Martha to get back from here by the middle of July, because the sickly season really commences here by that time, altho' the members of the government venture to remain til the last week of that month. Mr. and Mrs. P. Carr staid with me 5. or 6. days on their way to Baltimore. I think they propose to return in June. Nelly Carr continues in ill health. I believe they expect about the same time to get back to Dunlora.[1] I wrote Mr. Eppes yesterday. Be assured of my most affectionate and tender love to yourself, and kiss Francis for me. My cordial salutations to the family of Eppington when you see them. Adieu.   Th: Jefferson

1. Samuel Carr's home on the South Fork of the Rivanna River and a few miles north of Charlottesville. Eleanor Carr Carr (Mrs. Samuel).

To Anne Cary Randolph

Washington May 20. 1803.

It is very long, my dear Anne, since I have recieved a letter from you. When was it? In the mean time mine have been accumulating till I find it necessary to get them off my hands without further waiting. With them I send an A.B.C.[1] for Miss Cornelia, and she must pay you a kiss for it on my account. The little recipe about charcoal is worth your Mama's notice. We had peas here on Tuesday the 17th. and every day since. We had then also fullgrown cucumbers: but I suppose they had been forced. What sort of weather had you from the 6th. to the 10th. Here we had frost, ice

bodily pain was never capable of subduing. She sank at last in a
state of stupor however which seldom ever left her. She was as
certainly saved by bleeding[1] My Dear Father as others have been
killed by it. The evacutations instantly fell from 60 to 70 in the
24 hours down to 6. The complaint being thus sudenly and as it
were by magic arrested in it's progress. The fever gradually subsided untill it left her entirely but so debilitated that some little
indiscretion of diet brought it on her again and we have been very
much distressed by the danger which threatened her of it's ter-
minating in a slow fever the event of which we had too much
reason to apprehend might be fatal to one allready exhausted by
the dissentery. Thank god it has intermitted yesterday for the
first time and again this morning. At the time Ann wrote you the
crisis had taken place in consequence of the bleeding and my self
exhausted with watching, want of food which my stomach re-
jected and anxiety I had taken to my bed under a sever attack of
the same complaint but thanks to the very judicious and friendly
attention of Doctors Everet and Gilmer[2] who by sitting up with
Ellen relieved me from the fatigue and anxiety and also a fortunate management of the complaint in it's beggining it was speedily
terminated in me. I was not confined more than 5 days with it.
The fever and derangement of the stomach lasted perhaps 10.
Indeed to the false strength which that gave was I indebted for
the incessant attention night and day which it enabled me to pay
My Darling and by which perhaps she was saved. The others were
all of them sick at the same time. They required also unwearied
attention to their diet that they might not be suffered to get too
low. Jane[3] from home and not a female friend to assist me, I reflect
with horror upon that week that no language can paint. The
children are all getting better and my self well allthough greatly
debilitated. Adieu My Dear Father I must conclude for fear of
losing the post. When you send the groceries on will you remember
glasses, tumblers and wine glasses both are much want[ing here][4]
and again believe me with unchangeable love yours,   MR.

1. TJ did not believe in bleeding as an effective treatment for any ailment.
There is no record that he was ever bled, and this is the only recorded in-
stance in which any of the Monticello grandchildren were subjected to it.
    2. Doctor Charles Everett, later secretary to James Monroe, and Doctor
John Gilmer, son of Doctor George Gilmer.
    3. Jane Barbara Carr Cary (Mrs. Wilson) or Jane Cary Randolph Randolph
(Mrs. Thomas Eston).
    4. Original letter torn.

are wicked and impotent usually have. How much happier you in the midst of your family, with nobody approaching you but in love and good will. It is a most desireable situation, and in exchanging it for the scenes of this place we certainly do not calculate well for our happiness. Jerome Bonaparte[4] is to be married tomorrow to a Miss Patterson of Baltimore. Give my warm affections to my Maria and tell her my next letter shall be to her. Kiss all the fireside, and be assured yourself of my never-ceasing love.

TH: JEFFERSON

1. She was pregnant for the seventh time.
2. A midwife.
3. Federalists.
4. Napoleon's youngest brother. In 1803 he married Elizabeth Patterson, daughter of William Patterson, president of the Bank of the United States. The marriage was later dissolved by Napoleon, and Jerome returned to Europe without his bride. For additional information on the reaction of the bride's family and the international aspects of this marriage, see TJ to Robert Livingston, November 4, 1803, Lipscomb and Bergh, *Writings of Thomas Jefferson*, 10, 424–25.

TO MARY JEFFERSON EPPES

Washington Nov. 27. 03.

It is rare, my ever dear Maria, during a session of Congress, that I can get time to write any thing but letters of business: and this, tho' a day of rest to others, is not at all so to me. We are all well here, and hope the post of this evening will bring us information of the health of all at Edgehill and particularly that Martha and the new bantling[1] are both well: and that her example gives you good spirits. When Congress will rise no mortal can tell: not from the quantity but dilatoriness of business. Mr. Lillie having finished the mill, is now I suppose engaged in the road[2] which we have been so long wanting, and that done, the next job will be the levelling of Pantops. I anxiously long to see under way the works necessary to fix you there, that we may one day be all together. Mr. Stewart is now here on his way back to his family, whom he will probably join Thursday or Friday. Will you tell your sister that the pair of stockings she sent me by Mr. Randolph are quite large enough and also have fur enough in them. I inclose some papers for Anne; and must continue in debt to Jefferson a letter for a while longer. Take care of yourself my dearest Maria, have good spirits and know that courage is as essential to triumph in your case as in that of the souldier. Keep us all therefore in heart

Continue to love me yourself and be assured of my warmest affections.

1. TJ was referring to the Louisiana Purchase. The United States took formal possession of the Territory on December 20, 1803.

2. They were expecting the birth of Mary's child.

TO ANNE CARY RANDOLPH

Washington Jan. 9. 1804.

MY DEAR ANNE

I recieved last night your letter of the 7th. with your Mama's postscript. As your's was the principal the answer is due to you. I am glad to find you are pursuing so good a course of reading. French, History, Morals, and some poetry and writings of eloquence to improve the stile form a good course for you. How does Jefferson get on with his French? Will he let Ellen catch him? The American muse has been so dull for some time past as to have furnished nothing for our volume. I have here a pair of beautiful fowls of enormous size of the East India breed: and can get in the city a pair of Bantams. I should prefer sending you the latter, if an opportunity occurs, provided you will undertake to raise them, and furnish me a pair for Monticello. Tell your Mama I shall be extremely glad to have my chair brought by Davy Bowles, as it would be impossible for me to go home in my Phaeton in the spring, and I should have to perform the journey on horseback. I shall hope therefore to recieve the chair by Davy. I am glad to hear your Aunt Jane[1] is so near you. It will add exercise, and chearfulness to your enjoiments. Give my tenderest love to your Mama and Aunt Maria, and kiss all the little ones for me. I deliver kisses for yourself to this letter.   TH: JEFFERSON

1. Jane Cary Randolph Randolph (Mrs. Thomas Eston).

FROM MARTHA JEFFERSON RANDOLPH

Edgehill Jan. 14, 1804

MY DEAREST FATHER

It was so late the other day before I could write that I had only time to add a postscript to Anne's letter to inform you of Davy Bowle's intention of going to Washington, and the offer he made of carrying your chair if you wished it; he is still here and will be on thursday, so that your intentions with regard to it may be complied with if known, on that day. He leaves this sometime

to. My sister Jane[3] who held him during the last one he had two days only before Mary's birth mentioned it to me but the distress it might occasion his parents for such an idea to get abroad determined us to confine our suspicion within our own breast's. He may and I hope will outgrow them. Time only can shew what the event will be. My own children are remarkably healthy and freer from colds than common. Ann informed you of the acquisition we have made in Jane as a neighbour. We have walked back and fro repeatedly. She spends much of her time with us and her husband has been as attentive as an own brother could have been. He is a man of the purest heart and most amiable temper in the world. Adieu My Dearest Father. I must beg you to recollect that I write amidst the noises and confusion of six children interrupted every moment by their questions, and so much disturbed by [their][4] pratling around me that I catch my self repeatedly writing [their words] instead of my own thoughts. That will account for, and I hope [apologize] for any inconsistencies or repetitions in my letters. Perhaps it will be deemed some excuse for not writing oftener certain as I am that it is impossible for you to doubt for one moment of the warmth of my affection. I remain with unchangeable and tender love yours,   M RANDOLPH

Your letter to Anne has this moment come to hand having gone thro a mistake to Charlottesville. I wish it may not have come too late for enquiry. They tell me Davy Bowles contrary to his promise to me is gone to Richmond intending from thence to Washington. I shall hear more certainly presently and act accordingly. If St. Memin[5] comes to Washington will you remember your promise to Maria and Myself.

1. A slave. He was sold to John Perry a sometime Monticello carpenter for £ 125 on April 20, 1804. See Account Book for this date.
   2. Mary Stewart, the wife of William Stewart, the very able Monticello blacksmith. She is buried in the Monticello graveyard. See *The Annual Report of the Monticello Association* ([Charlottesville], 1940), 29.
   3. Jane Cary Randolph Randolph (Mrs. Thomas Eston).
   4. Bracketed words in this and the following sentence have been supplied, as originals are illegible.
   5. Charles-Balthazar-Julien Févret de Saint-Mémin was the French *émigré* artist. He did not delineate TJ until 1804, for which service TJ noted in his Account Book on November 27: "Gave St. Mémin order on bk US. for 29.50." For this payment he received the original crayon drawing, a small copper plate engraved from the drawing, and forty-eight small engravings struck from this plate. For further information, consult these excellent publications: Fillmore Norfleet, *Saint-Mémin in Virginia: Portraits and Biographies* (Richmond, 1942); Howard C. Rice, Jr., "Saint-Mémin's Portrait of Jefferson," *The Princeton University Library Chronicle*, XX, No. 4 (Summer, 1959), 182–92, and Alfred L. Bush, *The Life Portraits of Thomas Jefferson* (Charlottesville, 1962), 65–67.

be later than she has calculated, perhaps we may all be with her. Altho' the recurrence of those violent attacks to which Francis is liable, cannot but give uneasiness as to their character, yet be that what it will, there is little doubt but he will out-grow them; as I have scarcely ever known an instance to the contrary, at his age. On Friday Congress give a dinner on the acquisition of Louisana. They determine to invite no foreign ministers, to avoid questions of etiquette, in which we are enveloped by Merry's and Yrujo's families. As much as I wished to have had yourself and sister with me, I rejoice you were not here. The brunt of the battle now falls on the Secretary's ladies, who are dragged in the dirt of every federal paper. You would have been the victims had you been here, and butchered the more bloodily as they would hope it would be more felt by myself. It is likely to end in those two families putting themselves into Coventry until they recieve orders from their courts to acquiesce in our principles of the equality of all persons meeting together in society, and not to expect to force us into their principles of allotment into ranks and orders.[1] Pour into the bosom of my dear Maria all the comfort and courage which the affections of my heart can give her, and tell her to rise superior to all fear for all our sakes. Kiss all the little ones for me, with whom I should be so much happier than here; and be assured yourself of my tender and constant love.   TH: JEFFERSON

1. Following his precepts, TJ allowed his guests to enter the dining room pellmell or first come first served. This almost precipitated an international incident in the case of Anthony Merry, the British Minister, whose wife was overlooked in one of these scrambles. The Marquis de Casa-Yrujo also had a similar grievance and joined Merry in a strong protest. It was to no avail; republican simplicity prevailed. For TJ's reaction to the Merry protest, see his letter to James Monroe of January 8, 1804 (DLC). Irving Brant, in his *James Madison, Secretary of State 1800–1809* (Indianapolis, 1953), 163–69, gives an excellent account of this "etiquette quarrel."

TO MARY JEFFERSON EPPES

Washington Jan. 29. 04.

MY DEAREST MARIA

This evening ought to have brought in the Western mail, but it is not arrived. Consequently we hear nothing from our neighborhood. I rejoice that this is the last time our Milton mail will be embarrassed with that from New Orleans; the rapidity of which occasioned our letters often to be left in the post-offices. It now returns to it's former establishment of twice a week, so that

you will grant us this one favor. I am very much afraid you will be disappointed in getting your faeton. Davy Bowles went to Richmond intending to return here before he went on, but it is so long since he left us that as his wife is now staying in Richmond it is most probable he has hired himself there. Your acacias are very beautiful My dear Papa, there are eight of them very flourishing that have changed their foliage entirely. They have remain'd in my room to the warmth of which I believe they are indebted for their present flourishing state as they appear to be more delicate the smaller they are. I wish you could bring us a small piece of your Geranium in the spring if it is large enough to admit of it. Perhaps Mr. Eppes could more conveniently take charge of it than yourself. Adieu dearest Papa. We are all well here and all most anxious for the happy moment that will reunite us again after this long separation. Believe me with the tenderest love yours ever,   M EPPES

FROM ANNE CARY RANDOLPH

Edgehill Feb. 14 1804

MY DEAR GRAND PAPA

I received your letter on the 13th of Feb: and am much obliged to you for it and the poetry also. I will very gladly undertake to write to you every post. Jefferson is going to a very good latin school in the neighbourhood.[1] Mama is now in very good health and her apetite is quite restored. She has never been out yet for fear of catching cold. All the children send their love to you and Francis and we are all delighted to hear that we shall have the pleasure of seeing you soon. Adieu my Dear Grand Papa. Your most affectionate Granddaughter,   A C RANDOLPH

Aunt Virginia sends her love to you also.

1. Probably John Robertson's, which was located near the eastern slope of the Southwest Mountains.

FROM ANNE CARY RANDOLPH

Edgehill Feb 22 1804

I wrote to my Dear Grand Papa last post but I suppose he did not receive my letter or he certainly would have answered it. In my last letter I mentioned the changing my name to Anastasia but you did not say whether you approved it. I am afraid my letters

To Martha Jefferson Randolph

Washington Mar. 8. 04.

Your letter of the 2d. my dear Martha, which was not recieved till the last night has raised me to life again. For four days past I had gone through inexpressible anxiety. The mail which left you on the 5th. will probably be here tonight, and will I hope strengthen our hopes of Maria's continuing to recover, and Mr. Eppes's arrival which I presume was on the 6th. will render her spirits triumphant over her Physical debility. Congress have determined to rise on Monday sennight (the 19th). Mr. Randolph will probably be with you on the 22d. and myself within 3. or 4. days after. Maria must in the mean time resolve to get strong to make us all happy.[1] Your apologies my dear for using any thing at Monticello for her, yourself, family or friends, are more than unnecessary. What is there is as much for the use of you all as for myself, and you cannot do me greater pleasure than by using every thing with the same freedom I should do myself. Tell my dear Maria to be of good chear, and to be ready to mount on horseback with us and continue to let us hear of her by every post. If Mrs. Lewis be still with you deliver her my affectionate respects and assurances of my great sensibility for her kind attentions to Maria. Kiss the little ones for me, and be assured of my tenderest love to Maria and yourself.   Th: Jefferson

1. TJ recorded these vital statistics about Mary in his family Bible: "Mary
H M
Jefferson born. Aug. 1, 1778. 1 30 A.M. died Apr. 17. 1804. between 8. and 9.
A.M." The child survived.

To Martha Jefferson Randolph

Washington May 14. [1804]

My dear Martha

I arrived here last night after the most fatiguing journey I have experienced for a great many years. I got well enough to Orange C. H. the first day. The 2d. there was a constant heavy drizzle through the whole day sufficient to soak my outer great coat twice, and the roads very dirty and in places deep. The third the roads became as deep as at any season, and as laborious to the horse. Castor got into ill temper and refused to draw, and we had a vast deal of trouble and fatigue with him and obliged to give him up at last. I was from day light to sunset getting from Fauquier C. H.

in the stomach. The spasms were violent and came on with a desire
to puke which however produced nothing more than an insuperable distension of the breast at the moment and a difficulty of
breathing amounting allmost to suffocation. I was much allarmed
my self. Mr. Randolph has since affirmed it to have been hysterics
but I certainly know him to be wrong there. It was occasioned by
eating radishes and milk at the same meal both of which are un-
friendly to my stomach and the affection of the speech of which
I was very sensible at the time proves it to have been some thing
more serious than mere hysterics. I was relieved by pepper mint
repeating the dose till my stomach was brought to act again, but
it was several hours before I was sufficiently easy to sit or lye down.
I have been perfectly well since. I shall however allways stand in
dread of another attack of the same nature and which may not
be as easily checked the second time. Adieu Dearly beloved Father.
Believe me with a tenderness not to be expressed yours most
affectionately,   M. RANDOLPH

TO MARTHA JEFFERSON RANDOLPH

Washington July 17. 04.

It is a considerable time, my very dear Martha, since I have
written because I have been in expectation you were all at Eppington: and tho' I have not heard of your return to Edgehill, I presume it has taken place. I have some hope of being able to leave
this on the 23d. and to be with you on the 26th. but it is possible
I may not be able to get thro' my business. Mr. Gallatin and Smith
are gone. General Dearborne[1] and Mr. Madison will go in three
or four days. M. and Made. Pichon,[2] who have lately lost their
child are inconsoleable; and will pass the remainder of the season
in travelling about. They will pass some time with Mr. Madison
and us. I have written to my sister Marks to press a visit from her
and that I would send for her on my arrival. I hope the little ones
are all well and that you have left the family at Eppington, and
particularly our dear portion of it well, and in the intention of
visiting us. The necessaries for our comfort at Monticello have
been sent off long ago at two or three different times. Kiss the dear
children for me, and present me affectionately to Mr. Randolph.
My impatience to be with you all increases more as I approach
the moment of that happiness. God bless you my ever dear child,

To Martha Jefferson Randolph

Washington. Nov. 6. 1804.

MY DEAREST MARTHA

I send you the inclosed magazine supposing it may furnish you a few moments amusement, as well as to the reading members of your family. Mr. Randolph arrived here Sunday evening in good health and brought me the welcome news, that you were all well. Congress has as yet formed but one of it's houses, there being no Senate. My heart fails me at the opening such a campaign of bustle and fatigue: the unlimited calumnies of the federalists have obliged me to put myself on the trial of my country by standing another election. I have no fear as to their verdict; and that being secured for posterity, no considerations will induce me to continue beyond the term to which it will extend. My passion strengthens daily to quit political turmoil, and retire into the bosom of my family, the only scene of sincere and pure happiness. One hour with you and your dear children is to me worth an age past here. Mr. Eppes is here, with Francis in the highest health. He tells me he left our dear little Maria very well at Eppington, and all the family there. Tell Anne it is time for her to take up her pen. She shall have letter for letter. For Ellen I have a beautiful pair of little Bantams; but how to get them to her is the difficulty. In the spring I shall be able to send them. Kiss all the young ones for me, and be assured yourself of my tenderest unchangeable love.

TH: JEFFERSON.

From Martha Jefferson Randolph

Edgehill Nov 30, 1804

MY DEAREST FATHER

Lilly was here a fortnight ago to beg I would write to you immediately about some business of his, but a change in the post day disappointed me in sending the letters written to have gone by it. He says you desired him to part with 100 barrils of corn as more than you required, but he says he has got it on very good terms 16 and 16, 6 a barril and that there is not one bushell too much, on account of the heavy hauling he has to do. He says if the horses are not highly fed they will not be able to do the work and he thinks Anderson[1] from whom some of it was purchased will wait till the first of february for his money. After recieving your letter he went to see Moran[2] about the double payment that

him and Charles Smith for negro hire." (Account Book.) See Account Book for entries of January 7, 1802, February 8, 1803, and March 12, 1804. There are no other specific notations of payments to the Smiths.

4. This John obviously was a slave, and unfortunately nothing is known of how TJ finally acted in the matter.

5. Words supplied in brackets are unclear in original.

TO MARTHA JEFFERSON RANDOLPH

Washington Dec. 3 04.

MY DEAREST MARTHA

Taking for granted that Mr. Randolph writes to you regularly and much engaged by business and company myself, I have been more remiss. We are all well here, and our accounts from Eppington are favorable, and particularly that our dear little one there has two teeth. Francis is in remarkeable health: and I hope the objects of our affections with you are equally so. I send you some magazines which may amuse you and them. I have some poetry for Anne, but I reserve it for my answer to her first letter. Congress has scarcely any thing to employ them, and complain that the place is remarkably dull. Very few ladies have come on this winter, and we have lost Madmes. Yrujo, Pichon, Merry, and Law.[1] The theatre fails too for want of actors. You are happy to need none of these aids to get rid of your time and certainly they are poor substitutes for the sublime enjoiment of the affections of our children and of our cares for them. Mr. Burwell[2] being a member of the Virginia legislature has left us to attend it; and Mr. Isaac Coles[3] remains with me during his absence being this moment called off, I must here conclude with my kisses to all the dear children, and my tenderest and unalterable love to you.

TH: JEFFERSON

1. Mrs. Thomas Law was the wife of a Washington land speculator.

2. William Armistead Burwell, at one time TJ's secretary.

3. Isaac Coles was a son of John Coles of Enniscorthy and TJ's private secretary. The Coles family were neighbors and close friends of the Monticello family.

TO MARTHA JEFFERSON RANDOLPH

Washington Jan. 7. 05.

MY DEAREST MARTHA

A letter from Mr. Randolph to Mr. Coles informs him he shall bring you here but does not say if with or without the family. I shall rejoice my dear to recieve you here, and them, or as many of them as you can bring. I feel much for what you will suffer on

morning to hear you are perfectly reestablished. In the mean time this letter must go off by the post of this evening. Our last news from Eppington assured us of Maria's health, but Mrs. Eppes has been very ill. Francis enjoys as high health and spirits as possible. He wants only a society which could rub off what he contracts from the gross companions with whom he of necessity associates. He is a charming boy. Kiss all my dear little ones for me, and be assured yourself of my tenderest and unalterable love.

TH: JEFFERSON

To Martha Jefferson Randolph

Washington Jan. 28. 05.

MY EVER DEAR MARTHA

Your letter of the 11th. recieved here on the 15th. is the last news I have of you. Mr. Randolph having written to Mr. Coles that he should be here on the 15th. and not having come, and no letter from you by that post, I was thrown into inexpressible anxiety lest a relapse into your complaint should have called him to Edgehill. From this I was not relieved till three days ago when a letter from Mr. Burwell (in Richmond) to Mr. Coles mentioned incidentally that Mr. Randolph had been detained there longer than he expected. The continuance too of this dreadful weather is an additional cause of fear for you. The ground had just got uncovered with a snow which had covered it 24. days, when yesterday another fell of 6. or 8. I. deep, and the weather, tho' now fair, is very severe. I hope you will not expose yourself to a renewal of the inflammatory complaint. That of the stomach must be opposed by a strict attention to what you find it digests most easily, and to a course of exercise for strengthening the system generally and invigorating the stomach with that. I hope by the post of tomorrow morning to hear your recovery is confirmed, but at any rate to know your exact situation. Kiss our dear little children for me, among whom I wish so anxiously to be and be assured of my tenderest affections.

TH: JEFFERSON

From Ellen Wayles Randolph

Feb 22 1805

MY DEAR GRAND PAPA

I recieved your letter and am very much obliged to you for it, as it is very seldom that I get one. You cannot think how glad I

permits me to write only to you, to inclose you a poem about another namesake of yours, and some other pieces worth preserving. As I expect Anne's volume is now large enough, I will begin to furnish you with materials for one. I know you have been collecting some yourself; but as I expect there is some tag, rag, and bobtail verse among it you must begin a new volume for my materials. I am called off by company therefore god bless you, my dear child, kiss your Mama and sisters for me, and tell them I shall be with them in about a week from this time. Once more Adieu.

Th: Jefferson

From Anne Cary Randolph

Edgehill March 22 1805

This is the fourth letter I have written to My Dear Grand Papa without receiving an answer. I suppose you have not received them or else your business prevented your answering them. Mama has been very sick and two of the children but they are now quite well. We heard that you were to set of from Washington the 8 of March. I wish in your next letter you will let me know whether it is true. Adieu My Dear Grandpapa. Your most affectionate Grand daughter,   A C R

From Martha Jefferson Randolph

Monticello April 19 1805

My Dearest Father

Mr. Randolph's election is almost certain. The polls stand, Alb. TM.R 503 W.L. 140. Amh. TM.R. 390. WL. 474 which leaves Mr. Randolph a majority of 279, so that independent of his influence in Fluvanna which is great, he is safe.[1] We are all well, but I am moored here till Thursday as he merely stopped a day with us on his way to Fluvanna where he now is, of course I am obliged to stay till his return. The weather is very favorable to your new plantations but many of the thorns[2] I am told are certainly dead. Adieu My Dear Father. It is so late I am in danger of losing the post. Yours most tenderly,   MR.

1. Mr. Randolph was contesting with Walter Leake for a delegate's seat in the Virginia legislature from the counties of Albemarle, Amherst, and Fluvanna. He won, as Martha had predicted.

2. These were introduced in 1805 to surround the Monticello orchards. TJ's reason for not attempting live fencing sooner was the lack of a hardy plant of suitable size and strength and in sufficient quantity. Thomas Main,

To Ellen Wayles Randolph

May 21. 05.

1805. May 21. To a letter which ought to be written once in
every 3. weeks, while I am here, to wit
from Jan. 1. 1805. to this day 15. weeks   5.
CR.
Feb. 23. By one single letter of this day's date   1
Balance due from E. W. Randolph to Th: J Letters   4
                                                                    ——
                                                                    5
So stands the account for this year, my dear Ellen, between you
and me. Unless it be soon paid off, I shall send the sheriff after
you. I inclose you an abundant supply of poetry, among which
you will find Goody Blake,[1] which I think you wanted. I will thank
you if you will put on your boots and spurs and ride to Monticello
and inform me how my thorns live. This part of the country is
beautifying with them so fast that every ride I take makes me
anxious for those at Monticello. Your Papa in his last letter informs me that mumps have got into the family. Let me know who
have it and how all do. Kiss your dear Mama for me and shake
hands with all the little ones. Present me affectionately to your
Papa and accept mes baise-mains yourself.

TH: JEFFERSON

1. Unidentified. For other information on TJ's grandchildren's reading,
see James A. Bear, Jr., "Childrens' Books at Monticello," in press and to be
published in 1966 by the McGregor Library of the Alderman Library at the
University of Virginia.

To Martha Jefferson Randolph

Washington June 10. 05

MY DEAREST MARTHA

I have been a month now without hearing from Edgehill, Mr.
Randolph's letter of May 11. being the last I have recieved. Anne
then had the mumps which of course were expected to go thro'
the family, and heightens my anxiety to hear from you. Our post
is now I believe premanently established at three times a week.
The spring here continues sickly and cold, and poor prospects of
crops. We had yesterday cauliflowers and artichokes at table. The
40. days corn I mentioned to Mr. Randolph to have recieved and

TO MARTHA JEFFERSON RANDOLPH

Washington June 24. 05.

MY DEAREST MARTHA

I last night recieved a letter from Mr. Taylor of Baltimore informing me he had sent by the stage to this place the trunk of articles ordered by Mr. Kelly. I sent this morning to the Stage office; the trunk was arrived, and goes on this evening to Fredericksburg, where I shall desire Mr. Benson[1] to forward it by the first stage to Milton. I had paiment made here for transportation as far as Fredericksbg that no delay might happen on that account. Further could not be paid here, on account of it's being a different concern with which the stage-company here is unconnected. I hope you will get the trunk by the first stage. I have had here a considerable time ½ doz. pr. of shoes for Virginia and ½ doz. pr. for Anne, but am afraid to trust so small a parcel by the stage without a guardian. Perhaps it will not come on till I go myself which will be this day three weeks. I take for granted that Virginia's marriage[2] is to take place at Monticello, as we have so much more room there for our friends, and conveniencies of other kinds also. I will accomodate my trip to Bedford to the matrimonial arrangements. We have just heard from Capt. Lewis, who wintered 1600. miles up the Missouri; all well. 45. chiefs of 6. different nations from that quarter are forwarded by him to St. Louis on their way to this place. Our agent at St. Louis will endeavor to prevail on them to stay there till autumn and then come on. Should they insist on coming immediately they will arrive in July, and may derange my departure. I am glad to find the family has got so easily thro' the mumps, and hope you will discover that you have had them, as I think you had when very young. My love to every body; to yourself unceasing affection. Greet Mr. Randolph also affectionately for me.   TH: JEFFERSON

1. Benjamin Taylor was a Baltimore merchant, John Kelly a Milton merchant, and Benson a Fredericksburg innkeeper with whom TJ often lodged while traveling to and from Washington.
2. Virginia (Jenny) Randolph.

FROM ELLEN WAYLES RANDOLPH

recd. June 27. 05

DEAR GRAND PAPA

I now set down to write to you and hope you will answer my letter. I have often tried to do it before but never could succeed,

I did not put in my last letter, it is what is [the] seventh fine art? I know six of them, Painting, Sculpture, architecture, Music, Poetry, Oratory, but mama nor my self either cannot recollect the seventh. All the children have had the mumps except Mary who is the sweetest little creature in the world, always laughing talking and singing. She has a great many ideas and is a very forward child for her age. Cornelia begins to read very well; we have none of us deserved new books. We have not got half through those you gave us the last time you were at Monticello, but as far as I have got I am very much interested and we are going on with great spirit. Aunt Virginia Sister Ann and all the other children give their love to you. Give mine to Mrs. H Smith. Mama's health is daily improving. She has ridden out a good deal since you left us. Adieu my dear Grandpapa, believe me to be your affectionate Grand Daughter,   ELEOANORA WAYLES RANDOLPH

To ANNE CARY RANDOLPH

Washington July 6. 05.

MY DEAREST ANNE

I do not know whether it is owing to your laziness or mine that our letters have been so long intermitted. I assure you it is not to my want of love to you, and to all of those about you, whose welfare I am always so anxious to learn. But it is useless to discuss old bankrupt scores. We will therefore burn our old accounts, and begin a new one on the 1st. day of October next. I have expected to be able to set out for Monticello on Monday the 15th. but as I have not yet recieved Capt. Lewis's letters and the Western mail will not come in till Tuesday morning the 16th. very possibly I may not be able to set out till that or even the next day Wednesday. In the last case Ellen will not be able to go to bed for three nights, lest I should catch her there. It is possible the letters may come sooner in which case I see nothing to hinder my setting out on the Monday. You will be able to give me an account of your stewardship of the fowls. I expect but a short one from Ellen. I inclose a letter from Dr. Mitchell[1] in answer to one which accompanied a packet from your Papa. Deliver my endearments to all the family, and above all to your Mama: and accept kisses and salutations for yourself.

TH: JEFFERSON

1. Dr. Samuel Latham Mitchell was a Quaker who resided on Long Island, New York. He was also a chemist and botanist.

showed me a cane[1] which they said Buonaparte sent you. It is a very handsome one but I hope you never will have ocassion for it. It is made of fish bone I believe as it is too long to have been the horn of any animal, although it has that appearance. It is capped and pointed with gold very handsomely embost. You will certainly catch Ellen in bed for she is the laziest girl I ever saw and takes the longest to dress of any one I know. Adieu my Dear Grand Papa. Permit me to subscribe myself your most affectionate Grand Daughter, A C R

1. TJ owned several canes or walking sticks, but this description does not seem to fit any of them.

FROM MARTHA JEFFERSON RANDOLPH

Edgehill July 11, 1805

MY DEAREST FATHER

The trunk you were so good as to forward from Washington, arrived safe by the same post which brought your letter. It contained the wedding cloaths, which rendered it of so much importance to some of the family that I shall make no apology for the trouble it put you to. The marriage will take place at Monticello early in August entirely private except the old Gentleman and Lady and Aunt Carr.[1] There is however a possiblity of it's being delayed by the illness of Mrs. Cary's[2] youngest daughter whose situation is extremely critical and will be lingering, which ever way it terminates. I am afraid however the phisicians will *expedite* the business; a feeble constitution reduced as low as she is, is not apt to linger in their hands. I have this moment recieved a letter from Mr. Eppes informing me of the health of the children and a promise to see Francis early in August. The little Girl[3] not quite so soon, as My Aunt's attentions to her daughter Baker[4] will retard her motions. It will be the latter end of the month before we car expect to see her. I must beg your pardon for having omitted till this moment to inform you of the dismantled state of our tea equipage being reduced to *4 tea* cups. Of every thing else there is enough. The tea pots are too small consequently a large black one with 2 cream pots to match would add both to the comfort and appearance of the board, the plated ones being so much worn as to shew the copper. Coffee cups etc. we have in abundance. I am afraid having delayed so long will occasion you some trouble for which I am truly sorry but it slipt my memory till this moment and had like to have done it all together. Will you be so good as

To Martha Jefferson Randolph

Washington Oct. 13. 05

My dearest Martha

I performed my journey to this place without any accident or disagreeable circumstance except travelling half a day in a pretty steady rain, which I thought preferable to staying at Brown's.[1] I experienced no inconvenience from it. This place, which had been healthy thro' the summer is now rather sickly. Some cold mornings and frost after my arrival, it was hoped would remove all disease, but the present warm spell if it continues will probably produce a good deal of sickness. Two of our family are down with bilious fevers, one of them ill. As you did not propose to come till November, the frosts before that time will render every thing safe. As soon as you inform me of the time for your journey, every thing necessary shall be done on my part, and I insist you shall bring the whole family. Mrs. Madison is still at Gray's ferry.[2] Altho' the part affected is healed, it is thought as yet too tender to venture on the journey. But we hope to see her in a few days. I omitted to mention to you that I had agreed to lend Mr. Freeman[3] a mattras and straw bed till he could supply himself. From Mr. Strode's[4] character of him I am in hopes the disagreeable circumstances from him proceeded partly from his sickness, and had part of their colouring from the medium through which they passed. I inclose a paper for Ellen. My friendly salutations to Mr. Randolph and love to yourself and the children.   TH: JEFFERSON

1. Probably the Centreville, Fairfax County, inn where TJ on other occasions had lodged.
2. A ferry site north of Philadelphia.
3. John Holmes Freeman was a Monticello overseer who proved unsatisfactory and was replaced by Edmund Bacon.
4. Possibly Mr. Strode, the Culpeper innkeeper.

To Martha Jefferson Randolph

Washington Oct. 22. 05

My dearest Martha

I have been from home now three weeks without having heard from you or of you through any channel. This being our stage postday I had hoped for a line from some of the family. Knowing the uncertain state of your health this long silence makes me uneasy. I hope I shall soon be relieved by a letter. Your rooms will be in readiness for you here by the beginning of the month. Mrs.

desired, and they may be expected by the stage probably in a few days. I now inclose you an hundred dollars for your expences on the road, and you must consider every thing which yourself or the family will want here as to be furnished by me so that the visit may not at all affect Mr. Randolph's pecuniary arrangements. You have not told me in your letter whether I am to send a carriage for you half way or the whole way. Tho' there will be some reluctance in the carriage owners to undertake the whole way, yet we can effect it with two or three days notice. The stages and distances are as follows:
From Edgehill to Gordon's 16. miles to Orange C. H. 10. = 26. miles
   to Stevensburg 20. Herring's 5. Norman's ford 4. Elkrun church 9. = 38
   To Slate run church 14½. Brown's 5½ Centerville 9½ Fairfax C. H. 8. = 37½
      Wren's 7. Georgetown ferry 6. President's house 2 = 15 to dinner.
I think the sooner you come the better, as fine weather will be the more probable. You will not find Mrs. Madison here I expect, for tho' her recovery is pronounced to be compleated, yet the tender state of the part will induce her to continue there some time. Mr. Madison has been here near a fortnight. Let me hear from you immediately as to a carriage, and when you may be expected. Kiss all the young ones for me, and give Ellen the inclosed poetry. My best affections to Mr. Randolph and yourself.

TH: JEFFERSON

FROM ELLEN WAYLES RANDOLPH

Edgehill November 10 1805

DEAR GRAND PAPA

I expect you think I have forgotten the Promise I made you of writing to you every Post but I have not for I have tried several times but could not effect it for want of implements to do it. You must answer my letters for it would give me great Pleasure to keep up a regular Correspondence with you. I have no news to tell you except the report that prevails of Mrs. Trists marriage with Governor Claiborne.[1] I suppose you have heard it. It is time to finish my letter. I have written enough for this time. Sister Ann

your Mama and sisters and yourself, and my affectionate salutations to your Papa.   TH: JEFFERSON

1. Mrs. Richard Cutts was wife of the Maine congressman and sister of Dolley Madison.

TO MARTHA JEFFERSON RANDOLPH

Washington Nov. 25. 05

MY DEAREST MARTHA

I was uneasy at not hearing from you by the last post, that is to say, by the one which arrived Tuesday morning last, the 19th. I thought it certain I should recieve information as to sending a carriage. I take for granted I shall have a letter tomorrow morning; but in the mean time this goes out this evening. We find more difficulty than I had expected in getting a carriage. It seems that all Congress being to come on this week all the carriages are engaged for bringing them on. Joseph[1] was out on this business yesterday and will be to-day. If we fail here he will go to Alexandria where doubtless we shall succeed: so that you may count on the exactitude of our movements to your wishes, if we get them in time. You must come short stages, as it will be better to lodge badly than endanger being in the night in your situation,[2] and with so many in the carriage with you. Mrs. Madison sets off this day from Philadelphia but will probably not be here till the latter end of the week. My cordial respects to Mr. Randolph, kisses to yourself and the children.   TH: JEFFERSON

P.S. I hope you recieve my letter of the 7th with the remittance.

1. Joseph Daugherty was a Washington hostler and sometime servant to TJ while in the President's House.
2. She was expecting the birth of her eighth child, James Madison Randolph, who was to be the first child born in the President's House.

TO MARTHA JEFFERSON RANDOLPH

Washington Nov. 29. 05.

MY DEAREST MARTHA

The carriage goes off in the morning for Centerville, in time, if you should arrive there early and be so disposed, to bring you on to Fairfax court house in the evening. That will make your ride the next morning easy. But should you not leave Centerville till Sunday morning, you may with ease get here to dinner which we shall accordingly keep back for you till 4. oclock. If you could

almost without stopping in Albemarle. I shall probably be kept there a week or 10. days, laying the foundation of the house, which he is not equal to himself.[3] So that it will be near the middle of August before I shall be fixed at Monticello. Do you know anything of my Antenor's Travels?[4] I do not find them here. Perhaps they are lent out. I write this just at the commencement of an eclipse of the sun, total at Boston and 50 miles North and South of that, of 11¾ digits at Philadelphia, and I suppose at 11½ here and perhaps 11. with you.[5] Tell Ellen I shall acknolege her letter by the next post. Mr. and Mrs. Madison are still a little lamish. They will probably visit us also in September. Kiss all the young ones for me. Present my affections to Mr. Randolph and be assured yourself of my constant and tenderest love.

TH: JEFFERSON

1. John Wayles Eppes was courting an Annapolis lady who unfortunately remains unidentified. He was more successful in another quest, for in 1809 he married Martha Burke Jones of Halifax, N. C., and became the father of a family of four children — two sons and two daughters, who resided at Millbrook, in Buckingham County.

TJ remained on good terms with them and gave as a wedding present the epergne or "glass tree" presently standing on the dining table at Monticello. For additional information on Eppes, consult James H. Bailey, "John Wayles Eppes, Planter and Politician," unpublished Master's thesis at the University of Virginia.

2. William Short.

3. One of TJ's able carpenters. They were going to Bedford County to begin construction of the house on the Poplar Forest tract.

4. Antenor was a pseudonym. There are several editions of this work: *Les Voyages d'A. en Grece et Asie traduit par E. F. Lantier,* which could have been in the Monticello library. It is not included in Sowerby.

5. For an account of the eclipse as seen at Washington, see the Richmond *Enquirer,* July 1, 1806.

To ELLEN WAYLES RANDOLPH

Washington June 24. 06.

I learn with deep concern, my dearest Ellen, that the family has been unwell generally, that you have been ill and your Mama indisposed. Anne informs me you are getting better but does not say whether your Mama is so also. Yet, in the absence of your Papa, her health is doubly important because her care is necessary for you all. I hope this will find you all recovered. Your friends here are generally well. Mrs. S. H. Smith remains constantly in the country; and this place is duller than I ever saw it. I certainly have never been so tired of it; yet I do not at present expect to leave it till the 21st. of July, and on the 24th. shall expect to catch

unwell and very much reduced. There was a great Barbacue at Charlottsville to day at which Mr. Jones delivered an oration.[1] Aunt Jane has returned home and Aunt Lucy and Harriet with her. I got a letter from Miss Nicholson[2] and she told me that she was afraid that Mr. [and] Mrs. Gallatin would not come to Monticello this summer. Do you know whether they will or not? Aunt Carr has been to see us. She is a good deal better but still complains of a pain in her neck. All the children and Mama send their love to you. Adieu my Dear Dear Grand Papa. I cannot tell you how much I love and respect you. Believe me your most affectionate Grand daughter,   A C R

1. The Richmond *Enquirer* for July 26 reported the celebration by stating it began at 3:00 P.M., with Elijah Garth providing a handsome barbecue. The speakers were not identified. Mr. Jones may have been John R. Jones, a county resident.

2. Probably the daughter of Joseph H. Nicholson, a congressman from Maryland whose wife was Maria Gallatin, sister of Albert Gallatin.

FROM ELLEN WAYLES RANDOLPH

Edgehill Friday July 4 1806

I recieved My Dear Grandpapas letter with great pleasure and should have answered it last post but by some neglect it remained untill tuesday in the office and therefore I could not answer it as the post went out Saturday. We are all recovered now except Mary who is still unwell but she is now much better than she was a few days ago and I hope she will soon be entirely well. Aunt Jane has returned and with her Aunt Lucy and Aunt Harriot[1] who design to stay no longer than a month up the country. You must write to me very soon for I am allways exceedingly happy to get a letter from you. All the children give their love to you. Excuse this short letter My Dear Grand Papa. Adieu. Believe me to be your affectionate Grand Daughter.   E. W. RANDOLPH

1. Jane Cary Randolph (Mrs. Thomas Eston), Lucy Eppes Thweatt, and Harriet Randolph Hackley.

TO MARTHA JEFFERSON RANDOLPH

Washington July 6. 06.

MY DEAREST MARTHA

The last letter I have had from Edgehill was Anne's of June 20 that informed me that the family had been generally unwell,

TO MARTHA JEFFERSON RANDOLPH

Washington Oct. 20. 06.

MY DEAREST MARTHA

John delivered safely your letter of the 14th. I am sorry you did not continue at Monticello until your house was in compleat readiness for you. You will run the double risk of green plaister, and less perfect preparation of it for your winter's residence. I do not know what stores remained for your consumption, but it is always my wish you should take whatever does remain. Many of them will not keep, such as crackers, cheese, fish &c. Porter is so peculiarly salutary for your stomach, that I took a larger supply than usual that there might be some for you and in laying in the stores for the ensuing year, I never count on the fragments of the last. I beseech you therefore to consider every thing of that kind as intended for you, and to use any of the wines, and at all times, which you prefer to your own. Having been so long in the midst of a family, the loansomeness of this place is more intolerable than I ever found it. My daily rides too are sickening for want of some interest in the scenes I pass over: and indeed I look over the two ensuing years as the most tedious of my life. You will have with you in a few days a Mr. Brodie, an elderly English gentleman, who is seeking an asylum in this quiet country to bring his family to. He is a very worthy, inoffensive polite man. He turns his eyes to our neighborhood, and I have given him a letter to Mr. Randolph merely to prevent his being imposed on in any bargain. He has his eye on Henderson's and Overton's lands,[1] but of preference on the latter. I send in a separate package to Mr. Randolph 25. advertisements from Mr. Shoemaker[2] which we ask the favor of him to have set up in the most public places for 20. miles round, and without delay. By the return of Davy I shall send a piece of linen to be made up for me against March. Present me affectionately to Mr. Randolph and the young ones, and be assured of my constant and tenderest love.

TH: JEFFERSON

1. Mr. Brodie did not remove to Albemarle.
2. Johnathan Shoemaker was the miller at the Shadwell Toll Mill.

FROM ELLEN WAYLES RANDOLPH

Edgehill November 14 1806.

I am now preparing my self to write a short letter to my Dear Grandpapa and hope he will let me hear from him as soon as he

FROM ELLEN WAYLES RANDOLPH

recd Nov. 24. [1806]

DEAR GRAND PAPA

The post is going directly and I only have time to write a few lines to let you know that we are all well and I hope you are so. I wrote to you last saturday and shall wait impatiently to hear from you soon. I have not time to write any more to you now but I will very shortly make amends for this short letter. Mama and all the children send their love to you. Give mine to Mrs. H. Smith. Adieu my Dear Grandpapa. Believe me to be your affectionate Grandaughter,   E. W. R.

TO ELLEN WAYLES RANDOLPH

Washington Nov. 30. 06.

MY DEAREST ELLEN

I have recieved two letters from you since I left Monticello. By Davy I sent you a pair of Bantam fowls; quite young: so that I am in hopes you will now be enabled to raise some. I propose on their subject a question of natural history for your enquiry: that is whether this is the Gallina Adrianica, or Adria, the Adsatick cock of Aristotle? For this you must examine Buffon etc. Mr. Burwell asks in the name of your Mama, for a Nautical almanac.[1] She will find those of many years in the library at Monticello, in the press on the right hand of the Eastern outward door of the cabinet.[2] I send you inclosed much newspaper poetry. Adieu my dear Ellen: kiss your mama for me and all the young ones. For yourself recieve the kiss I give this paper.

TH: JEFFERSON

1. *The Nautical Almanac and Astronomical Ephemeris* was published in London. TJ purchased his first while in Paris in 1786.
2. The Cabinet is that room at Monticello opposite TJ's bedroom. It was one of the rooms of the library suite and where his chaise longue writing apparatus was situated.

TO ANNE CARY RANDOLPH

Washington Dec.8.06.

MY DEAREST ANNE

I owe you the acknolegement of your letter of Nov. 15. and I shall hope this evening to recieve one from some one of the

think them handsomer. I have no news to tell you for being in the country I seldom have any thing worth relating and that being the case I can never write long letters unless you suffer me to speak of myself. I have begun the Grecian History in which I am very much interested and have got to multiplication in arithmetic. I am going on with Dufief[1] and am reading Plutarque de la Jeuness in French[2] of which I read ten pages for my lesson sometimes more but not often less. I copyd the historical part of Lord Chesterfield's letters for a lesson in writing, all which is generally concluded by dinner time after which I play and at night sew while Sister Ann reads aloud to us. Adieu my Dear Grandpapa. Mama and the children join in love to you. Believe me to be your affectionate Grand Daughter,   E. W. R.

Mama says Buffon[3] cannot answer the question you propose to me.

1. Nicolas Gouin Dufief, *Nature Displayed, in her Mode of Teaching Language to Man* (Philadelphia, 1804), 2 volumes (Sowerby 4819), a popular French grammar of that day. Dufief presented Jefferson with the set; Volume I is now at Monticello. Dufief was also a book dealer and a correspondent of Jefferson's. For more on him, see Edith Phillips, *Louis Hue Girardin and Nicholas Gouin Dufief and Their Relations with Thomas Jefferson; An Unknown Episode of the French Emigration in America* (Baltimore, 1926).

2. Plutarque de la Terinesse. It is difficult to establish the specific title of Ellen's book. It might have been any of several abridgements, as: *Abrégé des Hommes, illustres de Plutarque, à l'usage de la jeunesse* . . . Beauvais, impr. de Des Jardins *an IV*; — *an V–IX, Beauvais l'auteur;* or *Abrégé des Vies de Plutarque, par M. Archer* . . . *Nouvelle Edition* . . .

3. Martha was correct; the solution was not in Buffon.

TO ELLEN WAYLES RANDOLPH

Washington Dec. 15. 06

MY DEAREST ELLEN

This is our postday, and I have been so engaged that the hour of dinner and company are arriving before I could begin a letter to you. I shall therefore merely say we are all well, and I hope we shall hear to-night that all are well at Edgehill. Tell your Mama, while you kiss her for me, that Rigden has returned and delivered me her watch neatly done which will be sent by your papa. I send you something for your collection. Kiss and bless all the young people for me, and be assured of my affectionate love.

TH: JEFFERSON

her in Milton. It will [be] a great addition to our neighbourhood. James[4] is very much grown and I think now is a very handsome and sprigtly child. Mama Sister Ann and the children are well and send their love to you. Give mine to Mrs. S. H. S. Adieu my dear Grandpapa. Believe me to be your affectionate Grand Daughter,   E. W. RANDOLPH
Your Grass looks very well.

1. James Ogilvie had been operating a school at Milton since January, 1806. See Richmond *Enquirer*, November 26, 1805, for his advertisement announcing its curriculum and opening date.
2. Mrs. Stewart Bankhead of Port Royal. She did not marry Ogilvie. Following her husband's death this much married lady took as her third husband Robert Gilchrist Robb of Gaymont, Caroline County.
3. A small tobacco port on the Potomac River in Caroline County.
4. James Madison Randolph, the second son of Martha and Thomas Mann Randolph, Jr., was born January 17, 1806, the first child to be born in the President's House. He was born during Martha's second visit to Washington.

TO ELLEN WAYLES RANDOLPH

Washington Feb. 8. 07.
MY DEAREST ELLEN

I believe it is true that you have written me 2. letters to my one to you. Whether this proceeds from your having more industry or less to do than myself I will not say. One thing however I will say that I most sincerely wish to be with you all and settle the point vivâ voce (if you do not understand these two Latin words you must lay Jefferson's Latin under contribution that you may know because they are often used in English writing). To return to our correspondence, you have a great advantage as to matter for communication. You have a thousand little things to tell me which I am fond to hear; for instance of the health of every body, and particularly of your dear Mama, every thing relating to her being of the first concern to me: then what you are reading, what are your other occupations, how many dozen Bantams you have raised, how often you and Anne have rode to Monticello to see if the Tulips are safe &c. &c. &c. However I shall be with you about the 11th or 12th proxima (more Latin, madam) and then we will examine the tulips together. Kiss your dear Mama a thousand times for me, and all the sisters, q.s.[1] (more Latin) and be assured yourself of my tender affections.   TH: JEFFERSON

1. An abbreviation for *quantum sufficit,* "as much as suffices." See Adriano Cappelli, *Dizionario di Abbreviature* (Milano, 1929), 314.

because it will carry a box of flower roots which I shall consign to her care, but not to be opened till we get to Monticello, and have every thing ready for planting them as soon as they are opened. I shall write by this post to your Mama, so I conclude with my kisses to you all.   TH: JEFFERSON

1. TJ had undoubtedly confused the title, which was *The Butterfly's Ball and Grasshopper's Feast,* a poem by William Roscoe. See George Chandler, *William Roscoe of Liverpool* (London, 1953), 118–19 and 410–11, for the words and early publication media. It is also worth noting that in the "Jefferson Scrapbook" (ViU), p. [69], there is a newspaper clipping of this poem.

TO MARTHA JEFFERSON RANDOLPH

Washington Mar. 2. 07.

MY DEAREST MARTHA

Tomorrow Congress will close; but I hardly expect to get away under a week. It will take that time at least to get all the laws put into a course of execution and some other matters settled. On Monday last Mr. Randolph and myself took a ride to Maine's to engage our thorns. The day was raw, he was without a great coat, and was before indisposed, as I had mentioned to you. That evening he[1] was taken with a chill and fever, which went off on Wednesday, but returned in the same evening. The last night he has had another intermission, and the return this morning is so moderate that we hope it will quit him finally this evening. He is considerably reduced and weakened and I shall endeavor to prevail on him not to attempt his return till I go; because I could keep him down to short journies, whereas, if alone, he might push so as to produce a relapse. He will return in my chair and, if with me, I should be with him and stay with him should he have any fever on the road. Mr. Burwell will leave this on Wednesday or Thursday and will call on you. Our obligations to him for his attentions to Mr. Randolph are infinite; and so also to Dr. Jones[2] who scarcely ever leaves him. He has decided absolutely not to offer again for Congress. In saying that I expect to get away in a week, I merely guess. It may be some days longer: so that I cannot fix the day when we shall call to take you on to Monticello. Adieu my beloved Martha, take care of yourself for my sake and every one's sake.   TH: JEFFERSON

1. Before Randolph had been in Washington two weeks he was so ill of a fever that it was feared he would not recover. "Jefferson evidenced great con-

me up with a fever one day. This indisposition will occasion me to be here some days longer than I expected, and indeed with the mass which is before me, I cannot fix a day at all for my departure. I think that it will take Mr. Randolph, as long, after his fever leaves him, to recover strength for the journey, as it will me to get thro' my business: so that you will see us both together, as certainly I shall not go till he is strong enough to accompany me. I shall write you by your stage mail which arrives on Thursday, and a horse post will now arrive at Milton every Monday morning. God bless you my beloved Martha, and all the young ones.

Th: Jefferson

1. Meriwether Lewis.
2. Isaac Coles.
3. Thomas Mann's body servant.

To Martha Jefferson Randolph

Monday Mar. 9. 07.

My dearest Martha

I have the happiness to inform you that Mr. Randolph is entirely well. His fever had left him at the date of my last but I did not then know it. He moved here on Saturday and Dr. Jones with him. He has now nothing but weakness to contend with. He was able to walk two or three times across the room to-day,[1] he eats with some appetite and sleeps tolerably. The Doctor will leave us tomorrow, as nothing is now wanting but care of our patient. But it will be many days before he will be able to set out on his journey. I would willingly compound for ten days. However he must not set out too soon. We shall detain the carts some days yet. As we have now two posts a week you shall hear from me every 3. or 4. days. God bless you my ever dear daughter and all our young ones.   Th: Jefferson

1. Mr. Randolph had finally yielded to TJ's entreaties and removed from his boardinghouse to the President's House.

To Martha Jefferson Randolph

Washington Mar. 11. 07. (Tuesday)

My dearest Martha

Altho' I wrote to you by post yesterday, yet as an opportunity offers by Capt. Clarke at noon to-day, and I know you will still be anxious, I write again to assure you that Mr. Randolph continues

some days longer danger would have supervened. On the 10th. day it abated evidently still more on the 11th. and went off on the 12th. which was the day I wrote you by Mr. Burwell. We are now at the 18th. day since he was taken. Adieu my dearest Martha. Kiss all the little ones for me. Should I by any post omit to write, do not be alarmed; for as he is quite well it is very possible my business may sometimes prevent my recollecting a post day.

TH: JEFFERSON

1. The Oval Room was on the second floor of the President's House and was used as a drawing room or study. William V. Elder, Curator of the White House, to James A. Bear, Jr., December 28, 1962.

To MARTHA JEFFERSON RANDOLPH

Washington. Friday afternoon. Mar. 13. 07.

MY DEAREST MARTHA

I wrote to you by the carts yesterday morning; but as you will not get that letter till Monday evening, and may recieve this written a day later on Monday morning, I again inform you that Mr. Randolph continues well. He rode yesterday 5. miles, without fatigue, was much exhilarated by it, and had a fine night's sleep. An Easterly storm having set in this morning will interrupt this salutary recruit to his spirits and health. He still looks to Monday sennight (the 23d) as the date by which he will be strong enough to set out on his journey: I think we may set out sooner. He is now so well, that I may possibly forget the post day sometimes, tho' I will not willingly. We both think it will be better for you to move over to Monticello a little before we get there; because as we shall probably not set out from Gordon's till 9. oclock in the morning, any stoppage at Edgehill might keep him out to an improper hour of the evening. But on this subject I shall have other occasions of writing to you. Accept my tenderest love for yourself and the children.

TH: JEFFERSON

From MARTHA JEFFERSON RANDOLPH

March 14. 1807

MY DEAREST FATHER

I have but a moment to return you a thousand thanks for your goodness in writing so regularly to me during Mr. R illness. I have been in a state of great anxiety upon his account. Thank

in a state not to be concieved. The carts have not arrived yet;
Davy broke down near orange court house[1] and past by on horseback to get the waggon to go down for his load. They could not
have proceeded but for the circumstance of being able to double
their team by being together. At the bad places some days they
only came 6 miles. To give you a still better idea of the *labours*
which await you, Mr. Carr[2] told me of their putting 9 horses to
one waggon; finally they had to take out the load and prize out 2
of the horses who *mired*. If you determine to venture your self
my dear Father which I think will be imprudent untill you feel
quite recovered yet would it be very improper for Mr. Randolph
whose fear of detaining you may make him venture upon it sooner
than prudence would authorise. If you come shortly pray advise
him to stay untill thoroughly recruited. I know it will put him
more at his ease and your servants are so attentive that he will be
as well attended to as if you were with him. I mention this merely
to put you both entirely at your ease. I know he would rather be
left than detain you one moment, or set off himself sooner than
entirely prudent. Pray take care of your self. Your constitution is
not adequate to the labours of your place. I look forward to the
2 remaining years with more anxiety than I can express. Those
past with what joy shall I hail that return which will be followed
by no sepparation. I make no exception when I say the *first* and
most important object with me will be the dear and sacred duty
of nursing and chearing your old age, by every endearment of
filial tenderness. My fancy dwells with rapture upon your image
seated by your *own* fire side surrounded by your grand children
contending for the pleasure of waiting upon you. Every age has
its pleasures, with health I do not know whether youth is to be
regretted. I have been very much delighted with a tract of Cicero's
upon that subject; he has certainly seen it in its true light, as a
harbour from the cares and storms of life to which the turbulence
of the passions expose us in youth. Adieu My Dearest Father.
Once more pray take care of your precious health and believe me
with unalterable tenderness yours,   M. R.

Isaac has just arrived. I think it will be better for us to go to
Monticello before you come. As soon as that is determined upon
I shall regulate my motions accordingly.   M. RANDOLPH

1. Orange Court House, the county seat of Orange County, was a stopping
point in traveling between Monticello and Washington. It was 25 miles north
of Charlottesville.
2. Probably Samuel Carr.

To Martha Jefferson Randolph

Washington Mar. 27. 07

MY DEAREST MARTHA

I presume Mr. Randolph writes to you and informs you he continues well. He has rode twice on horseback; and yesterday about 4. miles without feeling it. My fit of yesterday was so mild that I have some hope of missing it to-day. I write this in the morning, but will keep it open till the evening to add the result of the day. We both think we may very safely fix on Monday sennight for our departure, to wit, the 6th. of April, and that you had better move over to Monticello the first fair day after that, as we shall be there on the Friday to dinner. Should any thing derange our plan, we have still two other posts to write to you, to wit, those which will arrive at Milton on the 2d. and 6th. of April. Before this reaches you you will have heard of the arrival of Burr at Richmond for trial.[1] There may be a possibility of something connected with this circumstance arising which might detain me a little, but I do not foresee that that can be. Accept kisses for yourself and our dear children.   TH: JEFFERSON

P. S. Afternoon. I have scarcely had any sensation of a fit to-day: so that I consider it as missed.

1. Aaron Burr's trial for conspiracy to separate the western states from the United States. He was brought before Chief Justice John Marshall, who presided over the United States Circuit Court in Richmond beginning March 30, 1807.

To Martha Jefferson Randolph

Mar. 30. 07.

MY DEAREST MARTHA

I presume Mr. Randolph informs you himself that he is quite well. Indeed I have no doubt he could now very safely undertake the journey; but we continue to fix on Monday next for departure. As to myself altho' I have no actual head-ach, yet about 9. oclock every morning I have a very quickened pulse come on, a disturbed head and tender eyes, not amounting to absolute pain. It goes off about noon, and is doubtless an obstinate remnant of the head-ach, keeping up a possibility of return. I am not very confident of it's passing off. I shall write to you again on Friday, and should nothing have changed our purpose by that time, we shall hope you will be removed to Monticello so as that we shall find you there on the 10th. I send Ellen a little piece of poetry; yet I am not

gone on. My health has been constant since my return here. I inclose a newspaper for Mr. Randolph, a magazine for yourself, and a piece of poetry for Ellen. Tell her she is to consider this as a substitute for a letter and that I debit her account accordingly. I shall have a letter for Anne next week, by which time I am in hopes to recieve a report from her of the state of our affairs at Monticello. We had cucumbers here on the 20th. of May, strawberries the 24th. and peas the 26th. I am in hopes she has noted when you first had cherries and strawberries. Of small news in this place we have not much. Doctr. Bullas[1] and his family have left it for the Mediterranean. S. H. Smith proposes to give up his press. Whether he will remain here afterwards will probably depend on his obtaining office. It is thought he will offer as successor to Beckley.[2] Altho' we had fires on the 19th. 20th. and 21st. the summer seems now to have set in seriously. On the 30th. the thermometer was at $84°$. Will you tell Mr. Randolph that I have found here the pure breed of Guinea hogs, and shall endeavor to send on a litter of the pigs when my cart comes in autumn. Is there any thing here I can get or do for you? It would much add to my happiness if I oftener could know how to add to your convenience or gratification. Remember me affectionately to Mr. Randolph and the young ones, and be assured yourself of my tenderest love.

TH: JEFFERSON

1. Dr. John Bullus was later appointed as customs agent for the port of New York City.
2. Possibly John Beckley, author of *Address to the People of the United States; with an Epitome and Vindication of . . . TJ* (1800) and Clerk of the House of Representatives until 1797, when defeated for re-election; he was named Librarian of Congress in 1802.

To Anne Cary Randolph

Washington June 7. 07.

MY DEAR ANNE

I recieved last week from your papa information that you were all well except your Mama, who had still some remains of the pain in the face. I hope I shall hear this week that she also is restored to her health. From yourself I may soon expect a report of your first visit to Monticello, and of the state of our joint concerns there. I find that the limited number of our flower beds will too much restrain the variety of flowers in which we might wish to indulge, and therefore I have resumed an idea, which I had for-

tion a list of these shipwrecked packages. My tender love to you all, and to yourself above all.   TH: JEFFERSON

No. 1. a barrel. white Muscovado sugar.
2. cask. cheese and sundries.
3. do. raisins, rice, loaf sugar.
4. do. crackers.
5. do. brandy. double cased
6.7.8.9. four boxes. 200 bottles cyder
10.11.12. barrels of potatoes.
13. box. 36. beef's tongues

14.15. barrels of cyder for vinegar.
16. box. containg 12. boxes prunes, 4. do. figs
17. do. 18 bottles oil. 4. do. anchovies
18.19. boxes. 1. doz. Hungary wine in each.
20.21. boxes. 59 bottles syrup of punch.
22. box. horns, books, paper, prints
23. box. chimney facings.
24.25. boxes. ornaments in led.

TO ELLEN WAYLES RANDOLPH

Washington June 29. 07.

MY DEAR ELLEN

I believe I have recieved no letter from you since I came from Monticello, but perhaps there is one on the road for me. Hope is so much pleasanter than despair, that I always prefer looking into futurity through her glass. I send you some poetical gleanings. Our newspapers have been rather barren in that ware for some time past. Whether the muses have been taking a nap, or our news writers have been prevented from making their weekly visits to mount Parnassus,[1] by their occupations with Burr and the Chesapeake I cannot decide. But we will leave these idle ladies to their dreams in the Castalian valley, and descend to the more useful region and occupations of the good housewife, one of whom is worth more than the whole family of the muses. How go on the Bantams? I rely on you for their care, as I do on Anne for the Algerine fowls, and on our arrangements at Monticello for the East Indians. These varieties are pleasant for the table and furnish an agreeable diversification in our domestic occupations. I am now possessed of individuals of four of the most remarkeable varieties of the race of the sheep.[2] If you turn to your books of natural history, you will find among these 1. the Spanish sheep

because they keep up better at the heel and lower heels but otherwise exactly like the pattern.

To Martha Jefferson Randolph

Washington July 27. 07.

My dearest daughter

As it seems now tolerably probable that the British squadron in our bay[1] have not in contemplation to commit any hostile act, other than the remaining there in defiance, and bringing to the vessels which pass in and out, we are making all the arrangements preparatory to the possible state of war, that they may be going on while we take our usual recess. In the course of three or four days a proclamation will be issued for calling Congress on some day in October. These matters settled, I can leave this for Monticello some day I think from Friday to Monday inclusive, unless something unforeseen happens. I am endeavoring to persuade Genl. Dearborne to go and stay with me at Monticello; but I do not see much likelihood of prevailing on him. In expectation of being with you somewhere from Monday to Thursday I tender my best affections to Mr. Randolph and the family and my warmest love to yourself.
TH: JEFFERSON

1. They were anchored in the Norfolk Roads.

To Martha Jefferson Randolph

Washington Oct. 12. 07.

My dearest Martha

My journey to this place was not as free from accident as usual. I was near losing Castor[1] in the Rapidan, by his lying down in the river, where waste deep, and being so embarrassed by the shafts of the carriage and harness that he was nearly drowned before the servants, jumping into the water, could lift his head out and cut him loose from the carriage. This was followed by the loss of my travelling money, I imagine as happened on the Sopha in the morning I left Monticello, when it was given me again by one of the children. Two days after my arrival here I was taken with the Influenza, but it was very slight, without either fever or pain and is now nearly passed off. I send you a letter and pamphlet from your old acquaintance Dashwood, now Mrs. Lee,[2] who you will percieve not to have advanced in prudence or sound judgment.

that I may know what supplies to ask from Mc.Mahon[1] for the next spring. When Davy comes I shall send some Alpine strawberry roots, and some tussocks of a grass of a perfume equal to Vanilla, called the Sweet-scented Vernal grass, or Anthoxanthum odoratium. These I must consign to your care till the spring. I expect a pair of wildgeese of a family which have been natives for several generations, but they will hardly be here in time for Davy.[2] They are entirely domesticated, beautiful have a very musical note, and are much superior to the tame for the table. I have recieved from Capt. Pike[3] a pair of grisly bears brought from the head of the Arkansa. These are too dangerous and troublesome for me to keep. I shall therefore send them to Peale's Museum.[4] We have nothing new here except a new importation of Influenza by the Western and Southern members who take it on the road and bring it on. I am anxious to hear that you are all recovered from it. Convey my warm affections to your papa, mama and the family and be assured of them yourself.   TH: JEFFERSON

1. Bernard McMahon, the Philadelphia nurseryman and author of *The American Gardener's Calendar.*
2. A trusted slave who carted a great deal of TJ's supplies between Monticello and Washington.
3. Zebulon Pike.
4. An exhibition hall and museum in Philadelphia operated by Rembrandt and Charles Willson Peale.

FROM ELLEN WAYLES RANDOLPH

Edgehill November 6th 1807

I hope my dear grandpapa, will excuse my long silence, when he knows the reason of it which was that I had no paper, but now that papa has come from Richmond and brought some with him, I will gladly answer your letter. The song, which you sent me, I have always admired as a very beautiful and pathetic piece and am very glad that you sent it as it has always, been one of my favorites. Mama and all the children are well; James has grown a great deal, and begins to talk. He is a sweet child; Mama and Sister Ann send their love to you, give mine to Mrs. S. H. S. Adieu my dear Grandpapa. Believe me to be your very affectionate Grand Daughter.   E. W. RANDOLPH

expects to go down soon. Mama Aunt Virginia Sister Ann and all the children send their love to you. Give mine to Mrs S H Smith. Pray write to me when you have time. Adieu my dear Grandpapa. Believe me to be your affectionate Grand Daughter,

ELEONORA WAYLES RANDOLPH

TO MARTHA JEFFERSON RANDOLPH

Washington Nov. 23. 07.

MY DEAR MARTHA

Here we are all well; and my last letters from Edgehill informed me that all were so there except some remains of Influenza hanging on yourself. I shall be happy to hear you are entirely clear of it's remains. It seems to have gained strength and malignancy in it's progress over the country. It has been a formidable disease in the Carolinas; but worst of all in Kentucky; fatal however only to old persons. Davy will set out on his return tomorrow. He will carry an earthen box of Monthly strawberries which I must put under Anne's care till Spring, when we will plant them at Monticello. I have stuck several sprigs of Geranium in a pot which contained a plant supposed to be Orange, but not known to be so. We have little company of strangers in town this winter. The only ladies are the wives of Messrs. Newton, Thruston, W. Alston, Marion, Mumford, Blount, Adams, Cutts, and Mrs. Mc.Creary expected.[1] Congress are all expectation and anxiety for the news expected by the Revenge,[2] or by Colo. Monro,[3] whose immediate return however may be doubted. The War-fever is past, and the probability against it's return is rather prevalent. A Caucus of malcontent members has been held, and an organized opposition to the government arranged, J. R. and J. C.[4] at it's head. About 20. members composed it. Their object is to embarras, avoiding votes of opposition beyond what they think the nation will bear. Their chief mischief will be done by letters of misrepresentations to their constituents; for in neither house, even with the assured aid of the federalists can they shake the good sense and honest intentions of the mass of real republicans. But I am tired of a life of contention, and of being the personal object for the hatred of every man, who hates the present state of things. I long to be among you where I know nothing but love and delight, and where instead of being chained to a writing table I would be indulged as others are with the blessings of domestic society, and pursuits

house. I could say much about politics, our only entertainment here, but you would not care a fig about that. Now I recollect one thing which you will care about. Colo. Munroe left London Oct. 14. and probably sailed about the 20th. We may expect him therefore every hour and as it is probable he will come here first, he will not be with you till you will have heard of his arrival. Another recollection, new arrangement of the Western mail begins this day which will enable you to recieve to your letters written Saturday morning, the answers the Thursday following instead of the Thursday sennight. For fear of more recollections which might incroach on other pressing business I will here close with the addition only of my affectionate remembrance to your Papa Mama, and the others of the family, not forgetting yourself.

TH: JEFFERSON

TO MARTHA JEFFERSON RANDOLPH

Washington Dec. 29. 07

MY DEAREST MARTHA

I was taken with a tooth-ache[1] about 5. days ago, which brought on a very large and hard swelling of the face, and that produced a fever which left me last night. The swelling has subsided sensibly, but whether it will terminate without suppuration is still uncertain. My hope is that I shall be well enough to recieve my company on New Year's day. Indeed I have never been confined by it to my bed-room. This would not have been worth mentioning to you, but that rumour might magnify it to you as something serious. Present my warm affections to Mr. Randolph and the family and be assured of my unceasing love.

TH: JEFFERSON

1. One of the few instances of TJ's having trouble with his teeth or gums. The ailment began about Christmas Eve; the jawbone exfoliated, and a piece was extracted about January 5. For fear of complications he remained indoors for nearly a month. As late as February 23 there still was a small knot on his jawbone. Consult the "Medical Chronology."

FROM MARTHA JEFFERSON RANDOLPH

Edgehill Jan. 2, 1808

I am very much obliged to you My Dearest Father for your kindness in saving me from the anxiety which an exagerated report would have occasioned me. I am in hopes the swelling will go off

TO MARTHA JEFFERSON RANDOLPH

Washington Jan. 5. 08.

MY DEAREST MARTHA

I recieved yesterday yours of the 2d. My fever left me the day I wrote to you, and the swelling abated through the whole face, but still remains in a knot as big as a pigeon's egg, over the diseased tooth, which has now been suppurating so long that the Doctr. thinks he shall have to extract the tooth (altho' perfectly sound) to prevent a caries of the bone. A day or two will decide. In the mean time I am confined to the house, though without pain, and indeed in good health. I always apprehended that Mr. Randolph would be in great embarrasment between the imprudencies of some members of his father's family, and the necessity of taking care of a large one of his own, and knowing his liberal dispositions I thought it possible that present pressure might sometimes prevail over a prudent foresight of the future. If he keeps himself clear of engagements on their behalf, and only assists them with money when he has it, this will prevent any serious injury to himself. I never in my life have been so disappointed as in my expectations that the office I am in would have enabled me from time to time to assist him in his difficulties. So far otherwise has it turned out that I have now the gloomy prospect of retiring from office loaded with serious debts, which will materially affect the tranquility of my retirement. However, not being apt to deject myself with evils before they happen, I nourish the hope of getting along. It has always been my wish and expectation, that when I return to live at Monticello, Mr. Randolph, yourself and family would live there with me, and that his estate being employed entirely for meeting his own difficulties, would place him at ease. Our lands, if we preserve them, are sufficient to place all the children in independance. But I know nothing more important to inculcate into the minds of young people than the wisdom, the honor, and the blessed comfort of living within their income, to calculate in good time how much less pain will cost them the plainest stile of living which keeps them out of debt, than after a few years of splendor above their income, to have their property taken away for debt when they have a family growing up to maintain and provide for. Lessons enough are before their eyes, among their nearest acquaintances if they will but contemplate and bring the examples home to themselves. Still there is another evil against which we cannot guard, unthrifty

also the "Jefferson Scrapbook" (ViU) for evidences of the poetry of Peter Pindar in the Monticello family.

2. Henry Taylor was possibly one of James Ogilvie's students.

3. Evelina Bolling was the daughter of John Bolling and Mary Kennon and the granddaughter of Mary Jefferson Bolling (Mrs. John).

To Ellen Wayles Randolph

Washington Jan. 12. 08.

My dear Ellen

I send you some poetry, but am not sure whither I may not have sent you the same pieces before. My letters to your Mama will have informed you of my having been indisposed with a swelled face. It rose, suppurated, and has left me with a hard swelling still on the jawbone, which however I am in hopes will go down. It still confines me to the house for fear cold should affect it. Otherwise I am well. Your particular friends here are all well as far as I can recollect. Mr. Eppes has been confined a month by an Erysipelas. He went out yesterday for the first time. Francis is in good health and goes to school every day. He just reads. Mr. Rose's[1] delay on board his ship is still unexplained to us; but as you are no politician I shall add nothing further in that line. Kiss your dear Mama for me, and sisters. Present me affectionately to your papa, and be assured of my tender love for yourself. Adieu.

Th: Jefferson

1. George Rose was the special British envoy sent to adjudicate the *Chesapeake-Leopard* affair of June 22, 1807. See footnote 3 for TJ to Ellen Wayles Randolph, June 29, 1807.

From Ellen Wayles Randolph

Edgehill. January 15th 1808

Dear Grandpapa

I recieved your letter of the 12 yesterday and am very much obliged to you for the Poetry you sent me. I wrote to you the last post but I did not know when Jefferson went to the post office and he went without it. I inclose it to you now. I am sincerely sorry that you have that swelling on your face however I hope it will go down. How I long for the time that you are to come home to live and then we shall all go to Monticello to live with you. All is well here. James is well and begins to speak very plain. He is the sweetest little fellow you ever saw. Mama and Sister Ann send

Dear Father but I never can forgive my self for that unfortunate trip to Washington. I conjure you once more not to consider the children but secure your own tranquility and ours will follow of course.

Mr. Hackley has written to Mr. Randolph to know with certainty what he can count upon. He understood the promise of the consulship of Cadiz implied by an expression of yours "that if he was already there (in Spain) some thing might be done for him" where as Mr. Mead[2] tells him *he* expects it and has found powerfull friends to support his claim. Mr. Randolph begged me also to reccomend to your kindness a cousin of his (Tarlton Webb)[3] a grandson of Aunt Fleming's and one of a large family of beggared orphans. A midshipmans place is what they wish for the youth. Pardon me if I tease you. It is my misfortune to be so circumstanced as not to be able to avoid it allways as much averse to it as I am. Adieu My Dear Father. Remember that our happiness is so involved in yours as to depend upon it for never can I know peace if yours is disturbed. Yours devotedly,

MRANDOLPH

1. TJ at this time owned 4,164½ acres in the Poplar Forest tract in Bedford County.

2. A lieutenant in the United States Navy who hoped to obtain Don Joseph Yznardi's consular post at Cadiz. It later went to Richard S. Hackley.

3. A grandson of Tarlton Fleming and Mary Randolph, the latter an aunt of Thomas Mann Randolph, Jr.

FROM ANNE CARY RANDOLPH

Edgehill January 22 *1808*

I have intended to write to My Dear Grand Papa for several post's but we are so much engaged in our lesson's that I had not time. Ellen and myself are learning geography with which I am very much pleased indeed.

I read Coocks voyages in French and Livy in english besides a lesson in Dufief and my Arethmetic and writing every day.[1] I have not been to Monticello since we came from there but Jefferson was there the other day and says that the green house is not done. Both your ice house and ours are filled. I was at Mrs. Lewis's on my way from the North Garden. She told me she had saved some of the seed of the Cypress vine for you and some prickly ash trees. The Alpine Strawberries are doing very well. We were so unfortu-

From Martha Jefferson Randolph

Jan. 30 1808

I must beg the favor of you My Dearest Father to forward the inclosed, it is from Jane to her Sister and there is no mode of comunication at present unless through you.[1] I suppose you have heard of the loss of your dam.[2] Mr. Randolph begs particularly that you will transmit your orders about the repairs to *him*. He has nothing to do having two overseers to overlook his business and will do the dam with your own hands without it's costing you any thing; he thinks Bacon has not under standing and Shoemaker[3] wants honesty to do it properly. I know it will give him real pleasure to recieve any little commission from you and it can not possibly put him to the least inconvenience. Adieu My Dearest Father. We have no post yet I suppose from hight of the water courses. Yours sincerely,   M Randolph

1. Jane Randolph (Mrs. Thomas Eston) to her sister, Harriet Hackley (Mrs. Richard S.), in Cadiz, Spain.
2. A flood during the late summer of 1807 caused the loss of half of TJ's mill dam. See *Farm Book,* 367.
3. Isaac Shoemaker and his father Jonathan were the mill tenants at the Shadwell Mill. TJ had very unsatisfactory relations with both, and the mill instead of being an income-producer became a source of great trouble. *Farm Book,* 341ff.

From Cornelia Jefferson Randolph

recd Feb. 1. 08.

Dear Grandpapa

I do not know how to write myself but as I am very anxious to write to you I must get Sister Ellen to do it for me. I hope that I shall soon be able to do it myself and not to depend upon others. I am reading Sandford and Merton. Every day I get a peice of poetry by heart and write a copy. I have not begun arithmetic yet but I hope I soon shall. Virginia and Mary send their love to you. Adieu my dear Grand Papa. Believe me to be your affectionate Grand daughter,   Cornelia Randolph

To Martha Jefferson Randolph

Washington Feb. 2. 08.

My dearest Martha

The letter to Mr. Hackley shall go by a government vessel which sails for Cadiz the 10th. of this month: such a one will sail

year that I fear I shall be able to absent myself but little from this place. My spring visit will [I] apprehend be very short. Present me affectionately to Mr. Randolph, and kiss all the young ones for me. To yourself is devoted my unalterable love.

TH: JEFFERSON

1. Robert Smith was Secretary of the Navy in TJ's Cabinet.

TO MARTHA JEFFERSON RANDOLPH

Washington Feb. 6. 08.

MY DEAREST MARTHA

I wrote to you the last week, but a pressure of business at the time prevented my answering a part of your letter of the 16th. Jan. The regret which you there expressed at the supposed effect of your visit to this place on my ordinary expences, gives me real uneasiness, and has little foundation. Your being here with your family scarcely added any thing sensible to the ordinary expences of the house, and was richly compensated by the happiness I have when with you compared with the comfortless solitude of my general situation. I mean a solitude as to the objects dear to me, for of others I have more than enough. I mentioned my embarrasments merely as a reason for my having been unable to assist Mr. Randolph. The economies which I may practice this year with my crops of the last and present year, if the embargo does not deprive me of the proceeds, will not leave serious difficulties on my hands. That in going into private life I should return to a private stile of living is a thing of course: and this I shall be able to meet without interfering as you mention with the productions of Mr. Randolph's farms, which I wish he should be able to apply entirely to the easement of his own affairs. Indeed I know no difference between his affairs and my own. My only reason for anxiety to keep my property unimpaired is to leave it as a provision for yourselves and your family. This I trust I shall be able to do, and that we shall be able to live in the mean time in love and comfort. In proportion as the time of my rejoining you permanently approaches, every day seems longer, and the load of business appears heavier. But still every day shortens it. Kiss all the children for me, and be assured of my tenderest love.

TH: JEFFERSON

FROM MARTHA JEFFERSON RANDOLPH

Edgehill Feb. 20, 1808

This will be Delivered to you My Dear Father by Beverly Randolph[1] whom you may recollect to have seen at your house in the Spring 1806. Mrs. Madison has been so kind as to procure for him young Nourse's[2] place during his absence or untill some thing better offers. Enclosed is a little seal of My Mothers that I Must beg the favor of you to have mended and My watch key if it is possible to make it strong but as it is, it never will stand; the pin or the steel pipe continually breaking where it is bored. Adieu My Dear Father. I did not know of Beverly's intention to leave us to Morrow untill a few minutes ago or I should have written in the day, as it is I must leave you it being late bed time. Yours most affectionately,   MR.

1. Thomas Beverley Randolph was a son of William and Lucy Bolling Randolph of Chilower, Cumberland County. He was also a nephew of Thomas Mann, Jr.'s. TJ obtained for him an appointment to the military academy at West Point.
2. Charles Nourse was a son of Joseph Nourse, the registrar of the United States Treasury.

TO ELLEN WAYLES RANDOLPH

Washington Feb. 23. 08.

MY DEAREST ELLEN

I am several letters in your debt, but I am in hopes that age and occupation will privilege me against your counting letter for letter rigorously with me. The loss of your geraniums shall be replaced. I have this day planted a sprig in a small and very portable pot of earth. You give a bad account of the patriotism of the ladies of Williamsburg who are not disposed to submit to the small privations to which the embargo will subject them. I hope this will not be general and that principle and prudence will induce us all to return to the good old plan of manufacturing within our own families most of the articles we need. I can assure you from experience that we never lived so comfortably as while we were reduced to this system formerly; because we soon learnt to supply all our real wants at home, and we could not run in debt, as not an hour's credit was given for any thing. It was then we were obliged to act on the salutary maxim of 'never spending our money before we had it.' I expect it will not be long before you will spin me a dimity waistcoat. It is believed Congress will rise early in

From Anne Cary Randolph

Edgehill March 4 *1808*

MY DEAR GRAND PAPA

As I do not know when the ship goes to Spain I have written and inclose my letter to Aunt Harriet to you. Mr. Ogilvie has broken up his school in Milton and does not mean to keep one any where this year but to devote himself to public speaking. Papa has not determined where he is to send Jefferson yet. Mama intends to make him employ the time he stays at home in learning french Arethmetic Geography and reading history. Mrs. Barber the daughter of Mr. Strode has been trying to get a female boarding school in Charlottesville. I have not heard whether it is likely she will succeed or not. Evelina is certainly to be married after March court. Cousin Polly Carr left us to day. She spent a week with Aunt Jane and Mama. Poor Aunt Lewis I believe had a dreadful journey. Mr. Peyton [1] recieved a letter from them after they had been gone ten weeks and they were 4 hundred miles from the place to which they were going. All the children are well and send their love to you. Virginia and Mary are going on very well with their lessons and will be able to read before you come. Adieu my Dear Grand Papa. Your truly affectionate Grand daughter,   A C RANDOLPH

Jefferson has just returned from Milton and says that Mr. Ogilvie has made a fresh determination to continue his school. I wish it may be a firm one.

1. Craven Peyton was a son-in-law of Lucy Jefferson Lewis (Mrs. Charles), TJ's sister.

To Anne Cary Randolph

Washington Mar. 8. 08.

MY DEAR ANNE

I recieved yesterday your letter of the 4th. and as it said nothing of the health of the family, I presume all are well. Your letter to your aunt Harriet shall be taken care of. I wish Mrs. Barber may succeed in getting her school. She is a woman of extraordinary good sense, information and merit. Should Mr. Ogilvie discontinue his school, Jefferson cannot be better employed from morning till night than in reading French, and reading much to your mama in order to get the pronunciation. If he is not perfect master of French when he goes to Philadelphia he will not reap half the advantage of his situation. In fact there is not a science (medicine

will you soon answer her letter. She hopes the next you get from her will be in her own hand writing. Virginia sends her love to Francis, and yourself. We have not had such a thing as a ball for a long time in Milton and my dancing school is over so that I have not been to a dance for a long time however I never regreted the want of such kinds of amusement although I am fond of dancing I can always find employments infinitely more amusing and instructing. I am sorry there is so little poetry in the newspapers as my book is not full. If I can fill it sister Ann and myself will have together an excellent collection. We each have books in which we copy such poetry as we cannot get in newspapers. My dear Grandpapa will excuse this long catalogue but I have no news to tell him and rather than not write I will relate to him what passes among us which though dull and uninteresting to another will serve to show him that rather than not write at all I will this. All of us are in health. Mama since I have been writing has got up off the bed and feels a great deal better. My pen is shocking so that you must excuse the bad writing of this letter. Adieu my Dear Grand Papa. Believe me to be your most affectionate Grand Daughter,

E. W. R.

1. There was a riot at this time, but unfortunately there are no faculty or Board of Visitors minutes for the period. It was reported in the Virginia *Argus,* March 15, 1808, that the following students were expelled: "John Evins [Evans] . . . for disorderly conduct" and also "Andrew Holmes, John Goodall, John Ragland, William Taylor, William Buchanan, Joseph John Hill, William Tomlin and Thomas Hayes . . . for riotous conduct." See Thomas Todd to Charles S. Todd, June 4, 1808, and Albert Allmond (Allmand) to Andrew Reid, Jr., April 15, 1808, in *William and Mary College Quarterly Historical Magazine,* 1st Series, Vol. VIII (April, 1900), 222–23, and XXII, No. 1 (July, 1913), 22–23.

To Ellen Wayles Randolph

Washington Mar. 14. 08.

My dearest Ellen

Your letter of the 11th is recieved and is the best letter you have ever written me because it is the longest and fullest of that small news which I have most pleasure in recieving. With great news I am more than surfieted from other quarters, and in order that your letters may not be shortened by a bad pen of which you complain, I have got a pen for you which will be always good, never wearing or needing to be mended. Among my books which are gone to Monticello, is a copy of Madame de Sevigne's letters,[1] which being the finest models of easy letter writing you must read. If Anne

that I ever saw, Mr. Craven they say by means of his net has cought nearly three thousand. He kills some days 700 and seldom less than three or four hundred. He salts and barrels them like fish for his people. All the children send their love to you and are well but Mary who is a little indisposed. I am afraid the cider you got of Mrs. Clarke this year is bad ours is, and I hear great complaints of it in general. It is said that the summer was so wet that all the apples were watery and the cider also. Adieu my Dear Grand Papa. Your truly affectionate Grand daughter,

A C. R

I enclose you some white violets but fear they will lose their smell before they reach you.

1. Burwell was a trusted slave of TJ's.

FROM ELLEN WAYLES RANDOLPH

Edgehill March 18th 1808

I am glad my Dear Grandpapa expresses approbation at my writing about little things as I always shall have enough to say to you in my letters. I shall be much obliged to you for the pen. It will be very convenient and usefull to me as I have a great deal of writing to do. Pray in your next inform me what it is made of. I guess it is glass. I shall certainly read Madame de Sevigne's letters. I have heard they were the most elegantly written letters in the world. Cornelia has got in joining hand at last. She has begun arithmetic. Virginia goes on tolerably poor. Mary is sick. Mama is entirely recovered. I have not yet heard of cousin Evelinas marriage although I suppose it was yesterday as report says that the 17th was the day fixed on. Uncle William is with us now. Mr. Ogilvie has gone to Staunton. He is very much ashamed of the indecission he has shown concerning the breaking up of his school. He first said he would not then that he would then he was uncertain but at last he has gone away. Jefferson has changed his plan. He is to remain at home and carry on his arithmetic his geography History Latin and French. James has given the paper a kiss to be sent to you. The orange trees still look well. I am glad to hear that all your birds and flowers are well. We have had one or two violets in bloom and several persian Iris's. We all look forward with great impatience to the time when you are to come back to Monticello. How slow time passes away and how heavy it hangs on our hands when we expect to see any one whom we all love so tenderly as we do you. Papa has been to Monticello. He says

To ANNE CARY RANDOLPH

Washington Mar. 22. 08.

MY DEAR ANNE

My reason for desiring Ellen and yourself to write alternately was not that I did not wish to hear from you both oftener, but that I could not probably find time to answer more than one letter a week. I am sorry our strawberries are unpromising; however I trust they will put out soon. If some sand and stable manure were put on the earth, the waterings would carry both down into the clay and loosen and enrich it. But we had better not transplant them till we get them to Monticello, where we will take out the whole sod unbroken, and set it in the ground without having disturbed the roots. I ate strawberries from these plants last October after my return to this place. I inclose you some seed of the Beny, or Oriental Sesamum.[1] This is among the most valuable acquisitions our country has ever made. It yields an oil equal to the finest olive oil. I recieved a bottle of it, and tried it with a great deal of company for many days, having a dish of sallad dressed with that and another with olive oil, and nobody could distinguish them. An acre yields 10. bushels of seed, each bushel giving three gallons of oil. An acre therefore, besides our sallad oil, would furnish all kitchen and family uses, most of them better than with lard or butter. You had better direct Wormly to plant these seeds in some open place in the nursery, by dropping two or three seeds every 10. or 12. I. along a row, and his rows 2. feet apart. The plant grows somewhat like hemp. It was brought to S. Carolina from Africa by the negroes, who alone have hitherto cultivated it in the Carolinas and Georgia. They bake it in their bread, boil it with greens, enrich their broth etc. It is not doubted it will grow well as far North as Jersey, tho' McMahon places it among greenhouse plants. Adieu my dear Anne. Present my tender affections to the family.   TH: JEFFERSON

1. Oriental Sesamum (*Sesamum indicum* or *orientale*): used in salad dressings; was first cultivated in Africa and Asia. TJ usually referred to it as benne seed.

FROM ELLEN WAYLES RANDOLPH

Edgehill March 25th. 1808.

I shall write a few lines to inform my dear Grandpapa that all are well here except James and he is not very sick. All the plants are well. We have a great many flowers in bloom Narcissus's Daffa-

sincerely wish and hope that he will soon recover and come on to
see us all again. I will give another guess about the pen. It is
steel is it not? My bantam has hatched 8. pretty little chickens and
I shall follow your advice about her treatment. The orange trees
are well. Sister Ann is gone to Monticello to see about the flowers
and plant the Beny. 3 of your Alpine strawberries are flourishing.
Mr. Burwell has just sent me some of the seed of the Ice plant.
I am told it is a very beautifull flower. I cannot guess why an
et-caetera should be made in the manner you wrote the word.
If it is not that the figure represents the E. T. and the C. caetera.
Mama Sister Ann and all the children are quite well and send
their love to you. Adieu my dearest grandpapa. Believe me to be
(with the sincerest wishes for your health) your most affectionate
grand daughter,   E. W. RANDOLPH

TO CORNELIA JEFFERSON RANDOLPH

Washington Apr. 3. 08.

MY DEAR CORNELIA

I have owed you a letter two months, but have had nothing to
write about, till last night I found in a newspaper the four lines
which I now inclose you: and as you are learning to write, they will
be a good lesson to convince you of the importance of minding
your stops in writing. I allow you a day to find out yourself how to
read these lines so as to make them true. If you cannot do it in
that time you may call in assistance. At the same time I will give
you four other lines which I learnt when I was but a little older
than you, and I still remember.

> I've seen the sea all in a blaze of fire
> I've seen a house high as the moon and higher
> I've seen the sun at twelve oclock at night
> I've seen the man who saw this wondrous sight.[1]

All this is true, whatever you may think of it at first reading
I mentioned in my letter of last week to Ellen that I was under
an attack of periodical head-ach. This is the 10th. day. It has
been very moderate and yesterday did not last more than 3. hours.
Tell your Mama that I fear I shall not get away as soon as I
expected. Congress has spent the last 5. days without employing
a single hour on the business necessary to be finished. Kiss her
for me, and all the sisterhood. To Jefferson I give my hand, to
your papa my affectionate salutations. You have always my love,

TH: JEFFERSON

the post was the cause of your not recieving my letter of the first of the month. It goes out now much earlier than it formerly did. I am delighted to hear that your head-ach is over and that you are to come home so soon. Mr. Mrs. and the two Miss Lindseys[1] spent a few days with us; the young ladies, Sister Ann, and myself, went over to Monticello; I think the hall, with its gravel coloured border is the most beautifull room I ever was in, without excepting the drawing rooms at Washington. The dining room is also greatly improved. The pillars of the portico are rough cast and look very well. All the railing on the top of the house finished and painted. I wont say any thing of the flower beds. That is sister Anns part. The level is spoilt nearly. Mr. Bacon has made a mistake (I presume) and covered it with charcoal instead of manure; it looks rather dismal where ever the grass has not grown. It is quite black and is excessively dirty to walk on. It is not near as bad as it was but it is still disagreable and ugly. They are finishing your terrace now. The sheep eat up 4 orange trees and bit half of the finest besides, when we put them out; however I have 3 tolerably good though they are only 2 inches high. They are all mean little things except that which the sheep bit, but they are very young. The third of April snow drops bloomed. You have none I believe. They are very beautiful and I will give you mine if you want them, and have them set in your garden when we go to Monticello. We have had shad the latter end of march; we have got no asparagus beds here and I was so much taken up with looking at the house that I did not inquire about the vegetables at Monticello, besides we stayed but a short time. Aunt Virginia is well. All our family except James are well also. Cornelia was very much delighted with your letter, she easily found out the verse as she had seen many before of the same kind. Virginia and Mary send their love to you. I am reading Diodorus Siculus. I began to learn Spanish, but I have not said a lesson for a long time. I must take it up again for I wish to know it. I cannot read french entirely without a dictionary yet. Adieu my dearest Grandpapa, I am your most affectionate Grand Daughter,   E. W. RANDOLPH.

P S. I beg you to send the inclosed to Miss Forrest.

1. Colonel and Mrs. Reuben Lindsay were Albemarle friends and neighbors of the Monticello family. Reference here is to two of their three daughters, Sarah, Elizabeth, and Maria.

FROM ELLEN WAYLES RANDOLPH

Edgehill April 21st 1808.

My dearest Grandpapa must not imagine because he received no letter last post that I did not write for the post now goes out Friday and my letter was too late for it but I send it to him now. We have had blue and white lilacs blue and white flags and Jonquils. I found also in the woods a great many mountain cowslips and wild Ranunculus besides other wild flowers. I have got the seed of the Jerusalem cherry which I am told is very beautifull. Aunt Jane had asparagus the same time that you had. Will you fetch me a sprig of geranium when you come in. Your 3 strawberries look very well. All our family are in good health. How delighted we shall be when we see you drive up to the door. Uncle Randolph Jefferson [1] is with us and Cousin Nancy Neville [2] in the neighbourhood. You must excuse this short letter and the badness of the writing for my pen is horrible and I can scarcely see to subscribe myself. My dearest Grandfather your affectionate Grand Daughter.   E. W. R.

1. Randolph Jefferson was TJ's younger brother and a twin of Anna Scott Jefferson Marks (Mrs. Hastings). He resided at Snowden, a Buckingham County farm located across the James River from the present-day Scottsville in Albemarle County. Little is known of him, the best source being *Thomas Jefferson and His Unknown Brother Randolph* (Charlottesville, 1942), edited by Bernard Mayo. This contains a brief biographical sketch and a number of letters between TJ and Randolph.

2. Anna Scott Jefferson, a daughter of Randolph Jefferson, who married Colonel Zachariah Nevil of Nelson County, a one-time United States congressman.

TO MARTHA JEFFERSON RANDOLPH

Washington Apr. 25. 08.

MY DEAR DAUGHTER

Davy arrived last night with your letter of the 23d. and as he will stay some days and then return slowly with a lame horse I take advantage of this day's post to answer it. The recommendations for military appointment came too late. As it was impracticable for the Executive to select the best characters for command through all the states, we apportioned the men to be raised and the officers to command them among the states in proportion to their militia, then gave to each delegation in Congress all the recommendations we had recieved, and left to them to make the selection out of these or such better subjects as they knew. They in general distributed the appointments among their districts, and

that he did not take out the Baskerville Milton or Smith's wealth of nations,[3] because he had a Milton and Smith of his own, but was confident they would be found among his books. I sent off a few days ago a supply of groceries for Monticello. I did not send either coffee or tea, under an idea, I do not know whether recieved from you or not, that there is enough of those articles remaining to serve during the next visit. I must pray you to inform me immediately if this is not so, as there is yet time enough to forward a supply. The good health and calm of this place leaves us without news, except as to Mrs. Harrison, who is in an irrecoverable state of health. All doubt of the election of Mr. Madison has vanished, altho' some of the New York papers still keep up an useless fire. Present me affectionately to Mr. Randolph and to all our dear children, and be assured of my tenderest and unchangeable love for yourself.   TH: JEFFERSON

1. The home of James and Dolley Madison in Orange County.
2. Caesar A. Rodney was United States Attorney General from 1807 until 1809.
3. *Paradise Regain'd. A Poem, in Four Books* . . . Printed by John Baskerville . . . (London [1759]), or *Paradise Lost. A Poem in Twelve Books* . . . Printed by John Baskerville . . . (London [1758]). See Sowerby 4287, 4288, and 4289. Adam Smith, *An Inquiry into the Nature and Causes of the Wealth of Nations* . . . (London . . . [1784]). Sowerby 3546.

FROM MARTHA JEFFERSON RANDOLPH
Edgehill June 23 [1808]

Your conjecture with regard to the tea and Coffee was correct as we just began upon the last stock with out making any sensible impression upon them. I have no doubt therefore but there will be enough of both of those articles as well as of chocolate. Cooking wine will be wanting and the Madeira gave out before you left us. There was no white wine therefore but what was in the octagon cellars. I must beg the favor of you My Dear Father to pay a debt of Ann's very unintentionally contracted. She sent a pearl clasp to Mrs. Madison to exchange in some of the jewellers shop's for a gold chain. The price of the clasp was more than sufficient to pay for the chain, but Mrs. Madison informed me in sending the chain that she had been obliged to make a considerable sacrifice. From what she said I conjecture the chain to have cost perhaps 6 or 7 dollars more than she got for the clasp. Will you be so good as to ask her and discharge the debt. We have not heard of Colonel

TO ELLEN WAYLES RANDOLPH

Washington July 5. 08.

MY DEAR ELLEN

Your letter was safely delivered to Miss Forrest who was here yesterday well. I thank heaven that the 4th. of July is over. It is always a day of great fatigue to me, and of some embarrasments from improper intrusions and some from unintended exclusions. We have had such a week of hot weather as has never probably been known before in this country. My thermometer has been as follows:

Monday June 27. 93.
            28. 98 (95)
            29. 96
            30. 95
      July 1. 98½ (98½)
            2. 98   (98)
            3. 95½

Yesterday I took no observation. To-day it is quite moderate. I hope this severe spell will be an acquittal for us, at least till I get home, for which I shall leave this place about the 22d. inst. You have been before hand with us in roston ears. We had cimlings[1] yesterday. Kiss your dear Mama for me and all the young ones, and assure your papa of my constant affection. Be assured yourself of my tender love.   TH: JEFFERSON
P. S. 2. men died here on the 1st. instant drinking cold water. We shall probably hear of many more in other places.

1. A simlin was a white scalloped summer squash.

TO MARTHA JEFFERSON RANDOLPH

Washington July 11. 08.

MY DEAREST MARTHA

My last letters from Edgehill mentioned that you had been indisposed but had got the better of it. Having no letter from Edgehill by this mail I can only hope you continue well. In a conversation with you on the subject of Jefferson's going to Philadelphia[1] you mentioned that Mr. Randolph thought of declining it, and I do not know whether I inferred rightly from what you said that a supposed inconvenience to me might make a part of his reason. If a disapprobation of the measure or any other reasons prevail

incur a certain evil for a very uncertain benefit and perhaps the danger of giving expense for one who certainly has very little prospect at present of any thing more than bare competency. Ann is very much obliged to you for having discharged her debt to Mrs. Madison. I must beg the favor of you if such things are to be met with in Washington to bring me a little ivory memorandum book[1] such as you used to have. I find my chicken accounts troublesome without some assistance of the kind. Adieu My Dearest Father. I write in such haste that I am afraid you will scarcely be able to read My letter. Believe me with unchangeable tenderness yours,   MR

1. TJ had been able to procure such a memorandum book while in Paris, as attested by his Account Book entry for April 2, 1786: "Pd . . . a doz ivory leaves 12/." MHi.

To Martha Jefferson Randolph

Washington July 19. 08

MY DEAREST MARTHA

I drop this line merely to inform you that it is still doubtful whether I shall be ready to set off tomorrow or not till the next day. But indeed should the weather be as warm as it has been for some days I doubt whether I should venture on the road as I believe it impossible the horses should stand it or even ourselves. This day however is moderate, and if it continues so I shall have the pleasure of breakfasting with you on Saturday or Sunday at Monticello. I am glad to hear of Mrs. Trist's arrival. Present my affectionate salutations to her and tell her I shall hope to find her at Monticello and that she will make it her head quarters. All Georgetown and Washington have been searched and no such thing as an ivory book to be found. Salute Mr. Randolph and the family for me, and be assured yourself of all my love.

TH: JEFFERSON

To Martha Jefferson Randolph

Montpelier Sep. 30. 08.

MY DEAREST MARTHA

I forgot to bring with me the gravy spoons to be converted into Dessert spoons.[1] I must therefore pray you to send them to me. I think you mentioned a spare ladle. Two ladles I think are

omy as soon as you arrive that you may *use it* while attending the lectures in Anatomy. It is in 4. vols 8vo. and Mr. Peale will pay for it. Enter yourself for the lectures in Anatomy Natural history and Surgery all of which begin in November, and end in March. Mr. Peale will pay for the tickets amounting to 42. Dollars. The Botanical course does not begin till April. Then you must buy a Copy of Dr. Barton's botany, new edition.

TO MARTHA JEFFERSON RANDOLPH

Washington Oct. 18. 08.

MY DEAR MARTHA

I inclose you a letter for T. B. Randolph containing his appointment as a Cadet. But the lodgings at the Military school at Westpoint being entirely full, he cannot be recieved there till the 1st. of March. Indeed he could do nothing there sooner, as their vacation begins with November and ends with February. Genl. Dearborne proposed to me yesterday a new regulation respecting the Cadets. There is to be one to each company. And he proposes that those for whom there is as yet no room at the military school shall be attached at once to the company to which they are to belong and shall proceed immediately to do duty. In this case their pay and rations would commence immediately. Otherwise not till there is room for them at the school. Should we finally determine on this T. B. R.[1] will recieve instructions to repair to some particular company. If we knew in the mean time what particular captain he would prefer, perhaps we might be able to indulge his choice.

Jefferson left this on Friday. He would Stay Saturday and Sunday at Baltimore, and reach Philadelphia this day. While here he visited Maine's[2] thorn hedges, the hanging bridge,[3] Navy yard,[4] and Alexandria. When going to the latter I proposed to him to take a horse, but as he had never been in a sailing boat he preferred the packet. On his way down the river he took the masts of the vessels at Alexandria, which were in view, for Lombardy poplars, and at length asked the master of the packet if they were so. He will have a fortnight to sate himself with Philadelphia, before the lectures begin, which will be the 1st. of November. I am glad to hear that Benjamin's[5] eye is hoped not to be serious. Tell Anne that my old friend Thouin[6] of the National garden at Paris has sent me 700. species of seeds. I suppose they will contain all the fine flowers of

them examined untill you return. Your affectionate Grand Daughter,   ELEONORA WAYLES RANDOLPH

1. Actually Terme, a Bordeaux wine from the Château Marquis de Terme. According to the Account Book purchases, this was not one of TJ's favorite wines.
2. Possibly Oiry, a champagne from the Oiry district in the Marne Valley.

TO THOMAS JEFFERSON RANDOLPH

Washington, Oct. 24th, 1808.

DEAR JEFFERSON

I inclose you a letter from Ellen, which, I presume, will inform you that all are well at Edgehill. I received yours without date of either time or place, but written, I presume, on your arrival at Philadelphia. As the commencement of your lectures is now approaching, and you will hear two lectures a day, I would recommend to you to set out from the beginning with the rule to commit to writing every evening the substance of the lectures of the day. It will be attended with many advantages. It will oblige you to attend closely to what is delivered to recall it to your memory, to understand, and to digest it in the evening; it will fix it in your memory, and enable you to refresh it at any future time. It will be much better to you than even a better digest by another hand, because it will better recall to your mind the ideas which you originally entertained and meant to abridge. Then, if once a week you will, in a letter to me, state a synopsis or summary view of the heads of the lectures of the preceding week, it will give me great satisfaction to attend to your progress, and it will further aid you by obliging you still more to generalize and to see analytically the fields of science over which you are travelling. I wish to hear of the commissions I gave you for Rigden, Voight,[1] and Ronaldson,[2] of the delivery of the letters I gave you to my friends there, and how you like your situation. This will give you matter for a long letter, which will give you as useful an exercise in writing as a pleasing one to me in reading.

God bless you, and prosper your pursuits.

TH: JEFFERSON

1. John E. Rigden; Henry Voight, a one-time Philadelphia watchmaker and a coiner at the United States Mint in Philadelphia.
2. James Ronaldson, a member of the firm of Binney & Ronaldson of Philadelphia, the first successful type-founding company in America.

has left nearly one half of the Buffon. I presume the best way will
be to pack them and send them to Mr. Jefferson as he will have
occasion I suppose for all of them. It was *corks* and not bottles
that were wanting to bottle the rest of the wine. My orders were
that they should continue untill their corks gave out, which they
did not do for Ellen told me there were still some corks left but as
there were not enough for the whole cask they would not make a
begginning but prefered using 2 water casks that may or may not
answer. I shall send often to inspect them having been greatly
decieved in 2 of the same description once before. I am truly concerned to hear that your rheumatism has fixed in so dreadful a
part as the back. You will be obliged to try flannel next the skin
in which I have very great confidence, particularly as you have
never *abused* the use of it. Should the pain continue I am sure you
would find relief from it. Adieu My Dear Father. I am with tenderest affection your,   MRANDOLPH

TO MARTHA JEFFERSON RANDOLPH

Washington Nov. 1. 08.

MY DEAREST MARTHA

Mr. Bacon delivered your letter and every thing else safely. I
had ordered a gross of bottles to be bought: but I will now counter-
mand them. I send on corks by the stage, for I think that water
casks should be trusted no longer than necessary. The letter and
bundle for Jefferson shall be forwarded. Certainly the residue of
Buffon ought to be sent on to him to the care of Mr. Jefferson.
When he went to Philadelphia I gave him letters to some of my
friends, apprising them at the same time that I did not wish it
to be the means of drawing him into society so as to interfere
with the pursuits which carried him there and for which all his
time would be little enough. I have since recieved the inclosed
from Dr. Rush[1] which I send for your perusal and that of Mr.
Randolph and to be returned to me. I had advised Jefferson every
evening to commit to writing the substance of the two lectures he
will have heard in the day. If to that he adds the Doctor's advice,
he will be fully employed. As soon as my attak of rheumatism
came on, I applied flannel to the part, and toasted a great deal
before the fire. It carried it off compleatly in four days, and I am
persuaded the attack at Monticello might have been shortened in

send to N. York for one by the first of my acquaintance who goes there.

The lectures begin on the seventh and I have not been able to get Bells Anatomy nor is there a prospect of getting it shortly. I was therefore obliged to get Fifer for the present.[1] I am pleased with my situation and feel (contrary to my expectations) as happy here as I ever was, when I hear often from home. Yours affectionately,   THOMAS J RANDOLPH

1. John and Sir Charles Bell, *The Anatomy of The Human Body* (London, 1802–1804), and Andrew Fyfe, *A Compendium of the Anatomy of the Human Body* (Edinburgh, 1800), 2 volumes.

TO ANNE RANDOLPH BANKHEAD

Washington Nov. 8. 08.

MY DEAR ANNE

Not having heard of your departure[1] from Albemarle I address this letter to you expecting it will find you at that place. It covers one from Jefferson to Mr. Bankhead. In a letter I recieved yesterday from Jefferson he says 'I am pleased with my situation and feel (contrary to my expectation) as happy here as I ever was, when I hear often from home.' I hope this will stimulate yourself and Ellen particularly to write to him often, and as I shall be a safe channel of conveyance I may come in for a letter also occasionally. It will give me great pleasure to hear from yourself and Mr. Bankhead while at Port royal. I will make you returns in the same way whenever my business will permit. I trust it is Mr. Bankhead's intention to join us at Monticello in March and to take his station among my law books in the South pavilion.[2] Whatever field of practice he may propose, I do not think he can take a more advantageous stand for study. I hope therefore that he will consent to it, and that you will both ever consider yourselves as a part of our family until you shall feel the desire of separate establishment insuperable. Salute him and your Papa in my name. My love and kisses to your Mama, yourself, Ellen and the others,

TH: JEFFERSON

1. Anne Cary was married to Charles Lewis Bankhead at Monticello on September 19, 1808, by the Reverend Mr. William Crawford. Consult Albemarle County Marriage Record 1806–1808 in the county courthouse in Charlottesville, Virginia.

2. That small structure on the south side of the west lawn at the termination of the south terrace walk. His law books, as well as others, were stored here awaiting the completion of the library suite in the main house.

To Ellen Wayles Randolph

Washington Nov. 15. 08.

MY DEAR ELLEN

I recieved yesterday yours of the 11th. and rejoice to hear that all are well with you. I inclose a letter from Dr. Wistar the perusal of which will be agreeable to your Papa and Mama as it respects Jefferson, and to your Papa what relates to the Mammoth.[1] Return it to me. I am glad to hear that the sweet scented grass got safe, altho' the pot did not. The sooner you put it into a larger box the better. Perhaps your papa will take the trouble to separate the roots so as to spread without endangering them. It is the anthoxanthum odoratum of the botanists, and you must now become the botanist in addition to your charge over the basse-cour. This last department will be recruited when I come home by 6. wild geese born of tamed parents, 2. summer ducks, a pair of wild turkies, 6 grey geese, much larger and handsomer than the common race of which the ganders are white. For the former department I have 700. species of seeds sent me by Mr. Thouin from the National garden of France. What will you do under all this charge? And more especially as the geese ducks &c. will be very clamorous from daylight till visited. It is lucky for you that the milk pen and sheep-cote from their distance, cannot be ascribed to your care undercolour of their belonging to the field of Natural history. I sent by Mr. Bacon some corks to compleat the bottling our wines. Was my letter forwarded to Anne? Those to Jefferson will go on to-day. Affectionate Adieux to every body.

TH: JEFFERSON

1. TJ and Dr. Caspar Wistar, Curator of the American Philosophical Society, collaborated in classifying the fossil remains sent by William Clarke to Washington from the dig at Big Bone Lick, Kentucky. This was an archeological expedition directed by William Clarke and underwritten by TJ. For one of the best articles on TJ and fossils, see Howard C. Rice, Jr., "Jefferson's Gift of Fossils To The Museum of Natural History in Paris," *Proceedings of the American Philosophical Society*, Vol. 95, No. 6 (December, 1951), 597–627.

From Martha Jefferson Randolph

Edgehill Nov. 18, 1808

I gave the keys of the wine cellar in to Dinsmore's hands who promised to superintend the bottling of the wine. If the bottles and corks hold out would you wish them to begin upon any other

the letter and having explained the circumstance to Mr. Steptoe in the cover of the letter sealed, directed and sent it to the office.

1. Louis Dubroca, *Le ton de la bonne compagnie, ou régles de la civilité, à l'usage des personnes des deux sexes* (Paris, 1802). Martha's copy of this work is in the Alderman Library at the University of Virginia. It bears her signature, "M. Randolph Monticello." This is followed by "G W Randolph" in his handwriting.
2. Hugh Chisholm, a trusted employee of TJ's and literally a man of many trades. He worked for TJ from 1796 until 1824.
3. James Steptoe was clerk of Bedford County, a close friend of TJ's, and he resided near Poplar Forest.

FROM MARTHA JEFFERSON RANDOLPH

Edgehill Nov. 24, 1808

MY DEAREST FATHER

The small pox has broke out in Staunton and spread a general alarm, least through the medium of the stages it should be communicated. If it is easy to obtain the vaccine we should be greatly obliged to you to send us some as our three youngest children and many of our negroes have not been innoculated at all.

Looking over some of the literary magazines the other day we met with the beginning of a tale by Miss Edgeworth[1] which interested us so much that we are all anxious to see the end of it. Perhaps Mrs. H. Smith who is such a general reader may be able to tell you from what work of Miss Edgeworth's it is taken, and if not exceeding one volume in size I should be very much obliged to you to get it and send it to me. "The Modern Griselda" is the name of the tale, or novel, I do not know which, having read only as much as one number of a magazine contained and not possessing the following numbers. Old Col. Lewis[2] is confined to his bed and has lost the use of his hands entirely. Mr. Randolph went to see him last sunday and thinks from his general appearance that he can hold out but very little longer. Virginia leaves us to morrow.[3] They have obtained the old gentleman's consent to go to house keeping at Cary's brook next summer; Mr. Randolph proposed to Doctor Bankhead to purchase for his son *her* portion of the Bedford Lands, which will be laid off adjoining Ann's.[4] He has consented and by that means they will have near 1000 acres of the best land where they mean finally to settle, and Virginia's portion being converted in to *money* will enable Wilson to buy Miles's part of the Cary's brook estate.[5] So that nothing but a sad experience of the uncertainty of the fairest prospects of happiness, would

to advise or guide me, and recollect the various sorts of bad company with which I associated from time to time, I am astonished I did not turn off with some of them, and become as worthless to society as they were. I had the good fortune to become acquainted very early with some characters of very high standing, and to feel the incessant wish that I could even become what they were. Under temptations and difficulties, I could ask myself what would Dr. Small, Mr. Wythe, Peyton Randolph do in this situation? What course in it will ensure me their approbation? I am certain that this mode of deciding on my conduct tended more to it's correctness than any reasoning powers I possessed. Knowing the even and dignified line they pursued, I could never doubt for a moment which of two courses would be in character for them. Whereas seeking the same object through a process of moral reasoning, and with the jaundiced eye of youth, I should often have erred. From the circumstances of my position I was often thrown into the society of horseracers, cardplayers, Foxhunters, scientific and professional men, and of dignified men; and many a time have I asked myself, in the enthusiastic moment of the death of a fox, the victory of a favorite horse, the issue of a question eloquently argued at the bar or in the great Council of the nation, well, which of these kinds of reputation should I prefer? That of a horse jockey? A foxhunter? An Orator? Or the honest advocate of my country's rights? Be assured my dear Jefferson, that these little returns into ourselves, this self-cathechising habit, is not trifling, nor useless, but leads to the prudent selection and steady pursuits of what is right? I have mentioned good humor as one of the preservatives of our peace and tranquillity. It is among the most effectual, and it's effect is so well imitated and aided artificially by politeness, that this also becomes an acquisition of first rate value. In truth, politeness is artificial good humor, it covers the natural want of it, and ends by rendering habitual a substitute nearly equivalent to the real virtue. It is the practice of sacrificing to those whom we meet in society all the little conveniences and preferences which will gratify them, and deprive us of nothing worth a moment's consideration; it is the giving a pleasing and flattering turn to our expressions which will conciliate others, and make them pleased with us as well as themselves. How cheap a price for the good will of another! When this is in return for a rude thing said by another, it brings him to his senses, it mortifies and corrects him in the most salutary way, and places him at the feet of your good nature in the eyes of the company. But in

others to have these animals shaking their horns at you, because of the relation in which you stand with me and to hate me as a chief in the antagonist party your presence will be to them what the vomit-grass is to the sick dog a nostrum for producing an ejaculation. Look upon them exactly with that eye, and pity them as objects to whom you can administer only occasional ease. My character is not within their power. It is in the hands of my fellow citizens at large, and will be consigned to honor or infamy by the verdict of the republican mass of our country, according to what themselves will have seen, not what their enemies and mine shall have said. Never therefore consider these puppies in politics as requiring any notice from you, and always shew that you are not afraid to leave my character to the umpirage of public opinion. Look steadily to the pursuits which have carried you to Philadelphia, be very select in the society you attach yourself to; avoid taverns, drinkers, smoakers, and idlers and dissipated persons generally; for it is with such that broils and contentions arise, and you will find your path more easy and tranquil. The limits of my paper warn me that it is time for me to close with my affectionate Adieux.   TH: JEFFERSON
P. S. Present me affectionately to Mr. Ogilvie, and in doing the same to Mr. Peale tell him I am writing with his polygraph[1] and shall send him mine the first moment I have leisure enough to pack it.

1. Literally a machine for making several copies of writing at once. TJ owned several of the kind mentioned in this letter, which was the invention of a Mr. Hawkins, an Englishman, who at one time resided near Frankfort, Pennsylvania. This was the two-pen type and is the one TJ suggested improvements on to Charles Willson Peale. See correspondence between TJ and Peale in the Library of Congress and Historical Society of Pennsylvania.

FROM ANNE RANDOLPH BANKHEAD

Port Royal November 26 *1808*

I should have answered My Dear Grand Papas letter by the Last post but Mr. Bankhead wrote and as I have seldom time we agreed never to write to gether that you might hear from us often. On coming from Edgehill I left all the flowers in Ellens care, however I shall be with you early enough in march to assist about the border, which the old French Gentlemans[1] present if you mean to plant them there, with the wild and bulbous rooted ones we have already, will compleatly fill. Although no longer under

This scab is old, and therefore the Doctr. has not entire confidence in it. He will write to Baltimore this evening for fresh matter which you shall have by the next post. I have been delayed to the very moment of making up the mail, and must therefore close with my best affections to Mr. Randolph and the children, and my constant and tenderest love to yourself.

TH: JEFFERSON

1. Dr. Charles Worthington.

FROM THOMAS JEFFERSON RANDOLPH

Philadelphia Museum Dec 3 [1808]

DEAR GRANDFATHER

I recieved yours of the 24th and it gives me great pleasure to hear that sister Ann and her husband will live with us. I am aware of the dangers of my situation and of my own inexperience; I have heard much, and seen little of the vices and follies of the world and distrusting my own knowlegde of human nature, I have shuned all unnecessary intercourse with persons not previously recommended to my acquaintance, by some friend more experienced than myself; I go no where and I live in retirement amongst thousands; without your advice, Politics would have been, the rock upon which I should have split ere long; Although I never speak on the subject myself, yet when I hear these vile pensioners and Miscreants expressing Tory sentiments and abusing you, it is with difficulty I can restrain myself. You have no doubt expected a performance of my promise, I attempted it once, but it took me all day sunday and I could not finish in twelve what the professors expressed in fourteen. I however do it every night on Anatomy and chemistry, but on surgery I do not understand it sufficiently to do it regularly; when he (Dr. physick) lectures on the fresh subject I hope I shall understand it better.
Yours affectionately,   THOS. J. RANDOLPH
P S The cover of the letter you inclosed from Mother bore evident marks of having been broken open as likewise several others.

TO MARTHA JEFFERSON RANDOLPH

Washington Dec. 6. 08.

MY DEAREST MARTHA

I inclose you a letter from Jefferson which I presume will inform you he is well, and I send you one from Dr. Wistar which

therefore with courage and you will find it grows easier and easier. Besides obliging you to understand the subject, and fixing it in your memory, it will learn you the most valuable art of condensing your thoughts and expressing them in the fewest words possible. No stile of writing is so delightful as that which is all pith, which never omits a necessary word, nor uses an unecessary one. The finest models of this existing are Sallust[4] and Tacitus, which on that account are worthy of constant study. And that you may have every just encouragement I will add that from what I observe of the natural stile of your letters I think you will readily attain this kind of perfection. I am glad you are so determined to be on the reserve on political subjects. The more you feel yourself piqued to express a sentiment on what is perhaps said at you, the more the occasion is to be seized for preserving in silence, and for acquiring the habit of mastering the temptations to reply, and of establishing an absolute power of silence over yourself. The tendency of this habit too to produce equanimity and tranquility of mind is very great. On this subject perhaps I may say a word in some future letter. I must now close with my affectionate attachment.   TH: JEFFERSON

1. John McAlister.
2. James Pemberton, a Quaker merchant of Philadelphia who succeeded Benjamin Franklin as president of the Society for Promoting the Abolition of Slavery.
3. *The Commonplace Book of Thomas Jefferson*, Gilbert Chinard, editor (Baltimore, 1926). (Original DLC.) This includes only legal abstracts, etc., and is not as complete as the manuscript volume.
4. TJ was perhaps interested in this Roman historian because he was the first to use the monograph form.

TO ANNE RANDOLPH BANKHEAD

Washington Dec. 8. 08.

MY DEAR ANNE

Your letter of Nov. 26. came safely to hand, and in it the delicious flower of the Acacia, or rather the Mimosa Nilotica from Mr. Lomax. The mother tree of full growth which I had when I gave him the small one, perished from neglect the first winter I was from home. Does his produce seed? If it does I will thank him for some, and you to take care of them: altho' he will think it a vain thing at my time of life to be planting a tree of as slow a growth. In fact the Mimosa Nilotica and Orange are the only things I have ever proposed to have in my Green house. I like

together any way so as to prevent it from tumbling to pieces it will do. Many of the leaves are lost for it has seen hard service though not since I have had it. Col. Lewis died last Thursday night. The sweet scented grass looks very well. It was transplanted carefully in a larger box. My Bantams are very mischievous. They have pecked all the leaves off of some fine orange trees. They have increased very much. There are at least a peck of tuberose and 12 or 14 Amaryllys roots all packed in bran. The Geese and ducks shall be attended to when we go to Monticello. The seed I hope will succeed better than those which Sister Ann and yourself planted in the oval beds. The OERAS Wine which was in the little crazy casks is bottled off, there are not bottles enough to draw any other kind but it is no matter for All the rest is perfectly safe. When the book is bound I will thank you to return it for Cornelia to read. All the children send their love to you. Adieu dear Grandpapa. Believe me to be your most affectionate Grand daughter,   ELEONORA W. RANDOLPH

Mama says she will write next post. The watch, key and ring came safe but as the Vaccine was old Papa prefered waiting untill you got better.

FROM ANNE RANDOLPH BANKHEAD

Port Royal Dec. 19 *1808*

I recieved My Dear Grand Papas letters and in one of them he desires to know whether Jefferson ever had the small pox, he had it in Richmond at the same time that Aunt Virginia and myself did and was inoculated three times for fear of taking it in the natural way. I have not seen Mr. Lomax yet but make no doubt of geting the seed as I heard that he had some. He is very anxious to get one of your Likenesses by St. Memin and I promised to ask you for him, if you have another. I would be much obliged to you if you will send me in a letter some of the ice plant seed. A Lady here has Lost it and is to give me a few roots of the Lilly of the valley and a beautiful pink for it. I know it is to be had in Washington. Mr. Burwell got some there for Ellen. Adieu my Dear Grand Papa, your most affectionate Grand Daughter, A C B. It is so dark that I cannot see to write any longer. Nothing but the weather being too cold to travel in an open carriage has prevented our paying you a visit. Mr. Bankhead wished to hear the Debates in Congress.

where you may find what is good than Mr. Ronaldson to whom
you carried the fleece of wool for me. I am your's affectionately,
                                           TH: JEFFERSON
P. S. Do it up very close and hard in paper and send it by post.

To ELLEN WAYLES RANDOLPH

                                    Washington Dec. 20. 08.
MY DEAR ELLEN

   I recieved yesterday yours of the 15th. and I shall take care to
have your book bound. The letter to Jefferson went on direct.
I have not heard from him for sometime, but Doctr. Rush in a
letter just recieved says 'your grandson has not called upon me
as often as I expected, but I hear with great pleasure that he is
absorbed and delighted with his Anatomical and other studies.'
I have been expecting Vaccine matter from Dr. Worthington
here: but he has been disappointed, and I yesterday wrote to
Jefferson to get Dr. Wistar to send me some. I have been confined
to the house since 18th. of Nov. by a diseased jaw. An exfoliation
of the bone is taking place, and will in time relieve me. I feel
no pain from it, and the only inconvenience is the confinement to
the house, from the fear that a cold air might make the case
worse. Altho' you have been long silent, the muses have been
uncommonly loquacious. They have enabled me to send you three
of their effusions which do not want merit. I have written to
Jefferson if there is sufficient intermission in his lectures at
Christmas, to come and pass his free interval with us. Tell Cornelia I give her credit for her letter, and shall repay the debt
before long. Kiss your dear Mama and the little ones for me and
remember me affectionately to your papa. To yourself I am all
love.   TH: JEFFERSON

To CORNELIA JEFFERSON RANDOLPH

                                    Washington Dec. 26. 08.
   I congratulate you, my dear Cornelia, on having acquired the
invaluable art of writing. How delightful to be enabled by it to
converse with an absent friend, as if present. To this we are indebted for all our reading; because it must be written before
we can read it. To this we are indebted for the Iliad, the Aeneid,
the Columbiad, Henriade, Dunciad, and now for the most glori-

NB. When I had more time, I wrote more intelligible and more lengthy.

1. Thomas Jefferson Randolph was particularly interested in this insurrection in Amherst County because he was courting Jane Hollins Nicholas, who lived at Warren, not far removed from the site of the trouble.
2. Thomas Clarkson, *History of the Rise, Progress & Accomplishment of the Abolition of the African Slave-Trade* (Philadelphia, 1808).

FROM ELLEN WAYLES RANDOLPH

[1809]

I have sent a letter to be inclosed to Uncle Hackley which I beg you will forward by the first ship that sails to Spain.

E. W. R.

FROM MARTHA JEFFERSON RANDOLPH

recd. Jan. 1. 09

I enclose you another letter My Dearest Father, irksome as it is for me to add to your vexations of the kind Mr. R. thinks he can not refuse without danger of giving offense [to] friends who think they have a claim upon him. Mr. Hackley also wrote to beg him to mention his name to you. We recieved the vaccine safe and will innoculate our children immediately as well as our neighbours. Jefferson was innoculated with the small pox in Richmond With Virginia and Anne. Mr. Randolph recieved your letter in Milton and not having time by that mail to write to both wrote on to Jefferson to prevent his losing a lecture. Adieu My Dearest Father. You must excuse this hurried scrawl but I have been so closely at work for these 10 days past that I have never been able to take up My pen till the moment of the departure of the mail. Yours with unchangeable affection,   MRANDOLPH

Will you return Moultrie's letter[1] it has not been answered?

1. Relating to his appointment to West Point and that he would not be called until the spring.

TO THOMAS JEFFERSON RANDOLPH

Washington Jan. 3. [1809]

DEAR JEFFERSON

I had letters from home of last Thursday informing that all there were well. The disturbance among the negroes of which you

two things go on intimately together. I fear you are at present engaged in almost too much. However wonders may be done by incessant occupation, and refusing to lose time by amusements during the few months you have to pass in Philadelphia. You will be encouraged in this by the reflection that every moment you lose there, is irrecoverably lost. If you are obliged to neglect any thing, let it be your chemistry. It is the least useful and the least amusing to a country gentleman of all the ordinary branches of science. In the exercises of the country and progress over our farms, every step presents some object of botany natural history, comparative anatomy &c. But for chemistry you must shut yourself up in your laboratory and neglect the care of your affairs and of your health which calls you out of doors. Chemistry is of value to the amateur inhabiting a city. He has not room there for out of door amusements. I am your's with all possible affection.

TH: JEFFERSON

To MARTHA JEFFERSON RANDOLPH

Washington Jan. 10. 09.

MY DEAR DAUGHTER

I recieved yesterday your letter of the 5th. and Mr. Randolph's of the 6th. and I have this morning sent an extract of the latter to Mr. Nicholas.[1] I sincerely wish it success, but I am afraid Mr. Carr[2] has been misinformed of Mr. Patterson's[3] views, or, which is as likely, that Mr. Patterson has changed them. He has certainly concluded to settle on a tract of 5. or 600. acres which he gets from Mr. Nicholas about 2. miles from Warren. However we shall soon know the result of this offer. Joseph is now gone out in quest of the Imperial spelling book. If he gets it, and in time it shall go by this post. After being confined to the house about 6. weeks, I am now quite well. The diseased jaw bone having exfoliated, the piece was extracted about a week ago, the place is healed, the swelling nearly subsided, and I wait only for moderate weather to resume my rides. As the term of my relief from this place approaches, it's drudgery becomes more nauseating and intolerable, and my impatience to be with you at Monticello increases daily. Yet I expect to be detained here a week or 10. days after the 4th. of March. This will be unfavorable to our forwardest garden provisions. Can you have a sowing or two of the for-

FROM ELLEN WAYLES RANDOLPH

Recd. Jan. 23. 09

DEAR GRANDPAPA

I have not time this post but will certainly write the next. I am dear Grandpapa your affectionate grand Daughter.

E. W. R.

FROM ELLEN WAYLES RANDOLPH

Edghill January 26th 1809

DEAR GRANDPAPA

I would have written to you last post, if I had had time, but I am determined to do it this, although, I have not much to say, unless I talk about the plants; those in the large box were killed to the roots, but they are coming up all over the box; those in the small pot were killed also, but are putting out small fresh buds; the evergreens have lost all their leaves but one branch on each, which look lively enough; in the large pot, there is not the least appearance of life, but Mama preserved a little pod full of seed from it. Poor James has been inoculated with the Vaccine and is very unwell. Benjamin has had it but he did not have a fever. You must pardon this letter so full of mistakes, for it is written by candle light. I have been writing almost all day; give my love to Mrs. S. H. Smith, the children and mama send theirs to you. I am dear Grand Papa your most affectionate Grand Daughter,   ELLENORE WAYLES RANDOLPH

The sweet scented grass looks very badly although Mama seperated the roots and planted them with great care in a box of fine rich mould and the season in which it was done was warm and rainy. Yours affectionately,   E W R.

FROM THOMAS JEFFERSON RANDOLPH

Museum February 4 [1809]

DEAR GRANDFATHER

I have obtained permission to have a fire in the hall of the Philosophical Society[1] where I can study in solitude; Dr. Wistar and Mr. Peale have as yet made nothing of the Fleecy goat owing to the imperfection of the sample. All the lectures will end this Month and I wish very much to go to washington the 1st of

the application came. Pray let me know it by return of post, and
I will keep the place open a few days. Genl. Dearborne leaves us in
a few days; I have only time to add that Jefferson is well, and as
his lectures will finish this month he will come on here to see me
the 1st. of March, and return to commence the botanical lectures.
My affections to Mr. Randolph and the young ones and tenderest love to yourself.   TH: JEFFERSON

FROM MARTHA JEFFERSON RANDOLPH

Edgehill Feb. 17, 1809

MY DEAREST FATHER

The name of the young gentleman for whom the application
was made is Moultrie. The Christian name I do not remember
but it is probably mentioned in his Father's letter to Mr. Randolph which you told me had been filed with the papers of the
Office. If it is not to be found there, Mr. Randolph thinks it
probable that David R. Williams[1] may know it. He is the eldest
son of Doctor James Moultrie of Charlston S. Carolina. The inclosed I must beg the favor of you to send by the first vessel that
sails. This letter will be delivered to you by My Brother William's
son Beverley who will spend a day in Washington on his way to
west point. If you are not engaged when he arrives I would be
much obliged to you if you would ask him to dine with you any
little attention from you being particularly grateful to the family.
He will spend some days in Philadelphia where Jefferson will
spend as much of his time with him as is consistent with his
studies. The first of March he is obliged to be at west point. The
two little boys were *vaccinated* and had the disease finely. Benjamin's arm was very sore but he had no fever nor a moment's indisposition of any kind that we were sensible of with it. James on
the contrary had a very small place on the arm but was seriously
indisposed for several days. The Geraniums in the little pot have
come up from the root and are flourishing. The Arbre vitae is
budding out also and a box which I take to be the savory is very
flourishing. One more pot with a dead plant we have but of the
other boxes and plants you mentioned I have heard nothing. The
sweet scented grass that was sent on in the fall scarcely exhibits
the least sign of life. I some times think there is a little green
about the roots but am not allways certain even of that. I must
beg the favor of you to send Mary "the road to learning made

From Virginia Jefferson Randolph

Feb. 17. 1809

DEAR GRANDPAPA

I want to see you very much. I am reading a little book called Rosamond.[1] I have read seven books since december. The little geranium has grown a great deal. I had a good deal to say to you the other morning but I have forgotten it. Ben sends you a kiss. Cornelia is learning french. Sister Ellen sends her love to you and says she will write next post. I am spelling [words of] two syllables and [soon hope] to be in four. Adieu dear Grandpapa. Believe me to be your most affectionate Grand Daughter,

VIRGINIA RANDOLPH[2]

1. A child's book by Maria Edgeworth.
2. Letter written by Ellen W. Randolph.

To Ellen Wayles Randolph

Washington Feb. 20. 09.

MY DEAR ELLEN

My last letter to you stated the plants which had been sent, and I was in hopes, after you had been enabled to distinguish them, you would have informed me of their respective conditions. But no post has arrived for this week from Milton and consequently no letter from you. In about three weeks I hope to be with you, and then we shall properly be devoted to the garden. What has become of Mrs. Trist? I have not heard a word about her since I left Monticello. I inclose you a budget of poetry to be distributed according to their address. Tell your Papa that the ultimate decision of Congress is as uncertain at this moment as it ever was. I rather believe the embargo will be removed on the 4th. of March, and a nonintercourse[1] with France and England and their dependencies be substituted. But it is by no means certain. My affections to him, and kisses to your dear Mama and sisters. All love to yourself.   TH: JEFFERSON

1. The Non-Intercourse Act of March 1, 1809, repealed the Embargo, effective March 15, 1809; it reopened trade with all nations except France and Great Britain. The President was authorized by this act to resume trade with these nations if they should cease violating our neutrality rights.

TO MARTHA JEFFERSON RANDOLPH

Washington Feb. 27. 09

MY DEAR DAUGHTER

Your letters of the 17th. and 24th. are both recieved. Beverly T. Randolph[1] called at the hour at which I had rode out, and left your letter of the 17th. Taking for granted he was to stay a day as you mentioned, I wrote an invitation to him the next morning to come and dine with me. But he had already gone on. He called in like manner on his namesake Beverley here,[2] who being out did not see him. I had written a letter of introduction and recommendation to Colo. Williams, the superior of the whole institution, to be delivered by him in person: but as I did not see him, I sent it on by post. We have found the paper which gave Moultrie's Christian name, and his warrant was forwarded to him at Charleston 4. days ago: so Mr. Randolph can answer his friend on that ground. The schooner Sampson, Capt. Smith with the Campeachy hamocks &c. owned in this place, left N. Orleans for this destination about the 6th. of October, as the Captain's reciept, forwarded to me, shews: and has never been heard of since. No doubt remains here of her being lost with every person and thing on board her. Mr. Coles will leave this about the 9th. of March. Consequently if you will write to Botedour by the return of post, it will find him here, as it will myself. I send the two books you desired for Mary.

I am glad you have taken the resolution of going over to Monticello before my return, because of the impossibility of fixing the day of my return. I shall be able, I expect, to dispatch the waggon with the servants from hence, about the 9th. of March, and they will reach home about the 14th. But how many days after their departure I shall be detained in winding up here, I cannot determine. I look with infinite joy to the moment when I shall be ultimately moored in the midst of my affections, and free to follow the pursuits of my choice. In retiring to the condition of a private citizen and reducing our establishment to the style of living of a mere private family, I have but a single uneasiness. I am afraid that the enforcing the observance of the necessary economies in the internal administration of the house will give you more trouble than I wish you to have to encounter and I presume it is impossible to propose to my sister Marks to come and live with us. Perhaps, with a set of good and capable servants, as ours certainly are, the trouble will become less after their once understanding the regulations which are to govern them. Igno-

arrangements so as to relieve your self, and we shall all be happy if you are so. I assure you again and again that the possession of millions would not compensate for one year's sadness and discomfort to you. The trouble you speak of so far as it regards my self is nothing. You know "nothing is troublesome that we do willingly." Your difficulties will be a stimulus that would render *rest* the most intolerable of all cares to me. My health is good and exercise will still confirm it but I am afraid you will be very much disappointed in your expectations from Shoemaker. It is the opinion of the neighbourhood that it would be better for you to get the mill back upon any terms than to let him keep it. In the first place he is not a man of business his bargains are ruinous to himself and more over he has not one spark of honesty. His credit is so low that nothing but necessity induced any one to trust him with their grain; and the general complaint is that it can not be got out of his hands. He told Higginbotham that if *perfectly conveninient* he might perhaps pay the 500 $ on your order but not one cent more would he pay untill there had been a settlement between you. And it is the general opinion that he means to keep the mill and set you at defiance. From some circumstances I am afraid you have been decieved in the character of his Father. There are strong doubts of his honesty in the minds of many here. In short My Dear Father disagreeable as it is to tease you with tales of the kind I think it my duty to tell you the opinion of the whole neighbourhood of the man and your prospects from him. If the bargain was made with the Father perhaps you may secure your self though even that is *doubted.* As for the son your chance is I fear desperate for certainly a greater rascal or a more bitter personal enemy to you does not exist. They say farther that he will contrive to destroy the geer of the mill so as to make it scarcely hold out his time. You may depend upon it that I have not exaggerated the reports and I have reason to believe them too well founded. People allow your mill to be invaluable from its situation and if it was in the hands of a tolerably honest or indrustious man it would be a public benefit. As it is by the time his lease is out it will be totally destroyed as far as it will be possible to do it and you get nothing from him in the mean time. I should not have mentioned these things now, but that perhaps it may enable you to do something with the old man if your bargain is with him. As for the sons they have no character to maintain and never intended to comply with their contract. Excuse me again for intruding so disgusting a subject upon you. Nothing as I have al-

First Citizen of Virginia

To Thomas Jefferson Randolph

Monticello May 6. 09.

Dear Jefferson

Your's of the 28th. ult. came to hand by our last post. I have consulted your father on the subject of your attending Mr. Godon's lectures in mineralogy, and we consent to it so long as the Botanical lectures continue. We neither of us consider that branch of science as sufficiently useful to protract your stay in Philadelphia beyond the termination of the Botanical lectures. In what you say respecting the preservation of plants, I suppose you allude to Mr. Crownenshield's specimens which I shewed you. But I could not have promised to give you his method because I did not know it myself. All I know was from Genl. Dearborne, who told me that Mr. Crownenshield's method was, by extreme pressure (with a screw or weight) on the substance of the plants but that he could never make it adhere to the paper until he used garlick juice either alone or in composition with something else. I communicated to Mr. Randolph your wish respecting the specimens of antimony. But how shall we convey them. By an unintended omission in the act of Congress allowing my letters to be free, they omitted those *from* me, mentioning those *to me* only. It will be corrected at their ensuing session as the letters of my predecessors were privileged both *to* and *from*. And in truth the office of president commits the incumbent, even after he quits office, to a correspondence of such extent as to be extremely burthensome. To avoid the expence of postage to Mr. Peale, I inclose his letter in yours, that it may be paid out of your funds. I send you one also for Mr. Hamilton[1] open for your perusal. When read, stick a wafer in it before delivery. Attend particularly to the assurances of using his indulgence with discretion and to the study of his pleasure grounds as the finest model of pleasure gardening you will ever see. I wrote to Lemaire to

ings, that I could not expect to hear from them. Yours affectionately,   THOS J. RANDOLPH
PS I shall leave this place in four weeks.
NB Dr. Barton[2] has informed me the Lectures end the 12th of June.

1. Charles L. Bankhead was reading law at Monticello under TJ's direction.
2. Dr. Benjamin Barton was a Philadelphia botanist who taught at the College of Philadelphia.

TO THOMAS JEFFERSON RANDOLPH

Monticello June 20. 09
DEAR JEFFERSON

In the even current of a country life few occurrences arise of sufficient note to become the subject of a letter to a person at a distance. It would be little interesting to such an one to be told of the distressing drought of the months of April and May, that wheat and corn scarcely vegetated and no seeds in the garden came up; that since that we have had good rains but very cold weather, so that prospects are disheartening for the farmer and little better to the gardener &c. &c. Yet these circumstances excite a lively interest on the spot, and in their variations from bad to good, and the reverse fill up our lives with those sensations which attach us to existence, altho' they could not be the subject of a letter to a distant friend. Hence we write to you seldom, and now after telling you we are all well, I have given you all our news which would be interesting to you. But tho' we do not write we think of you, and have been for some time counting the days before you will be with us. The death of Dr. Woodhouse and loss of his lectures leave no inducement to protract your stay after the Botanical lectures are ended, for I do not think the mineralogical course important enough for that. We shall expect you therefore when the botanical course is finished. In the mean time it is necessary I should know the state of your funds. Before I left Washington I remitted to Mr. Peale what I supposed would suffice during your stay: but having made some draughts on you, and the one for Lemaire more considerable than I had expected there will probably be a deficiency. Your Mama desires you will get for Mary a little book she has seen advertised called the Adventures of Mary and her cat. Anticipating the pleasure of your return, and assuring you of the happiness it will give us to have you again among us, to the salutations of the family I add only my own affectionate Adieu.   TH: JEFFERSON

or less made little odds, but in our country economy, letter writing
is a hors d'oeuvre. It is no part of the regular routine of the day.
From sunrise till breakfast only I allot for all my pen and ink
work. From breakfast till dinner I am in my garden, shops, or on
horse back in the farms, and after dinner I devote entirely to relaxation or light reading. Hence I have not written to you. Still I
have wished to know what you have entered on, what progress you
have made, and how your hours are distributed. For it is only by
a methodical distribution of our hours, and a rigorous, inflexible
observance of it that any steady progress can be made. From what
I learn through the letter to your mother, I would advise you to
make the Mathematics your principal and almost sole object.
Consider Natural philosophy as quite secondary, because the
books will teach you that as well as any master can. Whereas
Mathematics require absolutely the assistance of a teacher. You
should therefore avail yourself to the utmost of your present situation, because of the uncertainty how long it may continue, and
the certainty that you will have no chance for another when this
fails. As you are entered with the class of Nat. philosophy, give to it
the hours of lecture, but devote all your other time to Mathematics, avoiding company as the bane of all progress. Mr. Jefferson is desired to furnish you all necessaries and to pay your tui-
tion and board. Of the two last articles give him punctual notice
at the end of every quarter that they may never be a day in arrear.

The family are all well, and late letters from Anne inform us
that she and Mary are so. But I presume you have lately seen
them as it was understood you meant to pass your Christmas with
them. Can you always, by the return of your father's boatmen
send us some oysters prepared as those you lately sent us. Robert
Hemings would I think prepare them for us, and call on Mr. Jefferson by your directions for the cost. I shall be glad to hear from
you from time to time, and be assured of my constant and affectionate attachment.   TH: JEFFERSON

To THOMAS JEFFERSON RANDOLPH
                              Monticello Mar. 14. 10.
DEAR JEFFERSON

I recieved by the last post your letter of 9th. expressing your
desire to study half the day in your own room rather than in the
school, if Mr. Gerardin's[1] consent should be obtained; and I
have consulted your father on the subject. We both find ourselves

to be particular as to it's quality. If fine I would be glad to have half a dozen quarts. If midling 2. or 3. bottles will do. If absolutely not good get a single bottle only to serve till I can get some from Philadelphia. Mr. Jefferson will be so good as to have it paid for, and I must get you to have it well packed, *in much straw,* and sent up by in a boat. Mr. T. Eston Randolph's[1] boat left Milton yesterday for Richmond, by the return of which you can send it. Your father's boats do not now come up this river. That the oil should be packed in *much straw* is to protect it from the heat of the sun.

We are all full of complaints against you for not writing to us. Independant of the wish to hear from you, I would advise you, as an exercise, to write a letter to somebody every morning, the first thing after you get up. As most of the business of life, and all our friendly communications are by way of letter, nothing is more important than to acquire a facility of developing our ideas on paper; and practice alone will give this. Take pains at the same time to write a neat round, plain hand, and you will find it a great convenience through life to write a small and compact hand as well as a fair and legible one. I shall probably see you in Richmond in May. The family is all well except Benjamin whose health is not good. Affectionately yours,   TH: JEFFERSON

1. Thomas Mann Randolph, Jr.'s brother-in-law and the husband of Jane Cary Randolph. He resided at Ashton, near Milton, where he was a merchant and, at one time, postmaster.

TO THOMAS JEFFERSON RANDOLPH

Monticello May 14. 10.

DEAR JEFFERSON

I have safely recieved the 4. bottles of oil you sent me and find it very good insomuch that I wish to get more of the same batch. For this purpose I inclose you 10.D. and pray you to get as much more as that will pay for, letting me know at the same time the price, and how much more of the same oil the person has: because if it be cheap, I may still lay in a larger stock of it. Send it up by some boat to Mr. Higginbotham. I cannot but press on you my advice to write a letter every day. It is necessary to begin the exercise of developing your ideas on paper. This is best done at first by way of letter. When further advanced in your education it will be by themes and regular discourses. Practice in this as in all other cases, will render that very easy which now appears to you

same stages as in my chair. And by losing myself the first day I made it 40. miles to Mr. Scott's.[1] I have sold my tobo. here for 7. Dollars: but my wheat is in an embarrassing situation. The dam of the mill in which it is has now broke a second time, and the Miller refuses to deliver my wheat back, altho he had promised in that event to redeliver it. It will take another month to mend his dam, by which time the price and the river both may fail us. I propose to make another formal demand of it, and if he refuses, I may have parted with my crop for a lawsuit instead of money. Besides that he is not able to pay all who are in my situation with him. I expect to obtain his final decision within a few days, and whatever it be to set out then on my return if the weather will permit. We have had 4. snows since my arrival here, one of 4. Inches, the others slight. They have put the roads into a horrible situation. I was two days ago at Belleplaine, Beaulieu, Bellavista, Mount Dougherty &c.[2] All well except a man (William) who is habitually otherwise. Slaughter[3] is much surprised that the two men expected are not yet arrived, and the more on my telling him they were to set out from Monticello the day after I left it now three weeks past. Kiss and bless all the fireside for me, and be assured yourself of my unceasing and tenderest love.

TH: JEFFERSON

1. C. A. Scott operated a ferry in Cumberland County on the James River. TJ lodged there on the night of January 28.

2. These several names have doggedly resisted complete identification. TJ departed Poplar Forest February 8 for Lynchburg, returned on the 9th or 10th and, according to his itinerary set down in his account book, remained at Poplar Forest until he left for Monticello on the 28th. The checklist of his correspondence at the University of Virginia lists letters dated the 13th and the above of the 17th, both written at Poplar Forest. This, coupled with his limited mobility, would have put him on February 15 no more than 30 to 40 miles, at the most, from his Bedford County seat. These places then were probably farm sites, possibly TJ's, in the vicinity of Poplar Forest.

3. Possibly Joseph Slaughter, a Bedford County farmer.

TO MARTHA JEFFERSON RANDOLPH

Poplar Forest Feb. 24. 11.

MY DEAR MARTHA

When I wrote you this day week, I thought I should have been with you as soon as my letter, so I think with respect to the present one. My whole crop of wheat had been put completely out of my power, and the miller who had recieved it has, by twice losing his dam, become insolvent and has delivered over his mill to a per-

for Mr. Bankhead and yourself the assurances of my cordial affection, not forgetting that Cornelia shares them.

TH: JEFFERSON

1. Probably the 1810 Philadelphia edition published by Joseph Milligan. 2. Anne Cary and Charles L. Bankhead had four children: John Warner, Thomas Mann Randolph, Ellen Wayles, and William Stuart Bankhead. For additional biographical information on these and other of TJ's children, grandchildren, and great grandchildren, consult "Collection of Papers to Commemorate Fifty Years of the Monticello Association of the Descendants of Thomas Jefferson," edited by Dr. George Green Shackelford and to be published in 1966.

To Cornelia Jefferson Randolph

Monticello June 3. 11.

My dear Cornelia

I have lately recieved a copy of Mrs. Edgeworth's Moral tales,[1] which seeming better suited to your years than to mine, I inclose you the first volume. The other two shall follow as soon as your Mama has read them. They are to make a part of your library. I have not looked into them, preferring to recieve their character from you after you shall have read them. Your family of silkworms is reduced to a single individual, that is now spinning his broach. To encourage Virginia and Mary to take care of it, I tell them that as soon as they can get III wedding gowns from this spinner they shall be married. I propose the same to you that, in order to hasten it's work, you may hasten home; for we all wish much to see you, and to express in person, rather than by letter. the assurances of our affectionate love.   TH: JEFFERSON

P. S. The girls desire me to add a postscript to inform you that Mrs. Higginbotham has just given them new Dolls.

1. *Moral Tales for Young People;* possibly the three-volume London edition of 1804.

From Francis Wayles Eppes

Millbrook Sep 2 1811

Dear Grandpapa

I wish to see you very much. I am very sorry that you did not answer my letter. Give my love to aunt Randolph and all of the children. Believe me to be your most affectionate Grandson,

FRANCIS EPPES

except overpassing their stage the 2d day, sleeping in the woods all night, without cover, and overwhelmed by a rain, in the center of which they were, while it did not extend 5 miles in any direction from them. The spinning Jenny is at work, well while with washed cotton, but very ill when with unwashed. At least this is Maria's[1] way of accounting for the occasional difference of it's work. The flying shuttle began a little yesterday, but owing to a variety of fixings which the loom required it exhibited very poorly. We hope to see it do better to-day. I am afraid I shall be detained here in getting Perry[2] off before I go away. If I leave him here I shall have no confidence in his following me. Still I shall not fail to be at home within a week or ten days from this date. Present me affectionately to Mr. Randolph and our beloved children, if Ellen will permit herself to be included under that appellation, and be assured yourself of all my love and tenderness.

TH: JEFFERSON

1. A Jefferson servant who was particularly adept at spinning and weaving.
2. Reuben Perry was a Poplar Forest workman.

TO FRANCIS WAYLES EPPES

Poplar Forest. Aug. 28. 13

MY DEAR FRANCIS

After my return from this place to Monticello in May last I recieved the letters which yourself and your cousin Baker wrote me. That was the first information I recieved of your being at school at Lynchburg, or I should certainly have sent for you to come and see me while I was here. I now send 2. horses for yourself and your cousin and hope your tutor will permit you both to come and stay with me till Monday morning then I will send you back again. I left your aunt and all your cousins well in Albemarle. In hopes of seeing you here immediately I remain affectionately yours,   TH: JEFFERSON

TO FRANCIS WAYLES EPPES

Poplar Forest Nov. 26.13.

DEAR FRANCIS

I have written to ask the favor of Mr. Halcomb to permit your cousin Baker and yourself to come and pass tomorrow and next day with me here. I send horses for you both, and will send you

To MARTHA JEFFERSON RANDOLPH

Poplar Forest June 6. 14.

My dear Martha

I have for some time been sensible I should be detained here longer than I had expected, but could not till now judge how long. Chisolm will finish his work in about 10. days, and it is very essential that I should see the walls covered with their plates, that they may be in a state of preservation. This will keep me 3. or 4. days longer, so that I expect to be here still about a fortnight longer. There have not been more than 2. or 3. days without rain since I came here, and the last night the most tremendous storm of rain, wind and lightening I have ever witnessed. For about an hour the heavens were in an unceasing blaze of light, during which you might at any moment have seen to thread a needle. They had been deluged with rain before I came; and the continuance of it threatens injury to our wheat, which is indifferent at best. I have not seen a pea since I left Albemarle, and have no vegetable but spinach and scrubby lettuce. Francis and Wayles Baker are with me. My journey was performed without an accident. The horses and postilions performed well. James will be an excellent driver, and Israel will do better with more strength and practice. You will always be perfectly safe with their driving. If Wormly and Ned should get through the ha! ha![1] and cleaning all the grounds within the upper roundabout, they should next widen the Carlton road,[2] digging it level and extending it upwards from the corner of the graveyard up, as the path runs into the upper Roundabout, so as to make the approach to the house from that quarter on the Northside instead of the South. Present me affectionately to all the family, and be assured of my warmest love.   TH: JEFFERSON

1. The idea for a ha-ha (a ditch or sunken fence) is found in TJ's "General ideas for the improvement of Monticello," circa 1804 (MHi). It was to run behind the Mulberry Row, being the boundary of the northern side of the vegetable garden terrace. There is no evidence this was ever constructed; in 1808–1809, however, a paling fence was erected along the same route as proposed for the ha-ha.

2. A Monticello road. See *Farm Book*, 70, for additional information on this road.

TO FRANCIS WAYLES EPPES

Monticello Sep. 9. 14.

My first wish, my dear Francis, is ever to hear that you are in good health, because that is the first of blessings. The second is to become an honest and useful man to those among whom we live. You are now in the high road of instruction for this object, and I have great confidence you will pursue it with steadiness and attain the end which will make all your friends happy. I shall carry with me to Poplar Forest the proper books for instructing you in French. Whether you can pass your time with me while there, and be employed in learning French must depend on the will of your father and of your tutor. I expect to go there within about three weeks, and to make a longer stay that usual. If that should be employed wholly on French, and you can afterwards pass your Christmas at Monticello where your aunt and cousins can assist me in helping you on, you will afterwards be able to proceed of yourself. In this you will be obliged to separate from your cousin who is too young for an undertaking to be pursued afterwards alone. In the hope of seeing you soon, and conveying to you the wishes of your aunt and cousins to be remembered to you, be assured of my affectionate love,

TH: JEFFERSON

FROM THOMAS JEFFERSON RANDOLPH

Timberlake,[1] Sep 9th 1814

MY DEAR GRANDFATHER

By accident I have obtained in this wretched country paper enough to write a letter upon. We arrived at camp (on the sixth) about two miles from West Point, in want of every thing necessary for the support of the army, both man and horse; we get some beef but never, enough, and that such as we find in the old field, not good, without salt and often without bread, the supply of which is allways precarious; our horses go often twenty four hours without food. We have nothing in abundance, but ticks and musketoes, not as many of the latter as we expected to find. If we remain here many days longer, we must depend entirely upon supplies brought from Richmond as the country between this and that place was found too poor to support us on our march. We

To Thomas Jefferson Randolph

Monticello Mar. 31. 15.

DEAR JEFFERSON

Ellen's visit to Warren [1] has been delayed by an unlucky accident. On Monday we heard that my brother was very sick.[2] Mrs. Marks wishing to go and see him I sent her the next morning in the gig with a pair of my horses, counting on their return the next day so that Ellen and Cornelia might have gone on Thursday according to arrangement. After Mrs. Marks had got about 7. miles on her road, one of the horses (Bedford) was taken so ill that she thought it best to return. He died that night, and no pair of the remaining three could be trusted to draw a carriage. Mrs. Marks going off again to-day to Snowden, I make Wormley take Seelah, and direct him to return by Warren and exchange him with you for the mare Hyatilda. She is an excellent draught animal, and with a match I have for her at Tufton will carry the girls very well; only that as it is sometime since she was in geer, it will be advisable to drive her in the waggon two or three days. In the mean time as your business will probably bring you to court the girls will have the benefit of your escort to Warren. This is the best arrangement it is in my power to make. Ellen is still unwell, and her face is tied up, which however she would not have permitted to disappoint her visit. The family here wish to be presented with respect to Mrs. Nicholas and the family of Warren. To our new friend [3] whom you have brought into so near a relation with us, give assurances that we recieve her as a member of our family with very great pleasure and cordiality and shall endeavor and hope to make this an acceptable home to you both. Ever affectionately yours,   TH: JEFFERSON

1. A small village in southern Albemarle County, on the James River.
2. Randolph Jefferson died on August 7, 1815, at the age of sixty.
3. Thomas Jefferson Randolph was married at Mount Warren, the Nicholas home in Albemarle County, on March 6, 1815, to Jane Hollins, a daughter of Wilson Cary Nicholas and Margaret Smith of the distinguished Baltimore family.

From Martha Jefferson Randolph

Monticello Aug. 13, 1815.

MY DEAR FATHER

The emergency of the occasion must apologise for the liberty I took in opening the enclosed. But as to morrow is Buckingham

Buckingham court, where I presume I shall meet Jefferson, and hear something from home. Indeed it would be a great comfort to me if some one of the family would write to me once a week, were it only to say all is well. I see no reason to believe we shall finish our work here sooner than the term I had fixed for my return. It is rather evident we must have such another expedition the next year. Remember me affectionately to the family and be assured yourself of my warmest and tenderest love my dearest Marth.

Th: Jefferson

1. A Buckingham County inn; TJ arrived there on August 20.
2. A Jefferson slave.
3. TJ referred to this natural formation in present-day Rockbridge County as "the most sublime of nature's works." He patented 157 acres of land lying along Cedar Creek, then in Botetourt County, in 1774, for 20 shillings under a grant from George III. The original deed is recorded in the courthouse in Fincastle, Virginia. For Jefferson's description, see William Peden, editor, *Notes on the State of Virginia by Thomas Jefferson* (Chapel Hill, 1955), 24-25.

To Martha Jefferson Randolph

Poplar Forest Nov. 4. 15.

My dearest Martha

We arrived here on the third day of our journey, without any accident; but I suffered very much both mornings by cold. I must therefore pray you to send my wolf-skin pelisse and fur-boots by Moses's Billy, when he comes to bring the two mules to move the Carpenters back. He is to be here on the 27th. by my directions to Mr. Bacon. In the closet [1] over my bed you will find a bag tied up, and labelled 'Wolf-skin pelisse,' and another labelled 'fur-boots,' wherein those articles will be found. The pelisse had better be sowed up in a striped blanket to keep it clean and uninjured; the boots in any coarse wrapper.

Mr. Baker called on me yesterday, and tells me Francis is gone to Monticello. I am in hopes Ellen will give him close employment. Mr. Baker is come to look for land in this quarter, and will return here this evening and start with me tomorrow morning to Mr. Clark's, [2] to examine his land which is for sale. It will place his family exactly under the sharp peak of Otter, [3] 20. miles only from hence, and along a good road. Lands of 2d quality are selling here now for 25. Dollars. I am this moment interrupted by a crowd of curious people come to see the house. Adieu my Dear Martha, kiss all the young ones for me; present me affectionately to Mr. Randolph, and be assured of my tenderest love.

Th: Jefferson

Bedford all April. The void you have left at our fire side is sensibly felt by us all, and by none more than your's with most affectionate love,   TH: JEFFERSON

P. S. My friendly respects to the President, and homage to Mrs. Madison and Mrs. Cutts.[5]

1. Margaret Smith Randolph was born at the Governor's Mansion in Richmond on March 7, 1816.

2. Mrs. Richard Randolph of Bizarre, Cumberland County.

3. Robert B. Streshley sold William D. Meriwether a tract of 312 acres lying along Moore's Creek and opposite the house of Charles L. Bankhead and approximately one mile down the mountain from the Thoroughfare Gap gate to Monticello. See Albemarle County Deed Book No. 20, page 122, Albemarle County Courthouse, Charlottesville.

4. Joseph Milligan was a Washington bookseller and friend of TJ's.

5. Mrs. Richard Cutts was the sister of Dolley Madison.

FROM ELLEN WAYLES RANDOLPH

Washington March 19th 1816

MY DEAR GRANDPAPA

Your letter of the 14th reached me yesterday and I hasten to return you thanks for this new proof of your affection. The remittance made to Mr. Barnes will indeed add considerably to my moyens de jouissance, and I need not tell you how gratefull I am for your kindness. I have no idea that my wants will exceed the 100. D. but if they should I will apply as you have directed. If I have not written to you hitherto it has been because I found myself unable to perform my promise of giving you the little news of Congress. I do not hear subjects of the kind much spoken of either at home or abroad. I have very little acquaintance with the members, who are not in the habit of visiting familiarly in the family; some of them attend the drawing rooms regularly, but these parties are always crowded, and the conversation consists of compliments, and common place observations made in passant. I did not know untill I came here, how much more amusement may sometimes be found in the solitude of one's own chamber, than in a gay circle. The election of the next President is a subject so interesting to every body, that even the most idle and indifferent think and talk a good deal about it. The merits of the candidates are discussed, and even the ladies of their families come in for their full share of praise or blame. Mrs. Monroe has made herself very unpopular by taking no pains to conceal her aversion to society, and her unwillingness to be intruded on by visitors. The English Minister and his lady and Mrs. Bagot[1] arrived in town

But, while you endeavor, by a good store of learning, to prepare yourself to become an useful and distinguished member of your country you must remember that this can never be, without uniting merit with your learning. Honesty, disinterestedness, and good nature are indispensible to procure the esteem and confidence of those with whom we live, and on whose esteem our happiness depends. Never suffer a thought to be harbored in your mind which you would not avow openly. When tempted to do any thing in secret, ask yourself if you would do it in public. If you would not be sure it is wrong: in little disputes with your companions, give way, rather than insist on trifles. For their love and the approbation of others will be worth more to you than the trifle in dispute. Above all things, and at all times, practice yourself in good humor. This, of all human qualities, is the most amiable and endearing to society. Whenever you feel a warmth of temper rising, check it at once, and suppress it, recollecting it will make you unhappy within yourself, and disliked by others. Nothing gives one person so great advantage over another, as to remain always cool and unruffled under all circumstances. Think of these things, practice them and you will be rewarded by the love and confidence of the world. I have some expectation of being at Poplar Forest the 3d. week of June, when I hope I shall see you going on cleverly, and already beloved by your tutor, curators, and companions, as you are by your's affectionately,

TH: JEFFERSON

1. Sowerby, in *The Library of Thomas Jefferson*, V, No. 4756, does not indicate which of the several listed titles TJ favored as a school text. She does state that a translation of *Elementa Linguae Graecae* . . . (Glasguae, [1795]) was one of the first books ordered by TJ after the sale of his library to Congress in 1815.

2. This is one of the oldest secondary schools in the United States that has continuously operated on a single site. It was chartered in 1795 and today is part of the Bedford County school system.

To MARTHA JEFFERSON RANDOLPH

Poplar Forest Nov. 10. 16.

We are all well here, my dear Martha, and thinking of our return home which will be about the 30th. or perhaps a day or two sooner. It is necessary therefore that the boys, Johnny and Randall with the mules should set off from Monticello on the 19th. or 20th. to take the cart and baggage. I must pray you to desire Mr. Bacon to let them have a good mule and geer in addition to Til-

not previously corresponded, but poor creature she is surrounded by ennemies and never in more need of the support of her family than at present. Adieu My Dearest Father we are All well but poor Ann. Mr. Bankhead[1] has returned and recommenced his habits of drunkeness. Mr. Randolph[2] has taken in to his own hands the mannagement of his affairs and if his family are much disturbed or endangered will take at once the steps necessary for their protection, as circumstances may require. Sending him to the mad house is but a temporary remedy, for after a few weeks he would be returned with renewed health to torment his family the longer. I really think the best way would be to hire a keeper for him to prevent his doing mischief, and let him finish him self at once. His Father is utterly in dispair, and told Aunt Marks that but for Ann and the children he never wished to see his face again. He so entirely threw off all respect for the old gentleman as to tell him he would be master in his own house and called for a decanter of whiskey and drank of two draughts to his face the more to brave him. Adieu My Dearest Father. With tender and unchangeable love Your affectionate Daughter,

MRANDOLPH

The large crown imperial root is for Mrs. Eppes, if you go that way. The smaller ones are not blooming roots yet, but will be in a year or 2. The tulips and hyacinths are mixed but Cornelia knows them all. I have sent you besides the first letter, 3 I believe of which I altered the direction. 3 packets enclosing many letters each the second via Richmond and the 3 went of[f] yesterday 19th before I recieved your letter, for they close the mail on Monday which will account for one packet going by Richmond. The mail being closed before my letters were sent to Charlottesville. I have also sent all the weekly registers as I recieved them.

1. Charles Lewis Bankhead, Anne Cary Randolph's husband. He had been visiting his family in Caroline County.
2. Thomas Mann Randolph, Jr.

TO MARTHA JEFFERSON RANDOLPH

Poplar Forest. Tuesday Dec. 3. 16.

We have been, my ever dearest Martha, now weather bound at this place since Sunday was sennight. We were then to have set off on our return home, but it began to rain that day, and we have had three regular N. E. rains successively, with intermissions of a single day between each. During the first intermission, Mr.

to be permitted to lay the first brick of the Central college. I do not know that I have authority to say either yea or nay to this proposition; but as far as I may be authorised, I consent to it freely. The inhabitants of Charlottesville deserve too well of that institution to meet with any difficulty in that request, and I see no possible objection on the part of the other visitors which exposes me to risk in consenting to it.[1]

Ellen and Cornelia are the severest students I have ever met with. They never leave their room but to come to meals. About twilight of the evening, we sally out with the owls and bats, and take our evening exercise on the terras. An alteration in that part of the house, not yet finished, has deprived them of the use of their room longer than I had expected; but two or three days more will now restore it to them. Present me affectionately to Mr. Randolph, the girls and family. I trust to Ellen and Cornelia to communicate our love to Septimia in the form of a cake. My tenderest love attends yourself.   TH: JEFFERSON

1. The Central College was the planned institution's name until a charter by the legislature altered it to the University of Virginia. The cornerstone of the first pavilion, the present-day Colonnade Club, was laid October 6, 1817, by the Widow's Son Masonic Lodge No. 60 and Charlottesville Lodge No. 90. Present were James Madison, James Monroe, and TJ, members of the institution's Board of Visitors. See Philip Alexander Bruce, *University of Virginia*, I, 183–90.

To Martha Jefferson Randolph

Poplar Forest Nov. 22. 17.

I arrived here, my dear daughter after a disagreeable journey, one day shut up at Warren by steady rain, the next travelling thro a good deal of drizzle and rain, and the last excessive cold, the road being full of ice. But all well in the end. Johnny Hemings had made great progress in his work. His calculation is that he may possibly finish by this day fortnight but possibly and almost probably not till this day three weeks. It is necessary therefore that Cretia's Johnny should be here this day fortnight with the cart for which purpose he must leave Monticello Thursday morning the 3d. of December. I shall be glad if you will send by him my old Rocquelo which will be found on the couch in the chamber. Mr. Burwell, and Mrs. Trist have staid a day with me and are now starting off after an early breakfast. I have time therefore only to add my affections to all and my most especiall love to yourself, inclosing a letter for Mr. Bacon on the mission of Johnny.

TH: JEFFERSON

very tired of a city life and indeed I think that there is a vast diference between the uproar and bustle of this place and our peaceful home in virginia, I feel the effects of confinement very much, Shut up within the walls of the college scarcely ever permitted to go out except when I am sent for by My Father. Greatly diferent from my past life and it is what I dislike very much. Thire is a gentleman here a Spaniard whom My Father intends to employ to carry on My Spanish but their is a great dificulty in procuring books. Believe me to remain with great respect your affectionate Grandson,   FRANCIS EPPES

TO FRANCIS WAYLES EPPES

Monticello Feb. 6. 18.

DEAR FRANCIS

I have deferred acknoleging the reciept of your letter of Dec. 28 in the daily hope of being able to speak with more certainty of the time when our Central college will be opened, but that is still undecided and depending on an uncertainty which I have explained to your father. I do not wonder that you find the place where you are disagreeable, it's character, while I lived in Washington was that of being a seminary of mere sectarism. The only question is how to dispose of yourself until the Central college opens. There is now at the N. London academy an excellent teacher, and that place is on a better footing than it ever has been. Indeed I think it now the best school I know. Dr. Carr[1] has also a school in our neighborhood, but I doubt whether you would find it as good, or as comfortable as the other. James[2] goes to that. If your father should conclude on N. London, you had better come here before the 15th. of April when I shall go to Bedford, and could carry you with me. If Dr. Carr should be preferred, come as soon as you please and I will endeavor to get a place for you with him. But this is not certain as he is very full. In all events I shall hope to see you here whenever your situation will permit, and that you will be assured of my constant love.

TH: JEFFERSON

1. Dr. George Carr operated a school at the east end of Main Street in Charlottesville.
2. James Madison Randolph, Martha's second son and seventh living child. He was born January 17, 1806.

FROM FRANCIS WAYLES EPPES

New London Academy August 2d 1818

DEAR GRANDPAPA

I found on my arrival here the day that we parted that the Trustees were assembling for the trial of Watts, after Spending most of the day in warm debate he was Suspended untill he should beg Mr. Dashiels pardon, and promise good behaviour in future, and this in the presence of the whole school. To my great surprise he agreed to these humiliating conditions and was admitted. All goes on now as before and a sullen calm has succeeded to the storm that was once threatening in its aspect. Mr. Dashiel is not as much respected I think by the Students as formerly.

By this time you have decided on the place for the University and I hope that the Central College is adopted, as the situation is an healthy one and the most eligible indeed in the state, and because it would afford me the greatest pleasure imaginable to finish my education there it being under your direction. I have commenced Xenophon, and Horace also, though I am afraid that I cannot get through the Arithmetic this Session. I have heard nothing from the Forest Since I saw you. Give my love to Aunt Randolph and the family. Believe me to remain your Affectionate Grandson, FRANCIS EPPES

TO MARTHA JEFFERSON RANDOLPH

Rockfish gap Aug. 4. 18.

MY DEAR DAUGHTER

All our members, except 3 who came not at all arrived on Saturday morning so that we got to work by 10. oclock, and finished yesterday evening.[1] We are detained till this morning for fair copies of our report. Staunton has 2. votes, Lexington 3. the Central college 16. I have never seen business done with so much order, and harmony, nor in abler nor pleasanter society. We have been well served too. Excellent rooms, every one his bed, a table altho' not elegant, yet plentiful and satisfactory. I proceed today with judge Stuart to Staunton.[2] Every body tells me the time I allot to the Springs is too short. That 2. or 3. weeks bathing will be essential. I shall know better when I get there. But I forsee the possibility and even probability that my stay there must be longer than I expected. I am most afraid of losing Mr. Correa's visit.[3] I shall write to him from the springs. Cooper[4] has failed in his election, Dr. Patterson having obtained the Chemical chair. I

Springs was approximately sixty miles. For an itinerary from Richmond to the Warm Springs, see *Johnson's Virginia Almanack* . . . *1807* (Richmond, 1806). A copy is in the almanac collection at the American Antiquarian Society, Worcester, Massachusetts.

TO MARTHA JEFFERSON RANDOLPH

Warm springs Aug. 14. 18.

MY DEAR DAUGHTER

I wrote to you by our last mail of the 8th. having been now here a week and continued to bathe 3 times a day, a quarter of an hour at a time. I continue well, as I was when I came. Having no symptom to judge by at that time I may presume the seeds of my rheumatism eradicated, and desirous to prevent the necessity of ever coming here a 2d time, I believe I shall yeild to the general advice of a three weeks course. But so dull a place, and so distressing an ennui I never before knew. I have visited the rock on the high mountain, the hotsprings, and yesterday the falling spring, 15. miles from here; so that there remains no other excursion to enliven the two remaining weeks.[1] We are at present about 30, and at the Hotsprings 20. Yesterday we were reduced to a single lady (Miss Allstone) but there came in 4. more in the evening. Mrs. Egglestone (Matilda Maury that was) left us yesterday for the Hotsprings, obliged to be carried to the bath in a chair, being unable to walk. The 2. Colo. Coles[2] came in last night, and John Harris the night before. Yesterday too Genl. Brackenridge[3] left us, who had accompanied me from the Rockfish gap, and who has been my guide and guardian and fellow lodger in the same cabin. We were constantly together, and I feel his loss most sensibly. He tells me you were at his house (in the neighborhood of Fincastle)[4] on your tramontane excursion. I have contracted more intimacy with Colo. Allstone than any other now remaining. He is father of the Mr. Allstone[5] who married Burr's daughter. The whole of the line of springs seems deserted now for the white Sulphur,[6] where they have 150. persons and all latter-comers are obliged to go into the neighborhood for lodging. I believe in fact that the spring with the Hot and Warm, are those of the first merit. The sweet springs retain esteem, but in limited cases. Affectionate remembrance to all the family and to yourself devoted love.   TH: JEFFERSON

1. The high mountain was probably the Warm Springs or Jackson's Mountain; others in the vicinity are not of great height. Hot Springs is in Bath County, as is Warm Springs, and about five miles southwest of it. TJ may

imposthume and eruptions which with the torment of the journey back reduced me to the last stage of weakness and exhaustion.[1] I am getting better, but still obliged to lie night and day in the same reclined posture which renders writing painful. I cannot be at Poplar Forest till the middle of October, if strong enough then. If you should have to go to another school, if you will push your Greek Latin and Arithmetic, there will be no time lost, as that prepares you for reception at the University on the ground of a student of the sciences. Altho' I now consider that as fixed at the Central College yet it will retard the opening of that till the spring, as the conveyance of all our property to the Literary fund[2] subjects us now to await the movements of the legislature. Be assured, My dear Francis of my affectionate and devoted attachment to you.   TH: JEFFERSON

1. TJ was at Warm Springs from August 8 to 27. While there he contracted an "erruptive complaint," undoubtedly boils or carbuncles, which he stated were treated with "unctions of mercury and sulphur." This would indicate only local medication, but in a letter to Henry Dearborn of July 5, 1819 (DLC), he infers that this treatment may have been internal as well: "The cause of the eruption was mistaken and it was treated with severe unctions of mercury and sulphur. These reduced me to death's door and on ceasing to use them I recovered immediately and consider my health as perfectly reestablished except some small effects on the bowels produced by these remedies." Whatever the causes of his indisposition, he was ill for about three months. See TJ to Lafayette, November 23, 1818 (DLC).

2. Established by the Virginia legislature in 1810, it formed the nucleus for the popular support of free education in the state. For a brief explanation of its history and activities, see Cornelius J. Heatwole, *A History of Education in Virginia* (New York, 1916), 104–9; also, Bruce, *University of Virginia*, I, 85–94.

FROM FRANCIS WAYLES EPPES

Millbrook Nov: 26th. 1818

DEAR SIR

You will no doubt be surprised at seeing the date of this letter, thinking that I have been at school for some time past. I have however been detained at home much longer than I myself expected by the indisposition of our family. A bilious Fever has been prevalent in our neighbourhood this fall and carried off many. It is now much abated. I set out this week at Furtherest for Mr. Bakers and will let you hear from me as soon as I arrive there. It is very uncertain whether Mr. Barbour will continue his school after Christmas, if he does not I shall pursue the course you recommended to me untill the Central College goes into operation.

or advise. Present my respects to Mrs. Eppes and be assured of my constant affection.   TH: JEFFERSON

1. Louis Leschot, a Charlottesville merchant and watch repairman. Tradition has it that TJ brought him to America, but there is no evidence to support this. Leschot and his wife Sophie were buried in the Monticello graveyard.

To MARTHA JEFFERSON RANDOLPH

Pop. For. July 28. [1819]

MY DEAREST MARTHA

I have just learned from the Enquirer the death of my old and valuable friend Cathalan [1] of Marseilles, an important loss to me, and at this time particularly requiring attention, as my orders are now on the way to him for the supplies of the year, and the money to pay for them. But I can do nothing without his papers which I request you to send me. In my Cabinet, and in the window on the right of my writing table you will see 4. or 5. cartoons of papers. The 2d. and 3d. of these contain a compleat set of alphabeted papers, and in the 2d where the alphabet begins you will find Cathalan's papers in one or more bundles, for I believe they are in more than one. The latest of these in point of date is the one I want. If it includes the present and last year or two it will be sufficient.[2] Be so good as to send it by the 1st. mail of which the girls apprise you. We should have felt great uneasiness at your sickness had not the same letter informed us of your convalescence. We have been near losing Burwell [3] by a stricture of the upper bowels; but he has got about again and is now only very weak. Bless all the young ones for me, and be blessed yourself.

TH: JEFFERSON

1. Stephen Cathalan, a Marseilles merchant with whom TJ had been doing business since his stay in Paris.
2. For TJ's filing method, see "Description of his presses and their contents," an undated manuscript (circa 1827) in a hand not identified (MHi).

FROM MARTHA JEFFERSON RANDOLPH

Monticello Aug. 7. 19

MY DEAREST FATHER

I found very readily the two bundles of papers which I enclose. Capt. Peyton [1] who has been with us lately says that he has your cement, and books, but that the river is so low that not a boat can

which Randolph was seriously wounded. Bankhead was arrested and then released after posting bond. He left the county, thus forfeiting his bond, and for some unexplainable reason was never brought to trial. Several years later he returned but was not called to account for his wounding of Randolph. See Joseph C. Vance, "Thomas Jefferson Randolph," 61–75, for an excellent account of the affair.

4. In 1817 TJ had applied to the Richmond branch of the Bank of the United States for a loan. An audit of his accounts revealed him in debt to the United States government as a result of his stay in France. The loan was granted, but an endorser was needed; Wilson Cary Nicholas, a member of the board of the bank, obliged TJ in this matter. Very shortly thereafter, TJ acted as an endorser for two of Nicholas' notes totaling $20,000. The following year (1819), one of these was protested, but Nicholas assured TJ that he would not suffer as a result. However, Nicholas was not able to meet the demand, and TJ informed the bank he would cover his own endorsement. This he was able to do by mortgaging his property. For additional details of this matter, consult the Jefferson-Wilson Cary Nicholas correspondence, March 26, 1818, through August 17, 1819, in the Jefferson Papers in the Library of Congress.

To Martha Jefferson Randolph

P. F. Aug. 24. 19.

My dear daughter

It is our purpose to set out from this place for Monticello on Monday the 13th. or perhaps on Sunday the 12th. of next month. As Henry, his mule and little cart will be necessary to carry our baggage, I would wish him to leave Monticello on Sunday morning the 5th. making stages at Tooler's on this side the river at Warren, at Noah Flood's, Hunter's and this place.

I am much recovered from my rheumatism,[1] altho' the swellings are not entirely abated, nor the pains quite ceased. It has been the most serious attack of that disease I ever had. While too weak to sit up the whole day, and afraid to increase the weakness by lying down, I long for a Siesta chair which would have admitted the medium position. I must therefore pray you to send by Henry the one made by Johnny Hemings. If it is the one Mrs. Trist would chuse, it will be so far on it's way, if not, the waggon may bring hers when it comes at Christmas. John or Wormly should wrap it well with a straw rope, and then bowed up in a blanket. Besides this, ticklenburg should be got from Mr. Lietch's[2] and a cover made for the cart. Wormly will see to it's being safely placed in.

We have nothing new here but comfortable rains which it is thought will make us half a crop of corn, sufficient for bread and perhaps for fattening some hogs. Present me affectionately to Mr.

TO FRANCIS WAYLES EPPES

Poplar Forest Sep. 21. 20

DEAR FRANCIS

I leave at Flood's with this letter a packet containing 3. small volumes of my petit format library[1] containing several tragedies of Euripedes, some of Sophocles and one of Aeschylus. The 1st. you will find easy, the 2d. tolerable so; the last incomprehensible in his flights among the clouds. His text has come to us so mutilated and defective and has been so much plaistered with amendments by his commentators that it can scarcely be called his.

I inclose you our measured distances expressed in miles and cents. We leave this tomorrow morning and shall be at Monticello the next night. From thence you shall hear from me about the end of the 1st. week of October. By that time I shall either see Doctr. Cooper, or know that I shall not see him. I was decieved in the weather the day we left Milbrook. We passed thro' 2. hours of very heavy rain, and got to Flood's at 11. oclock where we staid the day. We did not suffer ourselves but the servants got very wet. Present our cordial love to the family. Ever and affectionately yours,   TH: JEFFERSON

1. TJ maintained at Poplar Forest a small library of about seventy titles, chiefly for pleasurable reading. The Petit Format Library was a part of this. See *Catalogue of a Private Library . . . the Messrs. Leavitt, Auctioneers . . .* (New York, 1873), (NNP), the only record known of this library. The Petit Format Library is Item No. 647, and typical of the authors were Virgil, Tacitus, Ovid, Sophocles, Pindar, etc. There were 98 volumes in 12- and 32-mo. sizes, and they were principally from the Wetstein, Elzevir, and Jansonii presses.

TO FRANCIS WAYLES EPPES

Monticello Oct.6. 20.

DEAR FRANCIS

Your letter of the 28th. came to hand yesterday, and, as I suppose you are now about leaving Richmond for Columbia,[1] this letter will be addressed to the latter place. I consider you as having made such proficiency in Latin and Greek that on your arrival at Columbia you may at once commence the study of the sciences: and as you may well attend two professors at once, I advise you to enter immediately with those of Mathematics and Chemistry. After these go on to Astronomy, Natl. philosophy, Natl. history and Botany. I say nothing of Mineralogy or Geology, because I pre-

conduct them advantageously, nor any one more affectionately
yours.   TH: JEFFERSON

1. He was attending the South Carolina College, later the University of
South Carolina, at Columbia.

FROM FRANCIS WAYLES EPPES

Columbia Octbr. 31st. 20

DR GRANDPAPA

I waited untill this time (before writing) that I might be able to
give a more satisfactory, and circumstantial account, of the course
and regulations of this institution, which are pretty nearly the
same as those of the northern colleges, differing only in two points.
In the first place the course here is neither as full nor as comprehensive a one as that of Cambridge, secondly the discipline is more
lax and consequently better adapted, to the feelings and habits of
the southern students. This latter circumstance too is somewhat
surprising as the Faculty themselves (with the exception of Dr.
Cooper) are Clergymen. The objection too to their course is ob-
viated by the consideration of a college library the free use of
which is permitted to the students. They have four classes and
to the studies of each one year is allotted, so that the lowest
1. takes four years to graduate; in it Graeca Minora, Virgils AEneid,
2. and Arithmetic are the studies, those of the next in grade are, the
1st part of the 1st vol: of Graeca Majora, Horace, Algebra as far as
3d cubick equations, Geography. &c. Those of the junior are Blairs
Lectures, Watts's Logick, Kames's elements of Criticism, Paleys
Moral Philosophy, cubick equations, Geometry, Trigonometry &c.
Hutton alone is used, his demonstrations are much shorter than
4 Simpsons. The senior year Logarithms, conick sections and Flux-
ions, Cavallo's Natural Philosophy Butlers Analogy of Religion,
Chemistry. No one is allowed the privilege of entering as student,
without pursuing this course, unless he does under the Title of
Honorary, which besides being an unusual is moreover a disad-
vantageous standing. I have therefore entered as a regular student,
and am a candidate for the junior class, whose examination comes
on in two weeks. After it is over I will write again and perhaps may
be enabled then, to give you more satisfactory information concerning the elections of a President and Professor of Mathematics.
The only objection to Elliot who is talked of as President is his
not being a minister of the Gospel, this too is urged as a very

by reading hereafter without the aid of a teacher. As I do not know any professor at Columbia but Doctr. Cooper, request, in my name, his interest and influence to be permitted to adapt your studies to your wants.

Reviewing what you say are the courses of the 4. classes, I pass over the 1st. and 2d. which you are done with, and should select for you from the 3d. Algebra, Geometry, trigonometry and Natural philosophy, and from the 4. Logarrithms and chemistry to which I should add astronomy, Botany and natural history, which you do not mention in any of the classes. I omit Blair's Rhetoric, Watt's logic, Kaims, Paley, Butler &c. which you can read in your closet after leaving College as well as at it. And in Mathematics I do not think you have time to undertake either Conic sections or fluscions. Unless you can be indulged in this selection I shall lament very much indeed the having advised your going to Columbia because time is now the most pressing and precious thing in the world to you; and the greatest injury which can possibly be done you is to waste what remains on what you can acquire hereafter yourself, and prevent your learning those useful branches which cannot will be acquired without the aids of the College.

Whether our University will open this time, 12 month or be shut up 7. years, will depend on the present legislature's liberating our funds by appropriating 100,000 D. more from the Literary fund. If you watch the newspapers you will see what they do, and be able to judge what may be expected.

Ellen and Virginia are here with me. We leave this the day after tomorrow for Monticello, where we hope to meet your aunt, who will be returning at the same time from Richmond. We learn by your letter to Virginia that Wayles is with you. To him and to yourself I tender my affectionate attachments. To Dr. Cooper also give my friendly souvenirs. The difficulty with which I write puts that much out of my power.   TH: JEFFERSON

TO FRANCIS WAYLES EPPES

Monticello Jan. 19. 21.

DEAR FRANCIS

Your letter of the 1st came safely to hand. I am sorry you have lost Mr. Elliot, however the kindness of Dr. Cooper will be able to keep you in the tract of what is worthy of your time.

You ask my opinion of Ld. Bolingbroke and Thomas Paine.

you suppose. They authorized us to borrow another 60,000. D. pledging however our own funds for repayment. This loan enables us to finish all our buildings of accomodation this year, and to begin The Library, which will take 3. years to be compleated. Without waiting for that, it is believed that when the buildings of accomodation are finished, the legislature will cancel the debt of 120,000. D. and leave our funds free to open the institution. We shall then require a year to get our Professors into place. Whether the legislature will relingquish the debt the next session, or at some future one is not certain. In the mean time you cannot do better than to stay where you are until the end of 1822 confining your studies to Mathematics, Natl. Philosophy, Natl. History and Rhetoric. All other branches you can pursue by yourself, should we not open here by that date.

I note what you say of the late disturbances in your College. These dissensions are a great affliction on the American schools, and a principal impediment to education in this country. The source of discontent arising from dieting the students, we shall avoid here, by having nothing to do with it, and by leaving every one to board where he pleases. Nor do I see why this remedy might not have been resorted to in your late case, rather than that of making it a ground of difference with the Professors. There may have been reasons however of which I am uninformed.

The family here is all well, always remember you with affection, and recieve your letters with gratification. To theirs I add the assurance of very affectionate love.   TH: JEFFERSON

TO FRANCIS WAYLES EPPES

Monticello June 27. 21.

DEAR FRANCIS

Your letter of May 7. was recieved in due time, and in it you ask my opinion as to the utility of pursuing metaphysical studies. No well educated person should be entirely ignorant of the operations of the human mind, to which the name of metaphysics has been given. There are three books on this subject, Locke's essay on the human understanding, Tracy's elements of Idiology, and Stewart's Philosophy of the human mind,[1] any one of which will communicate as much on the subject as is worth attention. I consider Tracy as the most correct Metaphysician living; and I inclose you a small tract of his worth reading because it is short, profound, and treats an interesting question, to wit that on the certainty of

doubtful whether you would be permitted at Columbia to pursue those studies only which will be analogous to the views and purposes of your future life. It is a deplorable considn that altho neither your father nor myself have spared any effort in our power to press on your education, yet so miserable are the means of educn in our state that it has been retarded and baffled to a most unfortunate degree. And now that you have only a single year left, you cannot be permitted to employ that solely in what will be useful to you. Every instn however has a right to lay down it's own laws, and we are bound to acquiescence. There seems from your ltr. to be still a possibility that you may be permitted to remain as an irregular student. That is the most desirable event. If not, then to obtain from Dr. Cooper and Mr. Wallace the favor of attending them as a private student unconnected with the College. From them you can recieve every instruction necessary for you, to wit in Mathematics, Astronomy, Nat. Philosophy and Chemistry. If that cannot be permitted, there will remain nothing but the disastrous alternative of again shifting your situation. I know nothing of the plan or degree of instruction at Chapel-hill.[1] Perhaps you might be excluded there also by similar rules. If so, William & Mary is your last resource. There students are permitted to attend the schools of their choice, and those branches of science only which will be useful to them in the line of life they propose. The objection to that place is it's autumnal unhealthiness.

The thankfulness you express for my cares of you bespeaks a feeling and good heart: but the tender recollections which bind my affections to you, are such as will for ever call for every thing I can do for you. And the comfort of my life is in the belief that you will deserve it. To my prayers that your life may be distinguished by it's worth I add the assurance of my constant and affectionate love.　　　　　　　　　　　　　　　　TH: J.

1. Why TJ had such strong feelings against the college at Chapel Hill, North Carolina, are not clear. That he had them is evident in a letter from John Wayles Eppes to Francis Wayles Eppes: "I could not reconcile to my feelings going against your Grand Father and his prejudices against Chappell hill appear invincible." November 18, 1818 (MHi).

TO THOMAS JEFFERSON RANDOLPH

　　　　　　　　　　　　　　　　　　　　Mar. 15. 22.

TH: J to TH: J. R.

Do not give up the bonds to Morrison. Your right to them is sound. Colo. Nicholas covenated to assign certain bonds to Mor-

pended. This has brought me nearly through the Lectures on chemistry and so far in Nat. Philosophy that Mr. Wallace tells me I shall find no more difficulty, and may pursue the study to as much advantage at home. As to Astronomy the course taught here is scarcely better than that contained in every petty treatise on the use of the Globes, as it is an abridgement of the outline in Cavallo's Nat. Philosophy, by Brosius, and hardly worth perusal; so that I should not have gained much by staying for this. Had it so happened, I would have prefered staying until the Lectures on chemistry were quite over, but I have in a measure remedied this deficiency by studying the few remaining subjects in our text Book, which is an excellent one. Dr C's lectures will I expect certainly be over next week, and then Mr. Vanuxum begins with *Geological Mineralogy,* as the chair is entitled. Tomorrow I set off and in 10 days expect to reach Millbrook, when I hope to find your answer as I shall feel disatisfied until I know that you are not displeased with me for acting in the way that I have done. If you approve my intention I will turn in immediately to the Study of Law and divide my time between it and other studies.

Remember me to Aunt Randolph and family and accept this as testimony of my sincere love. Your affectionate Grandson,

FRS. EPPES

TO FRANCIS WAYLES EPPES

Monticello Apr. 9.22.

DEAR FRANCIS

Your letter of Mar. 22. did not reach me till a few days ago. That of Feb. 6. had been recieved in that month. Being chiefly a statement of facts, it did not seem to require an answer, and my burthen of letter-writing is so excessive as to restrain me to answers absolutely necessary. I think, with you, that you had now better turn in to the study of the law, as no one can read a whole day closely on any one subject to advantage, you will have time enough in the other portions of the day to go on with those essential studies which you have not as yet compleated. If you read Law from breakfast 4. or 5. hours, enough will remain before dinner for exercise. The morning may be given to Natural philosophy and Astronomy, the afternoon to Rhetoric and Belles lettres, and the night to history and ethics. The first object will be to procure the necessary law books for reading. They will come 25. per cent cheaper from England than bought here; and some indeed can

Reeves's history of the English law. 4.v. 8vo.
Jacob's Law dictionary by Russhead. fol.
Abridgment of Cases in Equity
Bridgman's digested Index of cases in Chancery. 3.v. 8vo.
Fonblanque's a treatise of equity. 5th. edition. 1819. 2.v. 8vo.

1. René Just Haüy, the well-known French mineralogist and author of *Traité de Minéralogie* (Sowerby 1089), and Biot, *Traité élémentaire d'Astronomie Physique.*

FROM FRANCIS WAYLES EPPES

Millbrook May 13. 1822

DR. GRANDPAPA

I merely write a few lines to inform you of the success of my negociation. Papa can only spare at present money for the purchase of two books, Bacons Abridgment, and Thomas's Coke Littleton, which I beg you will send for with yours. The money you have in your hands it will therefore be no trouble to retain a sum sufficient to purchase the books and pay their freight, and this my Father authorises me to say. I have a copy of Blackstone and a very good Law Dictionary and by the time that the others arrive will perhaps be enabled to send for more. Bad crops and bad prices, added to my Fathers ill health and the loss of 9000. wt. of tobacco by fire last winter have rendered it impossible to incur any other expences than those which are absolutely necessary. Knowing these circumstances and moreover in conversation having discovered that he had otherwise appropriated the greater part of the money we had calculated on, I forebore to ask any thing more than what I conceived essentially requisite. I am pursuing the plan you advised and have already made some progress in my Lord Coke: I do not find him any thing like as difficult as I had anticipated, and presume from this circumstance that the almost insuperable obstacles encountered by others were owing entirely to the want of arrangement in the old editions. I have as yet met with nothing that a little more, than ordinary attention could not master. My Father is still in very delicate health and at present almost a cripple in consequence of a wound in the arm by an unskilful bleeder; he desires to be affectionately remembered to you and requests that you and Aunt Randolph will take Millbrook in your way on your return in which request I most sincerely join. Accept the assurance of my constant affection,   FR: EPPES

thing trifling in comparison to this, will it not be better as my interest must be promoted by personal attention, to incur that likewise. With good security which I can give, the money may perhaps be obtained in Richmond on condition of its being returned in two years, one half the principal with interest the first, the remainder the next. Besides this, there is one other shift. My Father proposes that I shall join hands and work a plantation of his in Cumberland sharing the profits in proportion to the force of each. This would free me it is true from present expence, but reckoning on good prices, will yield only $800 which will not come to hand till april twelvemonth, besides the loss of labour in clearing anothers land while my own is lying idle, or yielding little profit. These are the circumstances to which I am reduced; and the different considerations which attend on either step appearing equally advantageous have brought me nearly to a stand. In this dilemma I apply to your better judgment and experience, and am determined to be guided by your advice. My Father had a severe attack on his journey, but in consequence of not being bled as the Physicians say, recovered speedily. He returned in much better health than when he left us and with his memory considerably improved. He is at present in Amelia, but expected back tomorrow. I obtained from Col. Burton[2] the address of several gentlemen who make the Carolina wine. He was much opposed to giving the information being willing and indeed anxious to procure it for you, but upon my insisting told me that Thomas Cox & co. Commission Merchants Plymouth, would be more likely to please than any others. The makers of the wine are persons in easy circumstances, who do not care to oblige, generally keeping the best for themselves. It was from Cox that your last and (I believe) my Fathers which you admired, were obtained. In case however, that you might still prefer the wine makers themselves, he informed me that Ebinezer Pettigrew P. O. Edenton, and George E. Spruel P. O. Plymouth make it best. The former will not always sell being very wealthy, the latter is not in as good circumstances, and owns the famous vine covering an acre of ground. Col. B. informed us that the vine does not grow from the slip, which accounts for the failure of yours.

If you can conveniently, I wish you would answer this as soon as it comes to hand. I am compelled to go down to Richmond on the 17th of novbr. at farthest, which will leave me two mails, the 14th and 16th. My *time* since I saw you, which I know you care most about, has been as well employed as circumstances would

extremely easy to rest contented with the continued assurances of your health recieved thro' the letters of my cousins. I now write in apprehension of some difficulties with the representatives of my late Father[1] both to obtain your advice, and to learn whether you may have in possession any letter of his expressive of his designs as to my settlement in life. Any written corroboration of intentions which I have affirmed and acted upon would be grateful to my feelings, as the executors seem disposed to wring from my grasp all that the law will allow. They now demand a copy of the conveyance made in August last of six negroes, with the intention of disputing the title, or of compelling me to take them in part of the reversionary interest. The deed is worded in consideration "of natural affection and of promises heretofore made;" without specifying what promise: you consulted Col. Barbour on this head but mentioned the former condition only. I thought it probable, that as the subject has on several occasions been in agitation between you (as to cite one, when the exchange of Pantops for land here was proposed) there might be some letter containing full and explicit views on the subject: some one at least that may serve to convince My Mother that the reversion of Pantops is not an ephemeral claim; an idea which seems to hang upon her mind. This month has been extremely cold and disagreable with us. We have had frequent storms of wind, often accompanied by rain, and several smart frosts. The fruit however is as yet safe. Crops of wheat are promising. Yours uncommonly fine; better than that of Mrs. Mosely, which is a great point in reputation and profit. Some recent sales of tobacco in Lynchburg as high as 10 and 11 dollars: one crop of eight hogsheads very fine averaged 8.50. The neighbours are all well, and make frequent enquiries about you. They hope that your visit will not be much longer protracted, and that you will give us a larger share of your time. I need not add how much it would gratify me. With my love to you all in which Elizabeth joins I must now conclude. Believe me ever and affectionately yrs.,   FRANS. EPPES.

P. S. If it will not be too troublesome I wish you to bring me a little bit of Pyracantha with the root to it. The method of propagation by rows is so tedious and uncertain that I am inclined to rely more on this tho' the season maybe unfavourable.

1. John Wayles Eppes resigned from Congress in April, 1819, because of failing health. He was only fifty when he died at Millbrook on September 5, 1823; he was buried in the family cemetery there. TJ's opinion of his will may be found under the date 1823 in the Ambler Papers (ViU).

bly detain me till the next month, when I hope I may be able to pay you a short visit. Give my love to Elizabeth and be assured of my best affections to yourself,   TH: J.

1. Specific boundaries for the acreage and house in the Poplar Forest planta-tion left Francis W. Eppes is recorded in TJ's will dated March 16–17, 1826. A copy is reproduced in Randall, III, 665–67; the original is in the Albemarle County Courthouse. See also Albemarle County Deed Book, 23, 253–54. The remainder of the Poplar Forest tract was reserved for the payment of TJ's debts.

2. This transaction is reflected in the account book notation for October 18, 1820.

To Francis Wayles Eppes

Monto. Feb. 17. 25.

DEAR FRANCIS

We heard some time ago indirectly and indistinctly thro' your friends at Ashton of the injury sustained by your house at P. F. and I have waited in hopes you would inform me of the particu-lars that I might know how far I could help you. I will spare J. Hem. to you and his two aids and he can repair every thing of wood as well or perhaps better than any body there. I understand that the roofs of the 2. NW rooms and Ding. room are burnt. Are the Portico and stairway burnt? The joists of the 3. rooms? The cornice of the Ding. room? The doors and windows destroyed? Let me know this and every particular. If the joists are burnt you will have to get others sawed at Capt. Martin's while his mill has water to spare. I used to cut and haul him stocks, and he sawed one half for the other. Those for the Dg. Room had better not be sawed till J. H comes up which will be as soon as I hear from you and he has finished a necessary job here.

Our last Professors from England are arrived in Hampton and we have announced the opening of the Univty. on the 1st. Monday of March.[1] All well here and at Ashton. Affectly yours,

TH: J.

1. These three professors were Robley Dunglison, Thomas Hewitt Key, and Charles Bonnycastle. They arrived at Norfolk on February 10.

From Francis Wayles Eppes

Poplar Forest Feb. 25.25.

I should have written to you sooner, My Dr. Grandfather, and given all the particulars of our late accidint, had I not supposed

P. S. If your catalogue for the university library is published I would be very much obliged to you for a copy.[2]

1. A Boston firm that supplied books for the University of Virginia Library See *Jefferson's Ideas on A University Library* (Charlottesville, 1950) edited by Elizabeth Cometti, for TJ's correspondence with William Hilliard.

2. It was not printed until 1828. See *1828 Catalogue of the Library of the University of Virginia, Reproduced in Facsimile with an Introduction by William Harwood Peden* . . . (Charlottesville, 1945).

TO FRANCIS WAYLES EPPES

Monto. Apr. [1825]

DEAR FRANCIS

The difficulty with which I write, my aversion to it, and the satiating dose which is forced upon me by an overwhelming correspondence have occasioned me to be thus late in acknoleging the rect of your letter of Feb. 24. I was glad to learn the damage to your house by the fire was less considerable than I had supposed. John Heming and his two aids have been engaged in covering this house with tin which is not yet finished. They shall repair to your assistance as soon as I can accompany them,[1] which shall be as soon as the roads become practicable. I would rather you should do nothing more than shelter by slabs or other temporary covering the uncovered parts of the house, any want of sawing which you can foresee had better be obtained while Captn. Martin's sawmill has waters for the terras, joists of the length and breadth of the former will be needed, but they may be 3.I. thick only as we can make the gutters in a different way which will for ever protect the joists from decay, pine would be the best timber, heart poplar will do. Oak is too springy. I will desire Colo. Peyton to send up tin for covering the dwelling house.

I will bring with me a plat of the land as you desire; but Mr. Yancey[2] knows so well the line between Cobb and myself, that I am sure he can point it out. So also can the surveyor who run the lines. The Catalogue of our library is not printed. Mr. Hilliard is now here and has brought on a collection of about 1000.D's worth of books, but chiefly of those called for by the schools. He will be able in abt. 3. months to furnish us with 30. copies of Thomas's Co.Lit. and his selling price will be 35.D. Your copy with all costs of importations cost me 30.91 and at that price I charged it to your father. If you prefer it's value in other books I would allow you the price which Hilliard will furnish it at, 35.D.

mense advantages of soil and climate which we possess over these
people, it grieves me to think that such great gifts of Nature
should have failed to produce any thing like the wealth and improvement which the New-Englanders have wrung from the hard
bosom of a stubborn and ungrateful land, and amid the gloom
and desolation of their wintry skies. I should judge from appearances that they are at least a century in advance of us in all
the arts and embellishments of life; and they are pressing forward
in their course with a zeal and activity which I think must ensure
success. It is certainly a pleasing sight, this flourishing state of
things: the country is covered with a multitude of beautiful villages; the fields are cultivated and forced into fertility; the roads
kept in the most exact order; the inns numerous, affording good
accommodations; and travelling facilitated by the ease with which
post carriages and horses are always to be obtained. Along the
banks of the Connecticut there are rich meadow lands, and here
New might, I should think, almost challenge *Old* England, in
beauty of landscape. From the top of Mount Holyoke which commands perhaps one of the most extensive views in these States,
the whole country as you look down upon it, resembles one vast
garden divided into it's parterns. There are upwards of twenty
villages in sight at once, and the windings of the Connecticut are
every where marked, not only by it's own clear and bright waters,
but by the richness and beauty of the fields and meadows, and the
density of population on it's banks. The villages themselves have
an air of neatness and comfort that is delightful. The houses have
no architectural pretensions, but they are pleasing to look at, for
they are almost all painted white, with vines about the windows
and doors, and grass plats in front decorated with flowers and
shrubs; a neat paling separates each little domain from it's neighbour; and the out-houses are uniformly excellent, especially the
wood-house, which is a prominent feature in every establishment,
and is, even at this season, well nigh filled with the stock for
winter's use. The school houses are comfortable-looking buildings,
and the Churches with their white steeples, add not a little to the
beauty of the landscape. It is common also to find the larger of
these country towns, the seats of colleges which are numerous
throughout the country.

The appearance of the people generally is much in their favor;
the men seem sober, orderly, and industrious: I have seen but one
drunken man since I entered New England, and he was a south
carolinian! The women are modest, tidy, and well-looking; the

of uncommon merit. Mr. Coolidge prays to be permitted to express his regard and veneration for you, and will attend immediately to your memorandum. Once more adieu my dear grandpapa, love to all and for yourself the assurance of my devoted love.

ELLEN W. COOLIDGE

1. She married Joseph Coolidge, Jr., of Boston, May 27, 1825, in the parlour at Monticello. See *The Annual Report of the Monticello Association Nineteen Hundred and Thirty-two*, page 11, for additional information on the wedding. For the story of their extended wedding trip, see Harold J. Coolidge, "An American Wedding Journey in 1825," *Atlantic Monthly* (March, 1929). They resided in Boston, where Coolidge was a successful merchant whose trade was chiefly with the Far East. Ellen died April 21, 1876, and her husband December 15, 1879.

To ELLEN RANDOLPH COOLIDGE

Monticello Aug. 27. 25

Your affectionate letter, my dear Ellen, of the 1st. inst. came to hand in due time. The assurances of your love, so feelingly expressed, were truly soothing to my soul, and none were ever met with warmer sympathies. We did not know, until you left us, what a void it would make in our family. Imagination had illy sketched it's full measure to us: and, at this moment, every thing around serves but to remind us of our past happiness, only consoled by the addition it has made to yours. Of this we are abundantly assured by the most excellent and amiable character to which we have committed your future well-being, and by the kindness with which you have been recieved by the worthy family into which you are now engrafted. We have no fear but that their affections will grow with their growing knolege of you, and the assiduous cultivation of these becomes the first object in importance to you. I have no doubt you will find also the state of society there more congenial with your mind, than the rustic scenes you have left: altho these do not want their points of endearment. Nay, one single circumstance changed, and their scale would hardly be the lightest. One fatal stain deforms what nature had bestowed on us of her fairest gifts. I am glad you took the delightful tour which you describe in your letter. It is almost exactly that which Mr. Madison and myself pursued in May and June 1791. Setting out from Philadelphia, our course was to N. York, up the Hudson to Albany, Troy, Saratoga, Ft. Edward, Ft. George, L. George Ticonderoga, Crown point, penetrated into L. Champlain, returned the same way to Saratoga, thence crossed

by the crowd of strangers who think themselves privileged to waste and misuse your time, intruding upon you at all hours, and sacrificing your comfort and even health without reflection and without remorse, we are always unwilling to add, by the introduction of new visitors, to the burthen which weighs so heavily upon you; but it is likewise difficult, sometimes almost impossible to refuse the recommendations which are asked of us. In this instance, I have yielded to the wishes of Mr. Brazer, taking care at the same time to let him know that your health is very feeble, and that his seeing you must depend upon your having a moment's respite from bodily suffering and extreme debility. Mama, or one of my sisters, will be so good as to receive him, and let him know whether you are well enough to admit of his visit to yourself. He is a man held in great esteem on account of the entire respectability of his character, and has a high reputation for talents and learning, being known among the literary men of Boston for his able articles in the North American Review and other periodical works of the day. He was formerly Latin Tutor in Cambridge University, and is the author of a criticism upon "Pickering on Greek pronunciation," and a review of Chalmers' "Christianity in connexion with modern Astronomy." Mr. Brazer tells me that he has had some correspondence with you upon the subject of his criticism on Pickering's Greek pronunciation, but as it was several years ago, he thinks you may have forgotten the circumstance.

Adieu my dearest grandfather. Mr. Coolidge offers his most respectful and affectionate regards, and from me you need no new assurance of my devoted love.   ELLEN: W: COOLIDGE

1. The Reverend Mr. John Brazer.

TO THOMAS JEFFERSON RANDOLPH

Oct. 21. 25

DEAR JEFFERSON

I inclose you a letter from N. H. Lewis as Secretary of the Rivanna company,[1] as also a copy of the interlocutory decree of Chancellor Brown for the appointment of Commissioners, which is the object of this letter. I have informed Mr. Lewis that I leave all further proceedings in this matter to you, and shall confirm whatever you do in it. Affectionately yours,

TH: JEFFERSON

1. A company chartered in December, 1806, to improve the navigation

We have heard of the loss of your baggage, with the vessel carrying it, and sincerely condole with you on it. It is not to be estimated by it's pecuniary value, but by that it held in your affections. The documents of your childhood, your letters, correspondencies, notes, books, &c., &c., all gone! And your life cut in two, as it were, and a new one to begin, without any records of the former. John Hemmings was the first who brought me the news. He had caught it accidentally from those who first read the letter from Col. Peyton announcing it. He was au desespoir! That beautiful writing desk he had taken so much pains to make for you! Everything else seemed as nothing in his eye, and that loss was everything. Virgil could not have been more afflicted had his Aeneid fallen a prey to the flames. I asked him if he could not replace it by making another? No. His eyesight had failed him too much, and his recollection of it was too imperfect. It has occurred to me however, that I can replace it, not, indeed, to you, but to Mr. Coolidge, by a substitute, not claiming the same value from it's decorations, but from the part it has *borne* in our history and the events with which it has been associated. I recieved a letter from a friend in Philadelphia lately, asking information of the house, and room of the house there, in which the Declaration of Independence was written, with a view to future celebrations of the 4th. of July in it, another, enquiring whether a paper given to the Philosophical society there, as a rough draught of that Declaration was genuinely so? A society is formed there lately for an annual celebration of the advent of Penn to that place. It was held in his antient Mansion, and the chair in which he actually sat when at his writing table was presented by a lady owning it, and was occupied by the president of the celebration. Two other chairs were given them, made of the elm, under the shade of which Penn had made his first treaty with the Indians. If then things acquire a superstitious value because of their connection with particular persons, surely a connection with the great Charter of our Independence may give a value to what has been associated with that; and such was the idea of the enquirers after the room in which it was written. Now I happen still to possess the writing-box [2] on which it was written. It was made from a drawing of my own, by Ben. Randall, a cabinet maker in whose house I took my first lodgings on my arrival in Philadelphia in May 1776. And I have used it ever since. It claims no merit of particular beauty. It is plain, neat, convenient, and, taking no more room on the writing table than a moderate 4to. volume, it yet displays it self sufficiently

count. We should be the better perhaps of your recipe for dressing both articles.

I promised Mr. Ticknor[5] to inform him at times how our University goes on. I shall be glad if you will read to him that part of this letter which respects it, presuming Mr. Coolidge may have communicated to him the facts of my former letter to him. These facts may be used ad libitum, only keeping my name out of sight. Writing is so irksome to me, especially since I am obliged to do it in a recumbent posture, that I am sure Mr. Ticknor will excuse my economy in this exercise. To you perhaps I should apologize for the want of it on this occasion. The family is well. My own health changes little. I ride two or three miles in a carriage every day. With my affectionate salutations to Mr. Coolidge, be assured yourself of my tender and constant love.

TH: JEFFERSON

1. A spirit of insubordination among the students had cropped out on June 22, August 5, and September 19. About ten days later the disorders began in earnest. At first they seemed directed principally at the European professors, that is, at Long and Key in particular, but soon came to include all the faculty. See Bruce, *University of Virginia*, II, 298–301.

2. This lap desk is now in the National Museum. TJ misspelled the cabinet-maker's name; it was Benjamin Randolph. See Margaret W. Brown, *The Story of the Declaration of Independence Desk and How It came to the National Museum* (Washington, 1954).

3. Simon Willard, the famed Boston clockmaker.

4. Marseilles merchants.

5. George Ticknor.

TO ELLEN RANDOLPH COOLIDGE

Monticello Nov. 26.25.

MY DEAR ELLEN

The inclosed letter (Nov. 14th.) has been written near a fortnight and has laid by me awaiting a pacotille which your Mama was making up of some things omitted to be sent to you with those so unfortunately lost. That is now made up and will be immediately forwarded to Richmond to the care of Colo. Peyton.

FROM ELLEN RANDOLPH COOLIDGE

Boston.Dec.26.25.

Your letter of Nov.14. and 26. my dearest Grandpapa, gave me a degree of pleasure only to be understood by those, who, like me, are far separated from the best and kindest of friends; it is some

liness of his fancy, all the vivacity of his thoughts and opinions. He converses with fluency and cheerfulness and a visible interest upon almost any topic; his manners are kind and courteous, his countenance animated, and his hearing so little impaired as to require only distinctness of articulation and scarcely any raising of the voice in speaking to him. He is surrounded by grand-children exceedingly attached to him, and watching over him with great care and tenderness, and altogether presented an image so venerable, so august even amid the decay of his bodily powers, as sent us away penetrated with respect and admiration for the noble ruin which time-worn and shattered looks still so grand in comparison with what is offered to us by present times. Mr. Adams might say with Ossian, "the sons of feeble men shall behold me and admire the stature of the chiefs of old." I am afraid our revolutionary worthies have been succeeded by a race comparatively small.

The weather has been, here, cold beyond the season; the Bostonians do not generally calculate upon anything as severe before January. I have not suffered as much as I feared I should, because great precautions are taken to guard against the inclemency of the climate. The houses are well built, with double doors, small close rooms, stoves and whatever contributes to keep out the general enemy, the intense cold; great stores of wood and other fuel are timely laid in, and against the open air, the females particularly, defend themselves by warm clothing. I find that with the wrappings generally made use of, I can walk or ride without inconvenience, and that it is not at all necessary to confine myself to the house more than I should do in Virginia. The New Englanders are so reconciled by habit to their climate as really to prefer it to a more [word omitted] one, a degree of philosophy which I do not think I shall very readily attain to. I have written a long letter, and in great part by candle-light, but I cannot close without saying that the brandy &c. will be shipped in about a week along with a piano built for Virginia, in this town, a very beautiful piece of workmanship, and doing, I think, great credit to the young mechanic whom we employed, and whose zeal was much stimulated by the knowledge that his work would pass under your eye. The tones of the instrument are fine, and it's interior structure compares most advantageously with that of the English-built pianos, having, we think, a decided superiority. The manufacturer believes that it will be to his advantage to have it known that he was employed in such a work for you, or what amounts to the

FROM THOMAS JEFFERSON RANDOLPH

Richmd Feb. 3d [1826]

[MY] DEAR GRANDFATHER

You will be disappointed in hearing [that] your bill[1] is not yet before the Legislature. Upon the [fact] being generally known that such an application would be made a panic seised the timid and indecisive among your friends as to the effect it might have upon your reputation which produced a reaction so powerfull that yesterday and the day before I almost dispaired of doing anything. But upon availing myself of the councils of Judges Brook, Cabell, Green and Carr[2] and their weight of character and soundness of views, to act upon gentlemen of less experience and decision. They have been again rallied to the charge and are now bold and determined, and assure me they will not again hesitate or look back and feel confident of success; they do not believe that the delay has been injurious. The policy of the state had been against lotteries as immoral and the first view of the subject was calculated to give alarm which it took time and reflection to remove.

We owe great obligations to the kindness and zeal of the Judges; particularly Brook whose tact and readiness and decision [letter torn] to us invaluable. The importance [letter torn] more urgent than ever. The Banks, with [letter torn] for us, without additional [illegible; letter torn] your friend; and which I properly [letter torn] ordered. If we fail I shall endeavor [to raise] money for pressing demands by pledging property [which will] give us time to sell ourselves. I do not anticipate [trouble, but] will not be unprepared to meet it. If you will preserve y[our health] and spirits and not suffer yourself to be affected by it; [your grandc]hildren will be so happy in that, that we shall never think of difficulties or loss of property as an evil. My own trials and struggles with the world have been so salutary, as to give me a decision of character and confidence in myself not to be dismayed at any difficulties which can arise. And if the worst happens we shall among us have a plenty for the comfort of my mother and yourself during your lives: and children that make the poverty of rich men, make the wealth of the poor ones. Peyton has been kind and true. He sees our difficulties and can wait for our crop

Most devotedly yours,   TH J RANDOLPH

1. Jefferson's financial plight in 1826 was almost beyond recovery: his debts amounted to something over $100,000; bankruptcy was impossible, for his lands were mortgaged to their limit. As disaster stared him in the face he snatched at a last straw: a lottery to dispose of his property. The consent of

brought in without fail; there will be opposition but wither by silent vote or active debate is not known; your friends are sanguine. There has been no pause or hesitation with them since I last wrote. By the next mail or by private conveyance if any offers earlier I can give you something decisive and certain. Ever affectionately yours,   TH: J. RANDOLPH

To THOMAS JEFFERSON RANDOLPH

Monticello. Feb. 8. 26.

MY DEAR JEFFERSON

I duly received your affectionate letter of the third, and perceive there are greater doubts than I had apprehended whether the Legislature will indulge my request to them. It is a part of my mortification to perceive that I had so far overvalued myself as to have counted on it with too much confidence. I see, in the failure of this hope, a deadly blast of all my peace of mind, during my remaining days. You kindly encourage me to keep up my spirits but oppressed with disease, debility, age and embarrassed affairs, this is difficult. For myself, I should not regard a prostration of fortune. But I am over whelmed at the prospect of the situation in which I may leave my family. My dear and beloved daughter, the cherished companion of my early life, and nurse of my age, and her children, rendered as dear to me as if my own, from having lived with me from their cradle, left in a comfortless situation, hold up to me nothing but future gloom. And I should not care were life to end with the line I am writing, were it not that I may be of some avail to the family. Their affectionate devotion to me (in the unhappy state of mind which your father's misfortunes have brought upon him,) I may yet be of some avail to the family. Their affectionate devotion to me makes a willingness to endure life a duty, as long as it can be of any use to them. Yourself particularly, dear Jefferson, I consider as the greatest of the god-sends which heaven has granted to me. Without you, what could I do under the difficulties now environing me? These have been produced in some degree by my own unskillful management, and devoting my time to the service of my country, but much also by the unfortunate fluctuations in the value of our money, and the long continued depression of farming business. But for these last, I am confident my debts might be paid, leaving me Monticello and the Bedford estate. But where there are no bidders, property, however, great, is no resource for the payment of debts.

as, I was able to consider, the gift, of no evil consequence to yourself, and as the equivalent of the land intended for my mother,
the possession was grateful both to my feelings, and to My sense
of propriety: but, now, when I learn that after the payment of your
debts, but little of your property will be left, I hope that under
such, or even better circumstances, you cannot do me the injustice
to suppose, that I could even consent to retain the smallest portion.
You have been to me ever, an affectionate, and tender Father, and
you shall find me ever, a loving, and devoted son, what that son
would do, I will, under all circumstances; and I now with the greatest allacrity relinquish, that competence which you so kindly gave
and I do assure you, if there be sincerity in human nature, that it is
with greatest satisfaction, and that I shall remain ever, as deeply
indebted, as though your kind intentions had been completely
fulfilled. As to myself it is sufficient to say, that I am still young,
healthy, and strong, and so being feel able to provide for myself,
and for those who depend upon me. In a few months more, with
the knowledge already acquired, I feel confident of obtaining
admittance to the bar, and in the time that intervenes between
introduction and practice, of perfecting that knowledge sufficiently for after occasions. Having held you ever in the light of a
Father, I could see no impropriety, while the gift was not preju-
dicial to yourself, in accep[ting] and retaining, whatever you were
pleased in your goodness, to give me; and deeming what you gave,
amply sufficient for all My wants, a life of quiet independence, and
of moderate but sure gains, suited my tastes better, than the all
engrossing, and laborious, study and practice of law. It afforded
too more leisure for the acquisition of general information, which
has always appeared to me preferable to that which is confined,
and particular: and the certainty of being always with my family
was no small addition to the considerations which swayed me.
But these views which may account for My want of immediate
preparation, I can easily forego; and I shall feel happy in so doing
only: and I am well assured that my attention once turned, and
rivetted, on another object, interest will soon render that most
agreable. Do not therefore, My dear Grandfather, from any
ill founded fears on my account, or from any other motive oppose
an act which setting aside its justice, is the necessary consequence,
of the filial tenderness with which my heart is over-flowing, do not
mortify me by refusing that which you own; and which if it were
not, I should think the same feelings which prompt the son to
offer, should compel the Father to accept. Forgive me if I have

FROM ELLEN RANDOLPH COOLIDGE

Boston March 8.26.

I enclose a bill for the brandy &c. my dearest Grandpapa, by which you will see that we save still a few dollars remaining of the sixty sent by Col. Peyton. There are also such receipts for dressing the fish and tongues and sounds as I could obtain, but these dishes, especially the latter, are scarcely ever brought upon table in Boston, owing, I suppose, to their being so easily obtained as to lose their value by their commonness. The salt cod is prepared the first day very much as we do our bacon and hams, soaked the over night and boiled a good deal to soften and freshen it; it is then eaten with hard boiled eggs melted butter, or oil, and various boiled vegetables as beets, carrots &c. Egg or anchovy sauce may be served with it and is prepared by some. The second day the fragments of the cold fish are minced very fine and mixed with boiled potatoes, and either eaten with a sauce or made into cakes and browned in a frying pan. With the tongues and sounds the principal care is to freshen them as much as possible by washing and soaking and they are oftenest boiled plain and served with a sauce. You will see that the brandy came to $1.30 by the gallon, it was the lowest price for which it could be obtained good. The merchant who supplied these articles exerted himself to get them of the best quality knowing for whom they were and anxious that they should give satisfaction. Any thing that we can do for you, my dearest grandpapa, will be so much gain for us, who look upon the power of serving you, ever in such trifles as these, as one of our great pleasures, and a privilege we would exercise wherever we may.

By the same mail with this letter I shall send a pamphlet directed to you but intended for Mr. Trist as the best answers to some questions of his concerning the schools of Boston. Having mentioned in one of my letters the circumstance that none but Bostonians were admitted to these schools, (a regulation so apparently illiberal,) I should have added that they are free schools, supported by a tax upon the townspeople, who of course would not be called upon to pay for the education of any children but their own and those of their fellow citizens. The sum of 70,000 Ds. is annually taken from the pockets of the Bostonians for the single purpose of maintaining the schools in their own city; and there is no tax paid with less reluctance, for not only does the public spirit and ambition, of the people generally, flow with it's

procure some slips of a cider apple which he understands you have and consider one of the best in the State. I presume it to be, not the Crab, for that is common in other parts of Virginia, but a red apple which I remember you prized for it's cider; and Horace Gray, who visited you some years ago, was the person who spoke of it to his brother in such a way as makes him anxious to obtain and propagate it here. Mr. Coolidge wrote to you about a week ago, and desires now to be affectionately remembered to you. With love to all my family circle I bid you adieu my dearest grandpapa, in the hope that no new assurance can be necessary of the unbounded veneration and affection of your devoted grand daughter.   ELLEN W. COOLIDGE

1. Probably Frederick R. Sears, whose son Frederick R., Jr., married Ellenora Randolph Coolidge, a great-great-granddaughter of TJ.

TO ELLEN RANDOLPH COOLIDGE

Monticello Mar. 19. 26.

MY DEAR ELLEN

Your letter of the 8th. was recieved the day before yesterday, and as the season for engrafting is passing rapidly by I will not detain the applecuttings for Mr. Gray, (but until I may have other matter for writing a *big* letter to you) I send a dozen cuttings, as much as a letter can protect, by our 1st. mail, and wish they may retain their vitality until they reach him. They are called the Taliaferro apple, being from a seedling tree, discovered by a gentleman of that name near Williamsburg, and yield unquestionably the finest cyder we have ever known, and more like wine than any liquor I have ever tasted which was not wine. If it is worth reminding me of the ensuing winter, I may send a larger supply, and in better time through Colo. Peyton. Our brandy, fish, tongues and sounds are here and highly approved. The Piano forte is also in place, and Mrs. Carey *happening* to be here has exhibited to us it's full powers, which are indeed great. Nobody slept the 1st. night, nor is the tumult yet over on this the 3d day of it's emplacement. These things will draw trouble on you; for we shall no longer be able to drink Raphael's *Imitation brandy* at 2. D. the gallon, nor to be without the luxury of the fish, and especially the tongues and sounds, which we consider as a great delicacy. All here are well, and growing in their love to you, and none so much as

will I think prevent any thing being done at present in that way. Altho it will not prevent the sale of tickets. Persons do not like to subscribe ten dollars where others have subscribed $500. The prospectus of the lottery will be published in the course of next week and tickets offered every where at once for sale. I am told by every body they will sell rapidly. Persons will purchase one, two or three who would not like to subscribe so small a sum. Every [thing] is as favorable as I could expect. I will write from Philadelphia by the 5 or 6 of next month when I hope to report progress. Most affectionately yours,   THS J RANDOLPH

FROM THOMAS JEFFERSON RANDOLPH

Philadelphia April 30th 1826

MY DEAR GRANDFATHER

I arrived here this morning from New York. Every thing is now ready to commence the sale of the tickets. But a movement has taken place in New-York promising some thing more in its effects than any thing of the kind heretofore. A meeting has been called (in pursuance of the request of individuals) by the Mayor to be held to morrow to take the subject into consideration. I had an interview previous to my departure yesterday with the Mayor, several Aldermen and leading republicans at their instance to inform them what course would be most agreeable to you. Much zeal was expressed and much confidence of success. At their special request I agreed to assist. 15 days or to the 15th of May to see the result of their operations before any tickets shall be sold. I do not doubt a rapid sale, if the N York movement should fail. In my next I may hope to be more certain upon the subject. I propose to remain here this week and spend ten days or a fortnight in Baltimore and Washington. If I find my services can then be dispensed with I shall joyfully turn my steps towards home. It is however possible I may find it necessary to return to N. York for a few days. Most affectionately yours,   THJ RANDOLPH

TO ELLEN RANDOLPH COOLIDGE

Monticello June 5. 26.

A word to you, my dearest Ellen, under the cover of Mr. Coolidge's letter. I address you the less frequently, because I find it easier to write 10. letters of business, than one on the intangible

water, but after removing the tin and making the sheeting perfectly tight, I found myself mistaken. A subsequent examination immediately after a hard rain, showed me, on the lowest side of every sheet of tin, spots of water on the sheeting plank. This water must have been drawn upwards, as there were no traces above: and that a few drops could be so drawn up, I could readily conceive; but the quantity is really incridible. The plaistering of the parlour is so entirely wet every rain, that I begin to fear it will fall in. Large buckets of water pass through it. Your room is nearly as bad and the others leak more and more every rain. The hall is in fact, the only dry room in the house. I have been so completely baffled in every attempt to stop the leaking, that I really feel quite at a loss; we have had here, in the last four weeks three of the most destructive rains ever known in this neighbourhood. The tobacco hills on flat land were entirely swept off. Mine were hilled over twice, and the third swept off soil and all. I count my loss equal to a good hogshead. Your loss would more than double that in first rate tobacco; for the land was heavily Manured, and nothing but the clay is left behind. The wheat is fairly buried in the mud every where. My love to all, my tenderest love to you My dear Grandfather.   F. EPPES

This is the last located Jefferson family letter, received less than two weeks before TJ's death. The old patriarch had been in noticeably failing health prior to the receipt of this letter, for on June 24 he had yielded to the entreaties of his family and asked Dr. Robley Dunglison, a professor at the University of Virginia and trusted physician, to come to Monticello. Dr. Dunglison recalled this visit in his "Memoirs": "I immediately saw that the affection was making a decided impression on his bodily powers . . . [and] was apprehensive that the attack [probably dysentery] would prove fatal. Nor did Mr. Jefferson indulge in any other opinion. From this time his strength gradually diminished and he had to remain in bed. The evacuations became less numerous, but it was manifest that his powers were failing." (Randall, III, 548.)

Jefferson died of the infirmities of old age aggravated by a severe visceral complaint at ten minutes before one o'clock on July 4, 1826, at Monticello. Here, in Jefferson's bedroom, a small group of family and servants had maintained a death vigil. Included were Jefferson Randolph, Nicholas P. Trist, and Martha

Index

A. B. C. book: for Cornelia, 245, 246n
Abraham. *See* Goulding, Abraham
Accomac County, Virginia: Bowman's
  Folly, Cropper property in, 128n;
  mentioned, 147
Acosta, José de, 81
Acrolophos (Dumbarton Oaks), Rob-
  ert Beverley home in Georgetown,
  Virginia, 385, 386n
Adam's Mill, 227
Adams, Abigail (Mrs. John), 4, 91,
  91n
Adams, John, 56n, 464, 465
Adams, John Q., 315, 316n
Adams, Mrs. John Q., 315, 316n
Adventures of Mary and Her Cat, 393
Aeneid, The, 373
Aeschylus: TJ on, 433
Albemarle County, Virginia: Ashton,
  Thomas Eston Randolph home in,
  397n; Belmont, TMR, Jr., home in,
  149; Birdwood, Trist home in, 157n;
  Blenheim, Carter home in, 125n;
  Colle, Philip Mazzei home in, 73n;
  drought in, 430; Dunlora, Carr
  home in, 230, 278n; Edgehill, TMR,
  Jr., home in, 95n; Ennisworthy,
  Coles home in, 265n; The Farm,
  Nicholas Lewis home in, 101n, 362n;
  Farmington, George Divers home
  in, 175; flood of 1807, 325n; Fourth
  of July celebration, 346n; Franklin,
  Dr. William Bache home in, 177,
  178n; Fredericksville Parish in,
  133n; hailstorm in, 205, 206; Henderson's lands in, 289; Milton (town
  in), 132, 133n; Monroe, Mrs. James,
  visit to, 189; Mount Warren, W. C.
  Nicholas home in, 132n, 409n; murder committed in, 189, 189n; Overton's lands in, 289; Pen Park,

Gilmer home in, 75n, 240n; TMR,
  Jr.'s return to, 297, 298n; St. Anne's
  Parish in, 133n; snow in, 292;
  Tufton, TJ farm in, 192n, 409;
  Viewmont, Edward Hill Carter
  home in, 135n; Warren, settlement
  in, 132n; mentioned, 289n, 343n
Alexander, Eli (tenant of TJ), 115n,
  127, 128n
Alexandria, Virginia: visit of TJR to,
  351; mentioned, 219, 269n, 351, 352n
Algerine pirates, 3, 39, 128
Algerine War: end of, 328
Alien and Sedition Acts: conditions
  under, 187; indictment of William
  Duane under, 187, 187n; trial of
  Thomas Cooper under, 187
Allen, Hancock, 191, 192n
Allen, Miss (schoolmate of Mary),
  250. *See* Livingston, Mrs.
Allen, Richard H. (owner of Bel-
  mont), 174, 175n
Allston, Col. Joseph (TJ friend), 425,
  426n
Allstone, Miss, 425
Alston, Mr. and Mrs. Willis, 315, 316n
American Philosophical Society:
  TJR's studies at, 379; mentioned,
  359n, 380n
Amherst County, Virginia: slave in-
  surrection in, 374, 375n, 376
Amonit, John, 38n
Amsterdam, The Netherlands: John
  Marshall to, 166
*Anacharsis (Voyage du jeune Ana-
  charsis en Grèce)*, 62, 62n, 81
Analostan Island, 286n
Anastasia. *See* Randolph, Anne Cary
Anderson, David, 263, 264n
Angola tract, 8n
Anna. *See* Randolph, Anne Cary